I0812300

RUISLIP

THROUGH TIME

Eileen M. Bowlt

Acknowledgements

I should like to thank the following for lending photographs and permitting their publication: Colleen Cox and Denise Shackell, for permission to use the map on page 5; Sally Crosher for the 1933 photograph of the Old House; Peter Musgrave for his 1998 picture of Ruislip Lido; Carolynne Cotton, Head of Heritage Services, Borough of Hillingdon, for lending old photographs from the Borough Collections and for her continued support of local history publications; my husband, Colin, who has so patiently and helpfully supported all my endeavours in the local history field, discussing ideas, checking the text and taking some of the modern photographs.

First published 2013

Amberley Publishing
The Hill, Stroud, Gloucestershire, GL5 4EP
www.amberley-books.com

Copyright © Eileen M. Bowlt, 2013

The right of Eileen M. Bowlt to be identified as the Author of this work has been asserted in accordance with the Copyrights, Designs and Patents Act 1988.

ISBN 978 1 84868 477 5 (print)

All rights reserved. No part of this book may be reprinted or reproduced or utilised in any form or by any electronic, mechanical or other means, now known or hereafter invented, including photocopying and recording, or in any information storage or retrieval system, without the permission in writing from the Publishers.

British Library Cataloguing in Publication Data.
A catalogue record for this book is available from the British Library.

Typesetting by Amberley Publishing.
Printed in Great Britain.

Introduction

Ruislip is first mentioned in the Domesday Book of 1086. The Domesday Book tells us that Wlward Wit owned the manor in the time of King Edward the Confessor and that Ernulf de Hesdin, a follower of William I, was the Norman lord. The short description of 'Rislepe' reveals a heavily wooded and thinly populated area with land for twenty ploughs. An unusual feature of the landscape was 'a park for woodland animals', the northern pale of which survives within the present Park Wood and is a scheduled ancient monument. As many of the fifty-three people mentioned in the survey would have been the heads of families, the population was probably between 200 and 250.

Manor and Parish

The area of the manor of Ruislip in 1086 is likely to have been the same as in later times, being bounded on the north by the boundary between the counties of Middlesex and Hertfordshire, and by the parishes of Northolt to the south, Harrow to the east, and Harefield and Ickenham to the west. The county boundary was set out in the eleventh century and the other places are all mentioned in the Domesday Book.

Manor court rolls from as early as the mid-thirteenth century show that Ruislip was divided into three vills: Westcote, Ascott and Norwood. The latter two survive as modern Eastcote and Northwood, but Westcote is now simply known as Ruislip and is the subject of this book. The church of St Martin, established in the eleventh century and rebuilt around 200 years later, served the whole area until Holy Trinity was built in Northwood in 1854. Ernulf de Hesdin granted Ruislip, with the exception of a portion west of Bury Street and between the River Pinn and the top of Mad Bess Wood, to the Norman Abbey of Bec around 1087. He gave the rest, which became known as St Catherine's, to the Abbey of Holy Trinity at Rouen. St Catherine's was part of the parish of Ruislip, but had different manorial lords.

The Abbey of Bec lost Ruislip early in the fifteenth century, and Henry VI gave it outright to his new foundation at Cambridge, King's College, in 1451. The provost and scholars finally severed their connection with Ruislip by gradually selling off much of the land for suburban development in the early twentieth century.

Westcote

The manorial and ecclesiastical centres (Manor Farm and St Martin's) were in Westcote, close to a crossing place on the River Pinn. The wooded hillside rose behind to the north, and the open fields where corn, peas and beans were grown lay on the flatter, primarily clay lands to the south. The inhabitants lived in hamlets, Great & Little King's End, Field End, Silver Street Green, The Withies and Park Hearne, scattered along the lanes (now Ickenham Road, West End Road and Bury Street) that led from the village centre. Some had strips of land in the open fields, others small fields near their houses. The open fields were enclosed by Act of Parliament between 1804 and 1814, leading to the creation of a few new farms and a gradual change-over to producing hay, rather than peas and beans, owing to the proximity of London with its huge number of hungry horses.

By 1861 the population of Westcote had reached 633. Some 68 per cent of the working population were employed in agriculture. The great change to suburban life came in the wake of two major events in 1904: the opening of the Metropolitan Railway station in Ruislip, and the formation of the RNUDC (Ruislip-Northwood Urban District Council). The major landowners, the provost and scholars of King's College, Cambridge, wished to develop their property on garden suburb lines and were ably assisted by the RNUDC, which determined to introduce a town plan under the terms of the 1909 Town & Country Planning Act that would ensure that the whole area would be built up according to the same principles.

This book tells the story of the Westcote and St Catherine's part of Ruislip, showing how the character of the village and its surrounding hamlets has changed over the last 150 years, and allowing readers to judge for themselves how far the college and the council succeeded in their aims.

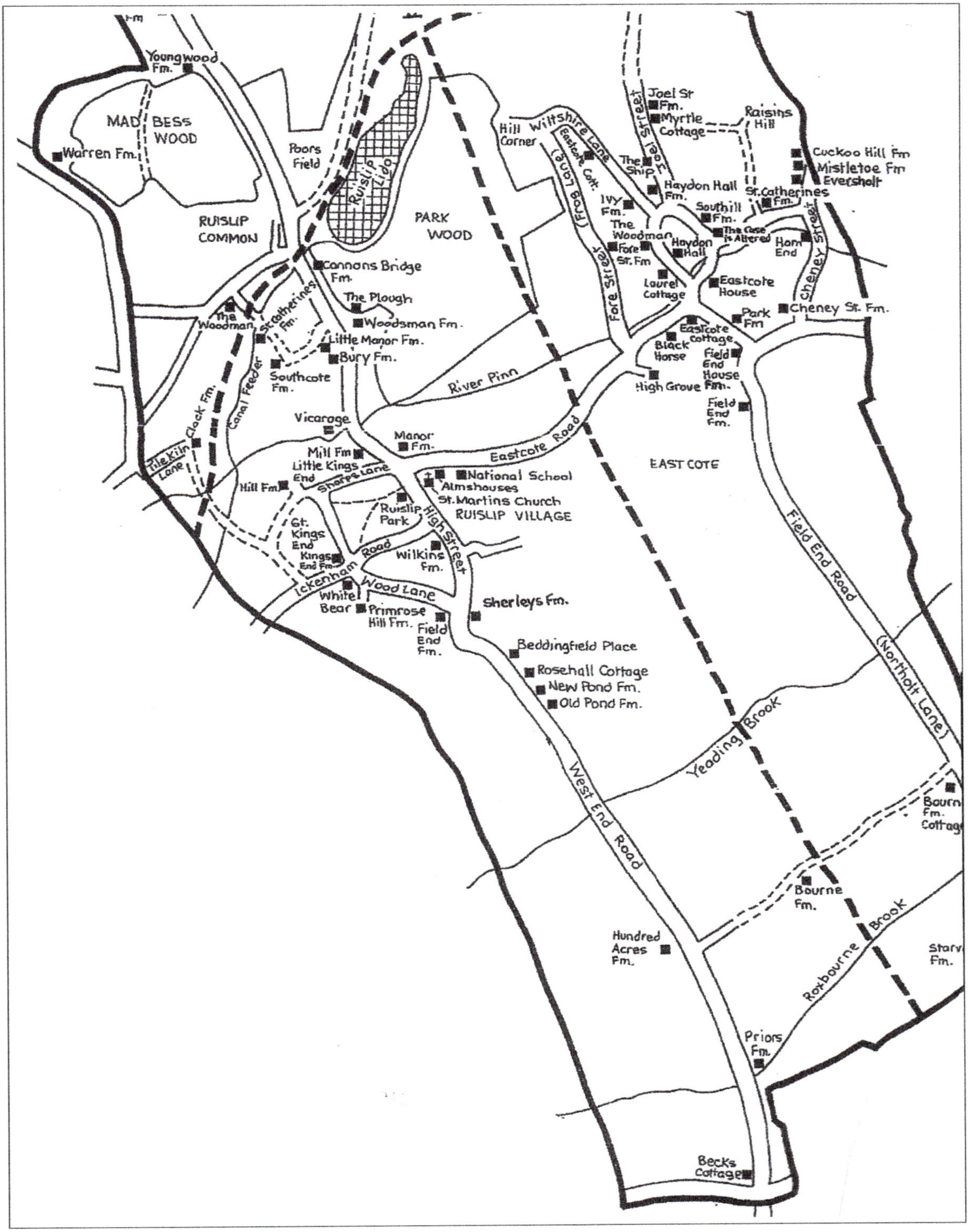

Map of Ruislip

Ruislip (Westcote and St Catherine's) before the Metropolitan Railway came.

The Village

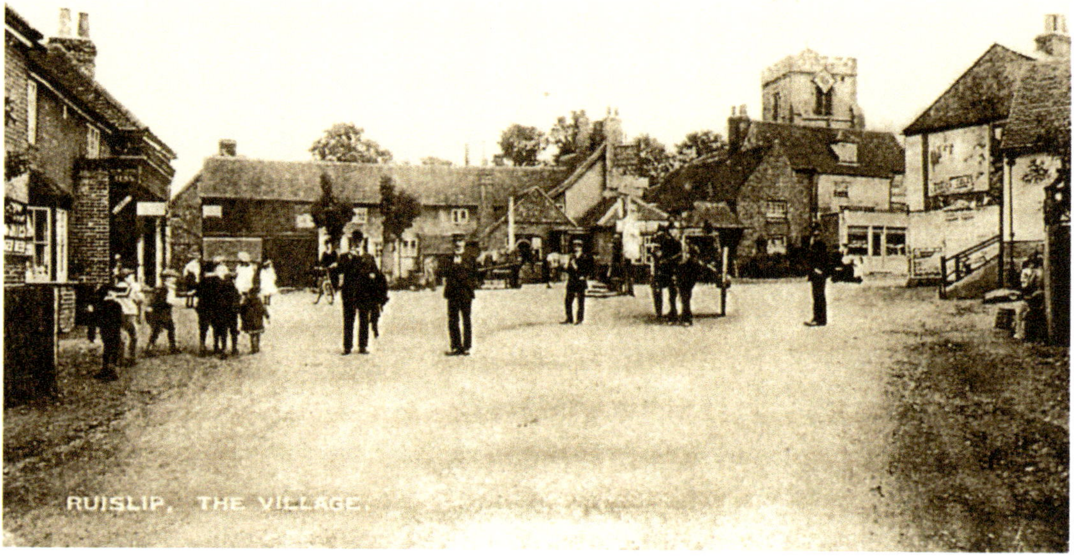

Ruislip Village Centre, *c.* 1907 and 2012
Manor Farm lies behind the buildings on the left, and St Martin's church tower dominates the scene. The open space at the junction of High Street, Bury Street and Eastcote Road is surrounded by inns, a baker's shop and the village post office. Crowds gathered here for fairs, sports and communal festivities. Now, in 2012, the inns and shops are mainly restaurants, a barn has been lost, but the other buildings remain.

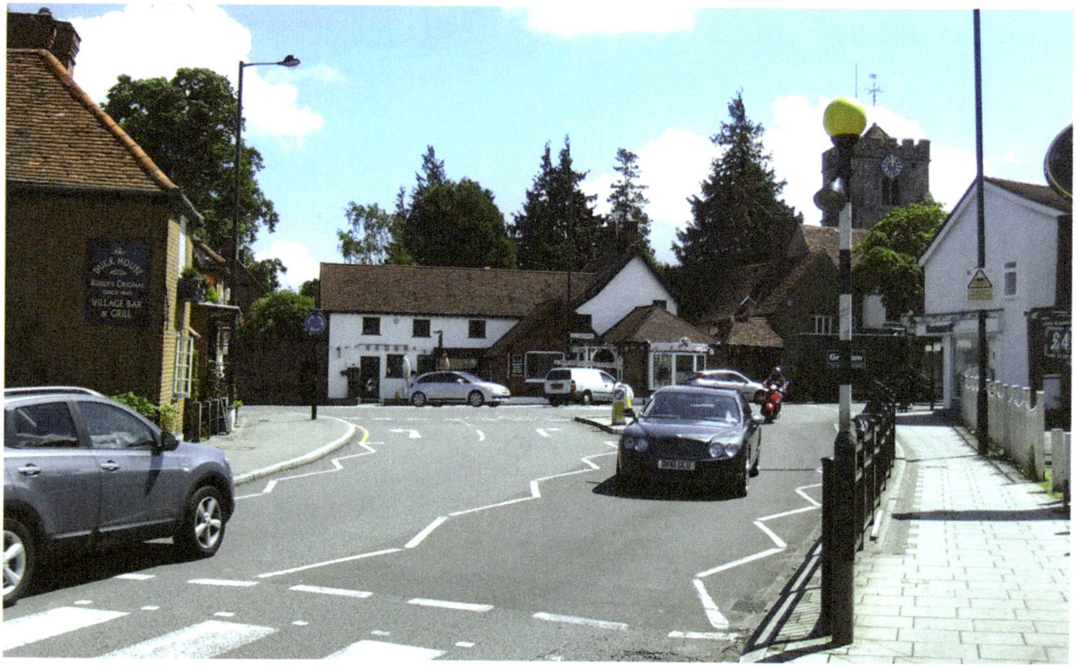

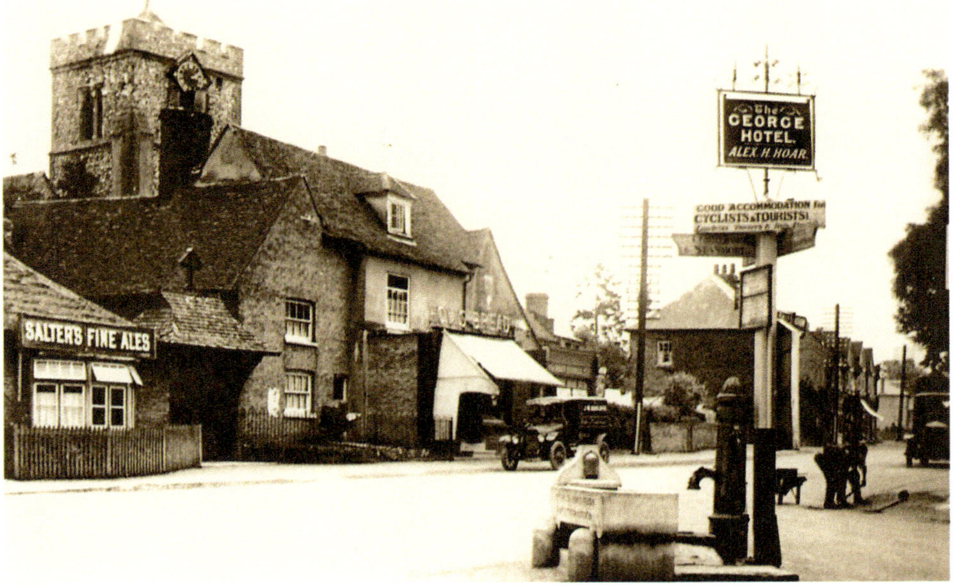

The Old Bell, Church Cottages and the Police Station, *c.* 1920

Salter's Brewery owned the Old Bell, seen on the left of the picture. The Hovis bread sign is above Mr Moulder's baker's shop. Washing is hanging out in the gardens in front of Church Cottages. There are newly built lock-up shops beyond the square building of the police station. The drinking trough was erected beside the pump in 1916 by the Metropolitan Fountain & Cattle Trough Association. In 2012 the pump has been moved for safety into the former cottage gardens and shops occupy the site of the police station.

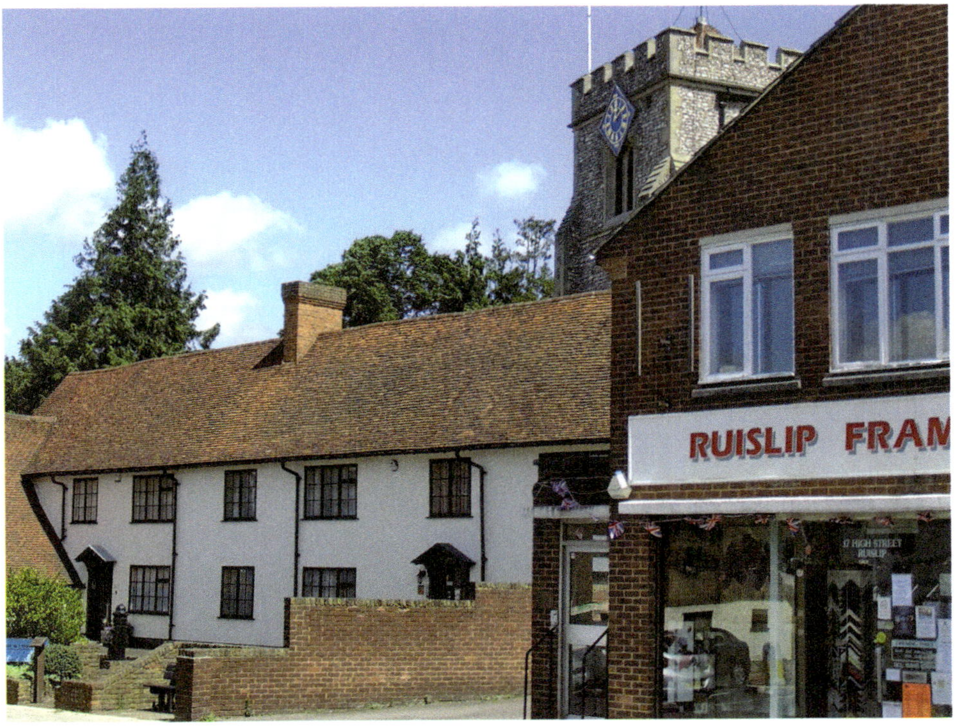

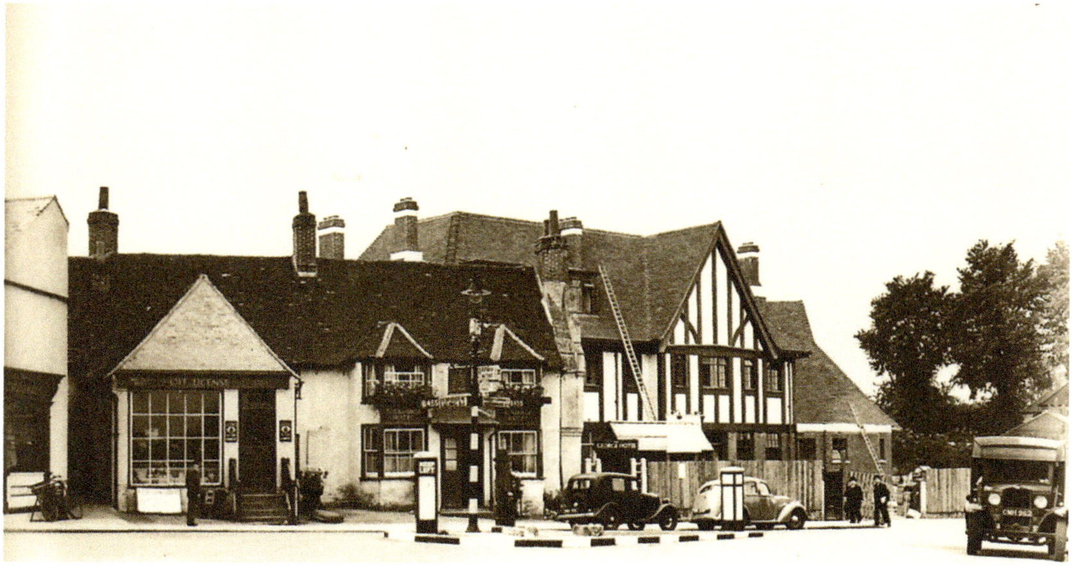

The George, 1939 and 2012

The old George, licensed in 1760, was declared unsafe, and a new building complete with an assembly room was erected in 1939, considered more suited to the sophisticated tastes of the incomers who had caused the population of Ruislip-Northwood to triple since 1931. This picture shows the increased size of the new George compared with the old. The off-licence was originally a butcher's shop, reminding us that a village publican needed a second occupation to make a decent living.

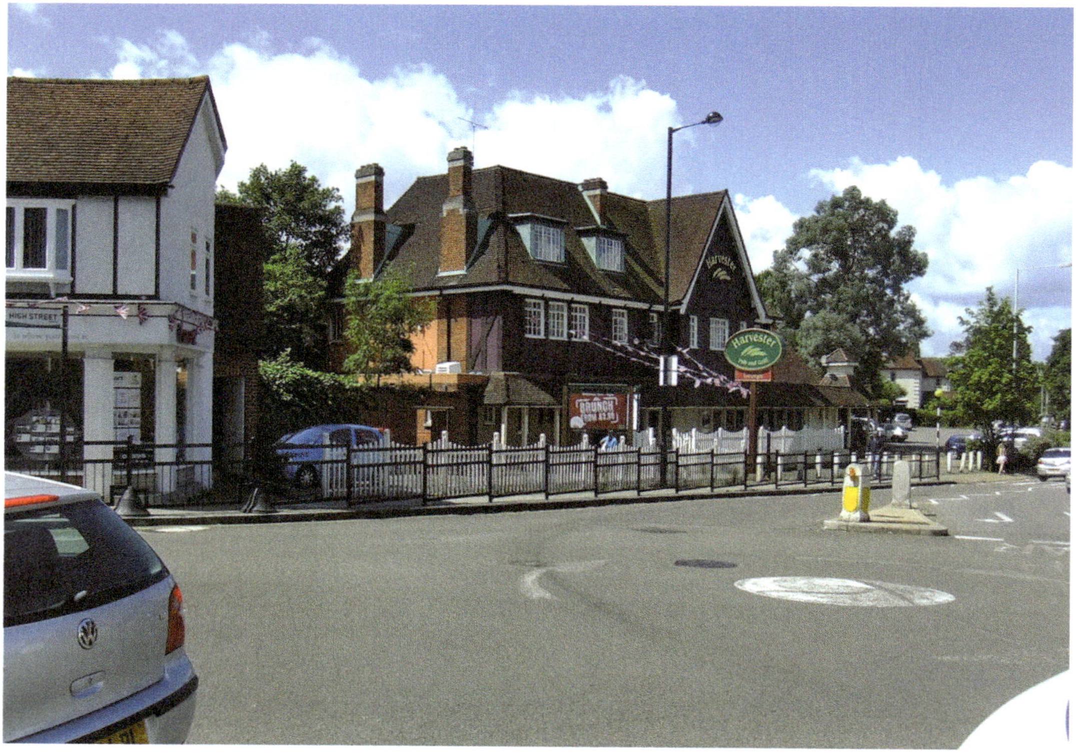

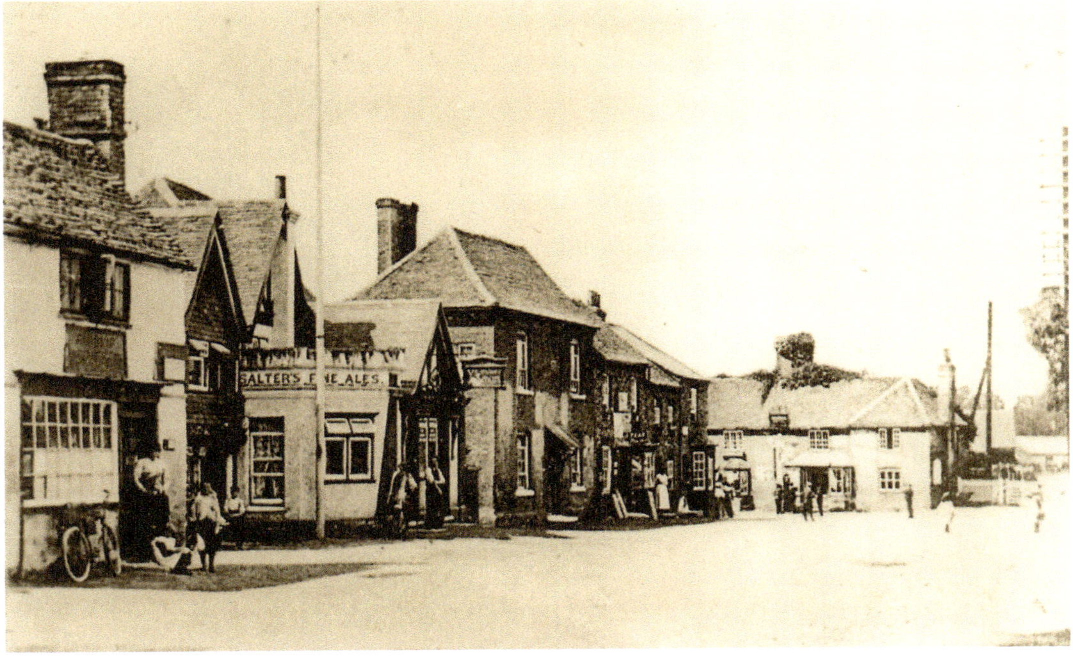

The Village, *c.* 1905 and 2012

Mr Puddick's post office on the left – later Mrs Gooderson's shop – was demolished in 1930 to widen Swan Alley. The Swan remains, albeit now a restaurant, but Naylor's Cottage beside it has gone. Mrs Riddle's general store and Crookall's butcher's shop are now an estate agent's premises. Hailey's shop, facing down the High Street, has also become a restaurant. The end of the Little Barn and the stables can still be seen down the trackway to Manor Farm.

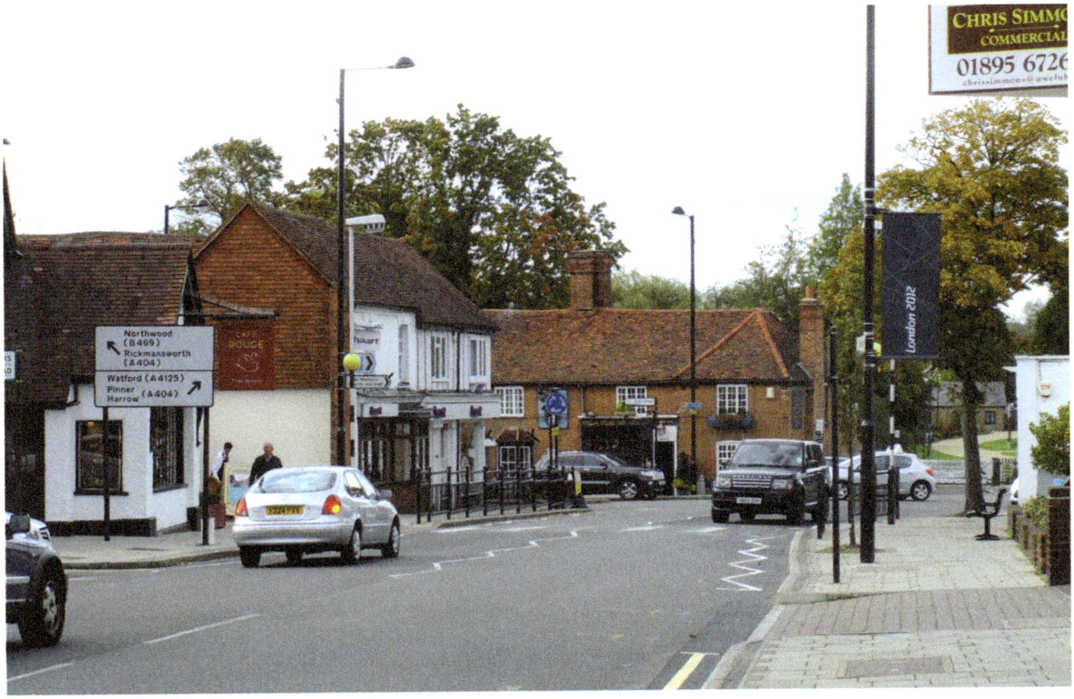

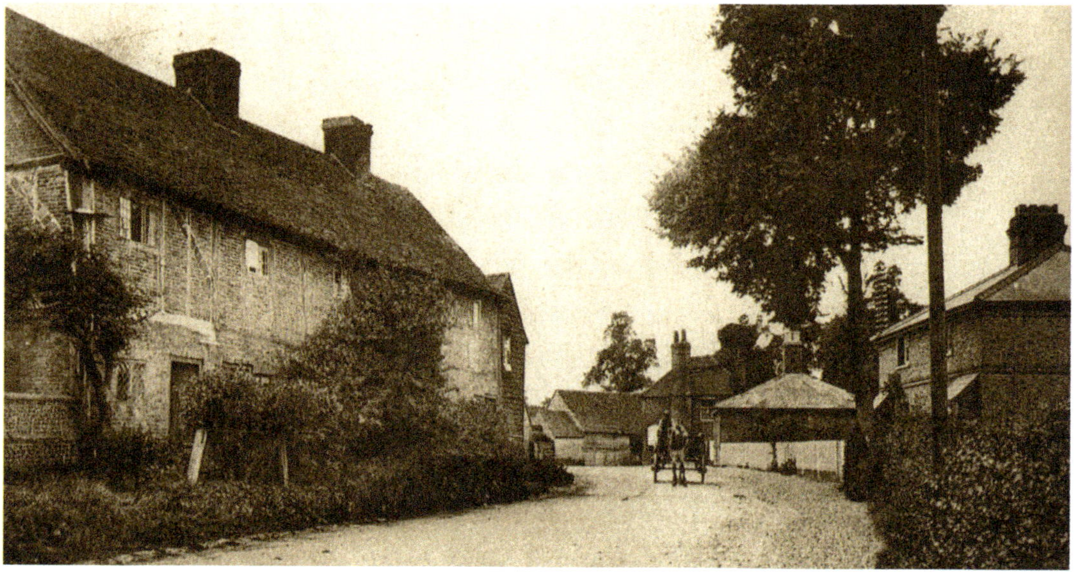

The Church House, Now Called the Almshouses, Eastcote Road, *c.* 1905 and 2012

The Church House, built as a private dwelling *c.* 1570, was converted into ten cottages to house the poor in 1616/17. A notable resident was 'Granny' Tobutt, who used to cook dinner over her open fire for her grandchildren, who passed the door each day in the 1920s on their way to the National School further along Eastcote Road. The Almshouses were restored in 1980, converted into four flats and one maisonette, and are leased to a housing trust.

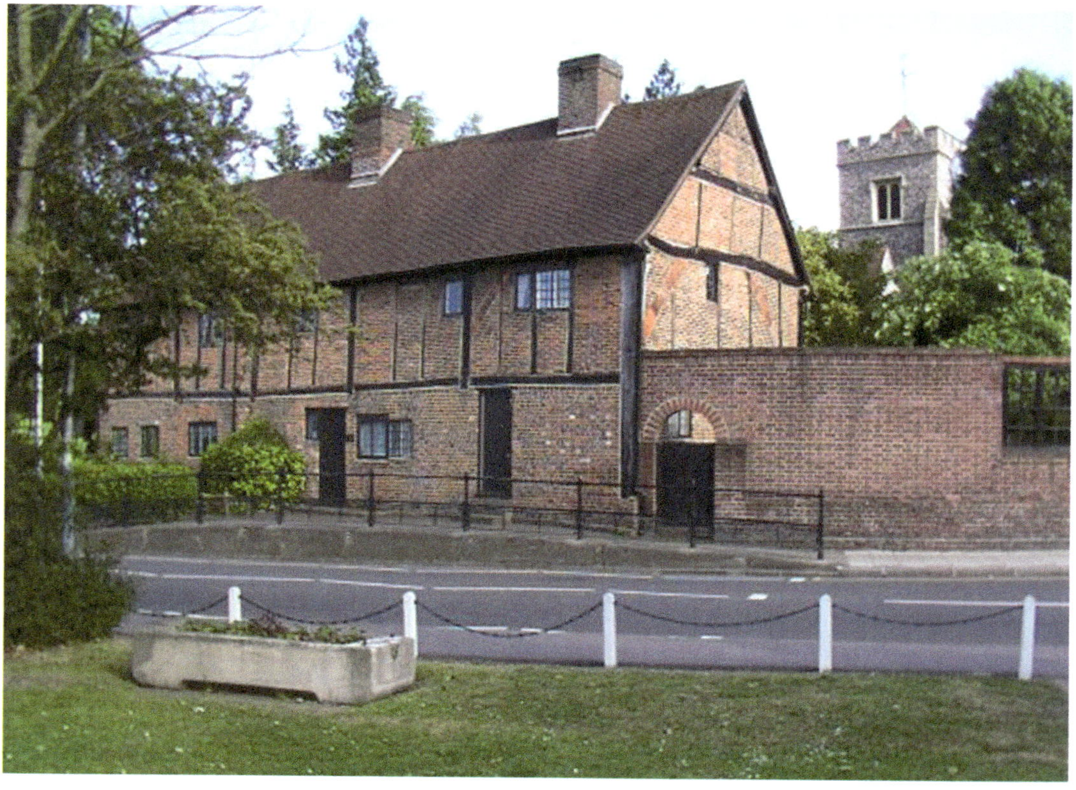

Park Lane Cottages, 1904, and the Lane Widened in 1930

Cissy Bell and Lucy Allen are standing outside Park Lane Cottages with their grandfather Bell, who worked as a shepherd at Wilkins Farm along the High Street. The view from the houses was restricted by the high brick wall of the Park estate on the right. The lane was renamed The Oaks after it was widened in 1930, as seen in the lower picture. Ruislip police station can be seen next to Church Cottages on the High Street. The Metropolitan Police rented the house from Richard Ewer of Hill Farm in 1869 and purchased the copyhold four years later. It contained living accommodation for a police sergeant and his family, a charge room, parade room and cells. There was stabling at the back, but the police had bicycles in the early twentieth century. The police moved to a purpose-built station in The Oaks in 1961.

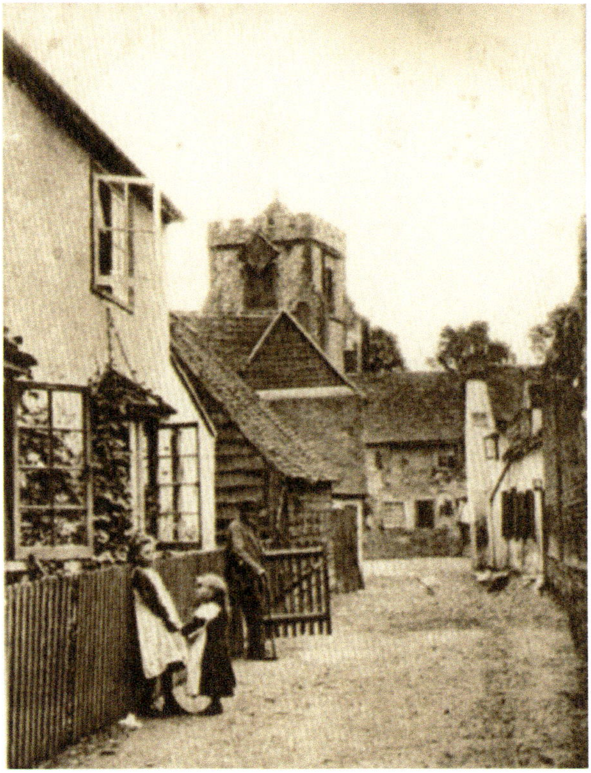

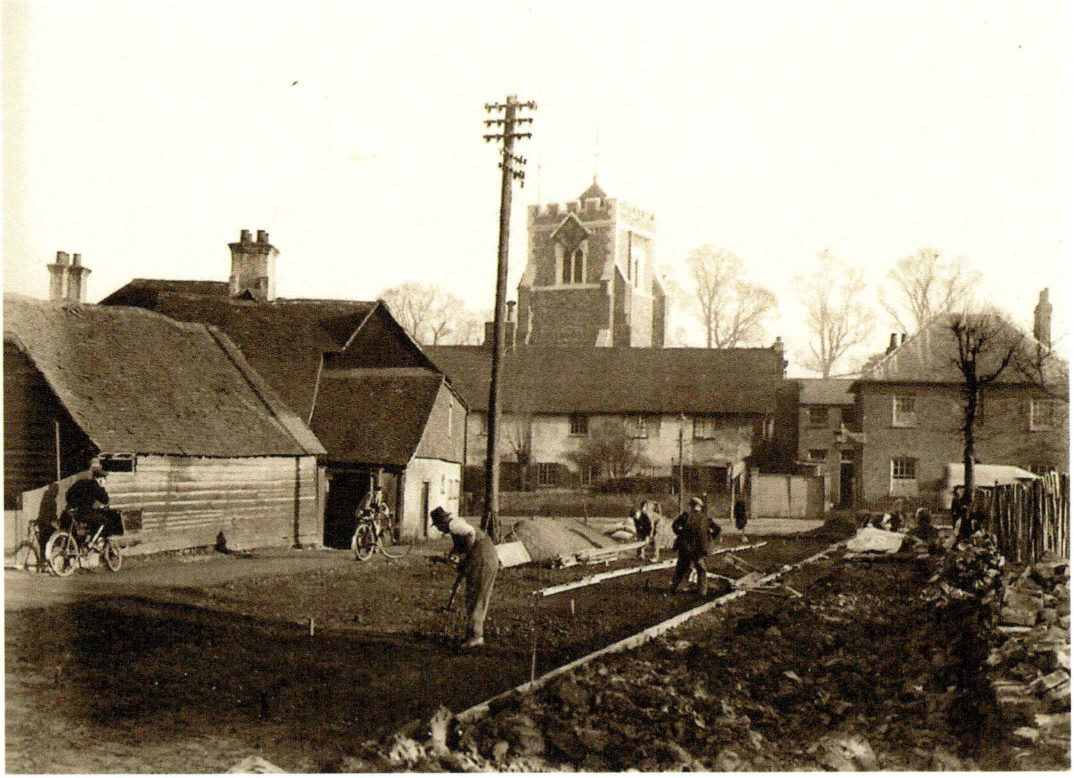

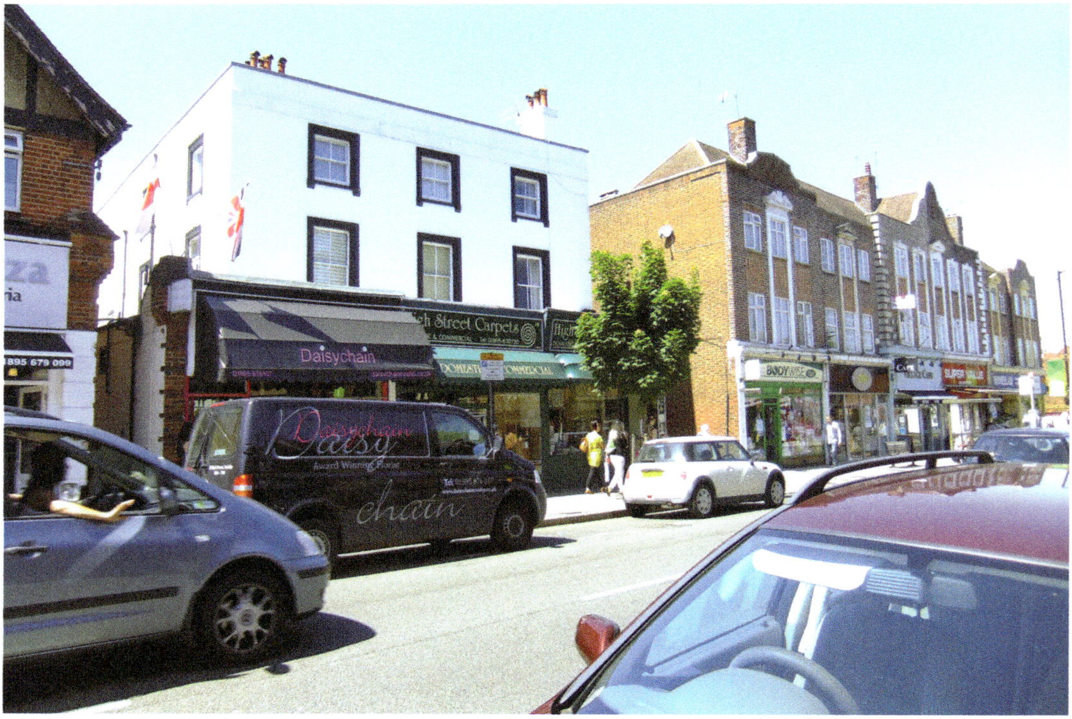

Park House in its Grounds and Amid Modern Shops

Harry Edgell, a barrister, bought an old farmhouse on Ruislip High Street around 1790 and gradually acquired properties around it, finally achieving a compact 40-acre estate, complete with a lodge, winding drive, shrubbery and two sheets of ornamental water. He improved the dwelling, giving it a fashionable stuccoed façade and pretty iron veranda. It now stands end-on to the high street between shops, those on the left built in 1927/28, and those on the right in 1934. The Royal British Legion Club rented Park House from 1930 and purchased it in 1946.

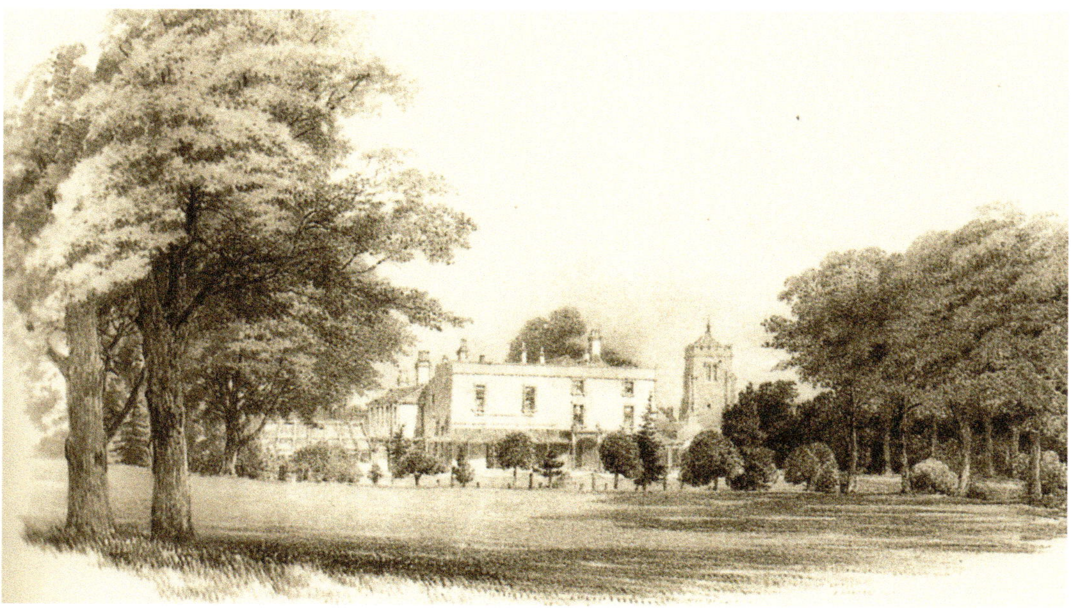

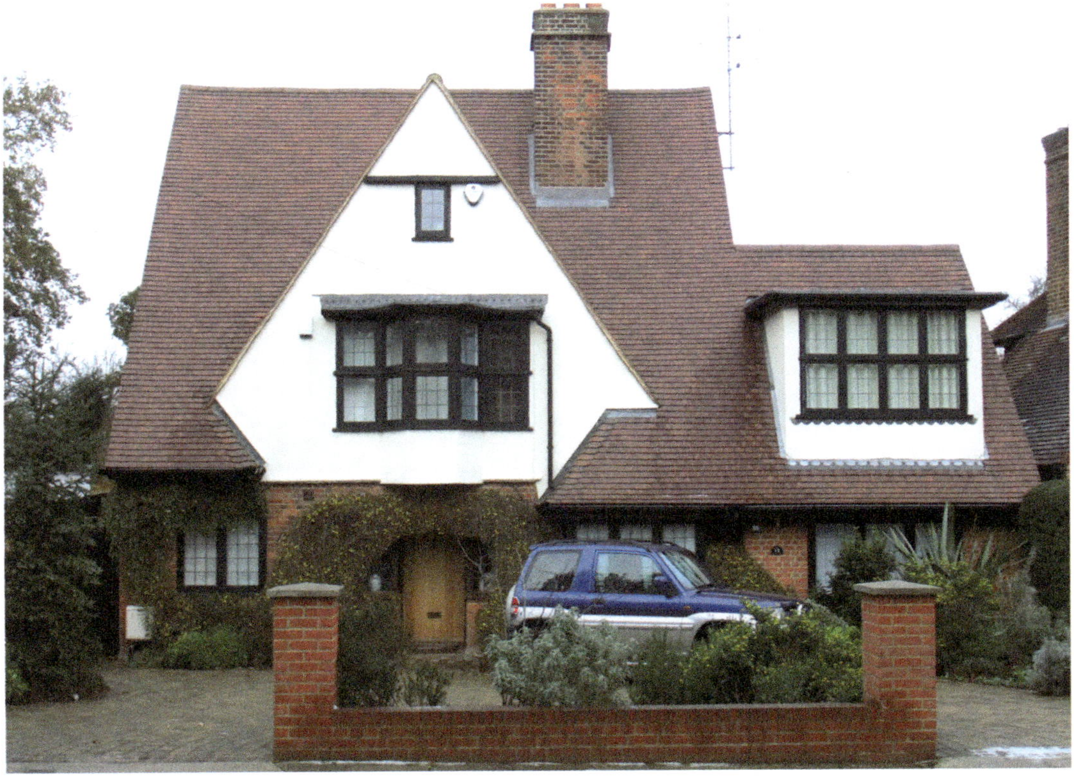

New Houses on the Park Estate, Dulce Domum and Kelvin House

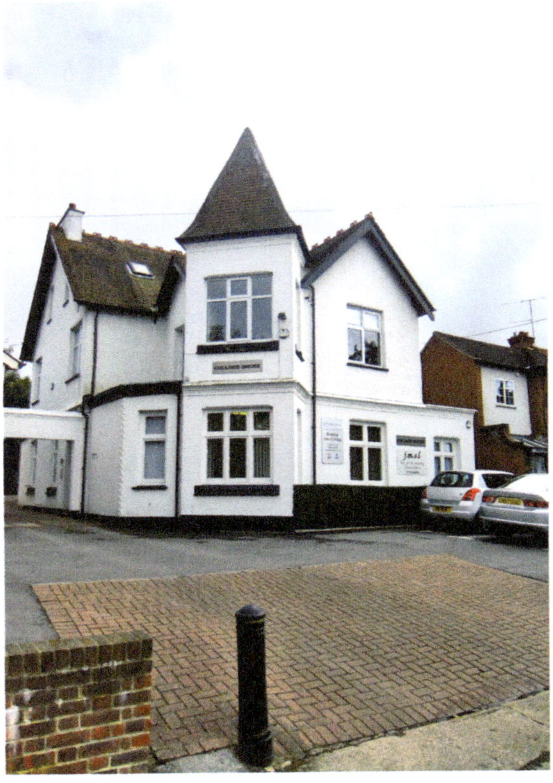

The Park estate was bought by Dickens and Welch in 1906. Manor Road and Church Avenue replaced existing footpaths and King Edward's Road was created. The area was divided into generously sized building plots, put up for auction in 1906 and again in 1911, when sales improved. Dulce Domum (Sweet Home) was built in 1911 for Miss Bigwood and her companion, independent-minded women, and the only females on the Board of Ruislip Manor Cottage Society. Kelvin House was occupied by a High School for Girls, with a preparatory department for boys going on to public schools. It was owned by Mrs Aileen Todd, wife of a clergyman, in 1914, and in 1934 by Mrs Charis Weare Brophy, wife of John Brophy, the novelist and critic. It was one of several establishments that provided education for the children of the newcomers, mainly professional people, for whom the National School's elementary education was insufficient.

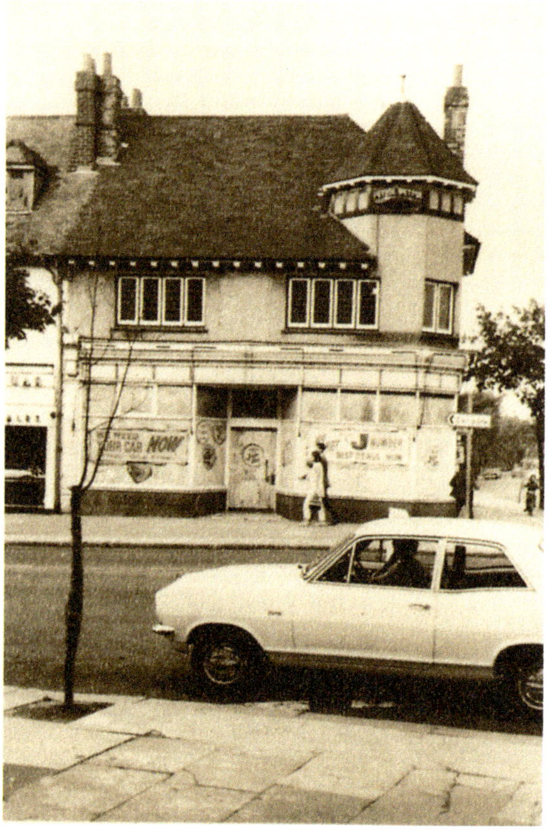

The High Street at the Top of Midcroft, 1969 and 2012

The building with the tower, shown in the earlier picture, was built in 1922 as a grocer's shop, with rooms above where Mr Fabb, formerly butler at Highgrove in Eastcote, ran a restaurant. The young people of Ruislip held meetings of the FORTY Club (For Others Rather Than Yourself) there around 1930. Formerly Howard Roberts' grocer's, it had become Budgen's by 1969. The sign on the turret is advertising the petrol sold by Inwards motor car dealers next door.

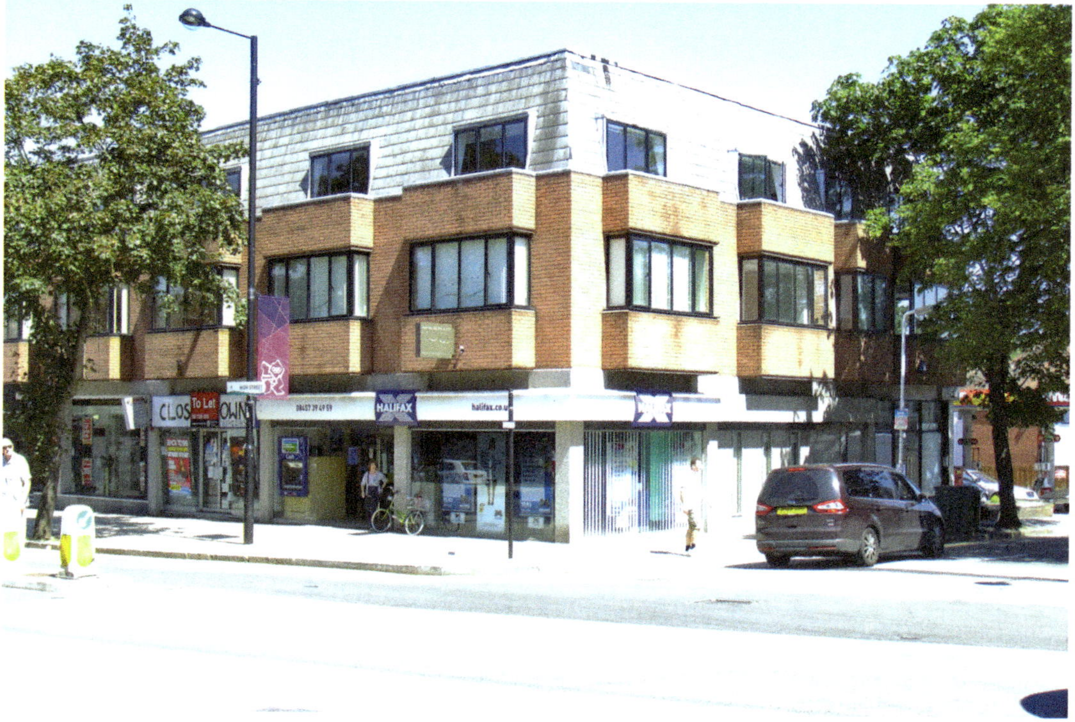

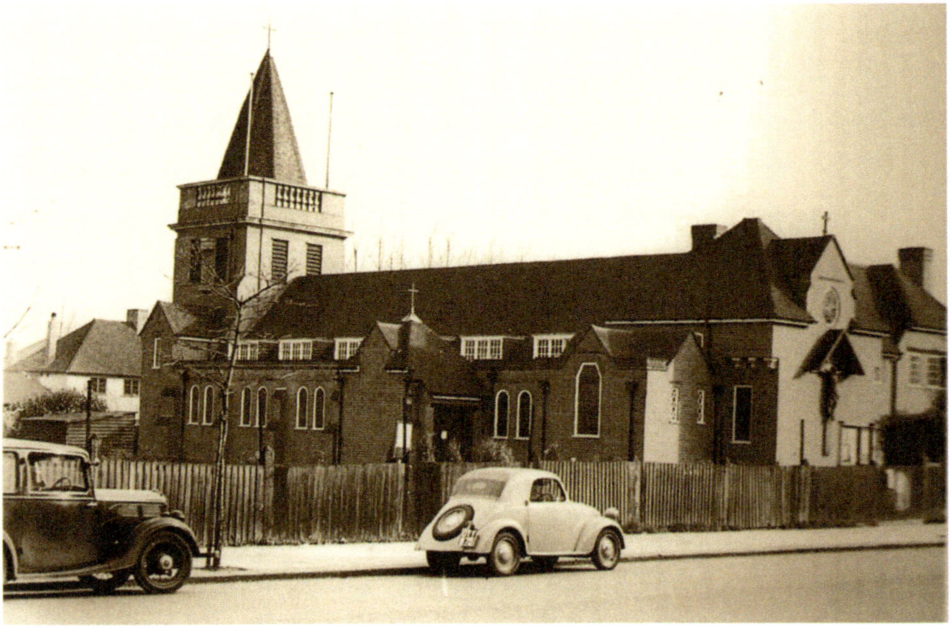

Church of the Most Sacred Heart, 1921–39 and 2012
The church was the gift of Miss Eleanor Warrender of Highgrove, who converted to Roman Catholicism during the First World War. It occupied a prime site in the middle of the developing suburban High Street and was sold in 1938. A new church was erected nearer to Ruislip Manor, where the bulk of the increasing Catholic population by then lived. Lyttons, Burtons, and Home & Colonial Stores (now Saunders, M&S and small shops) were built in 1939.

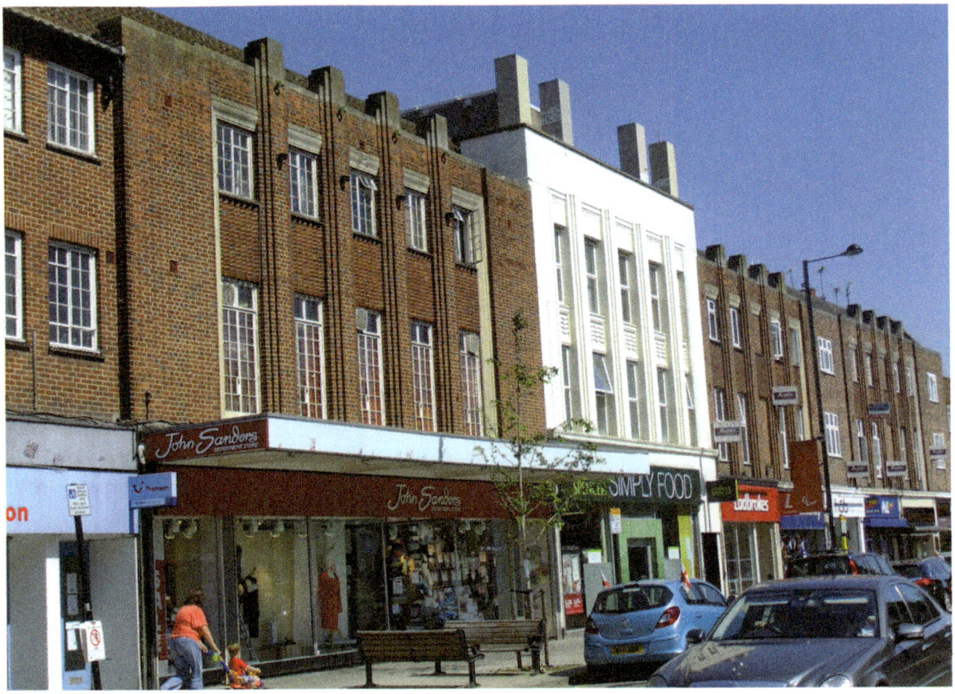

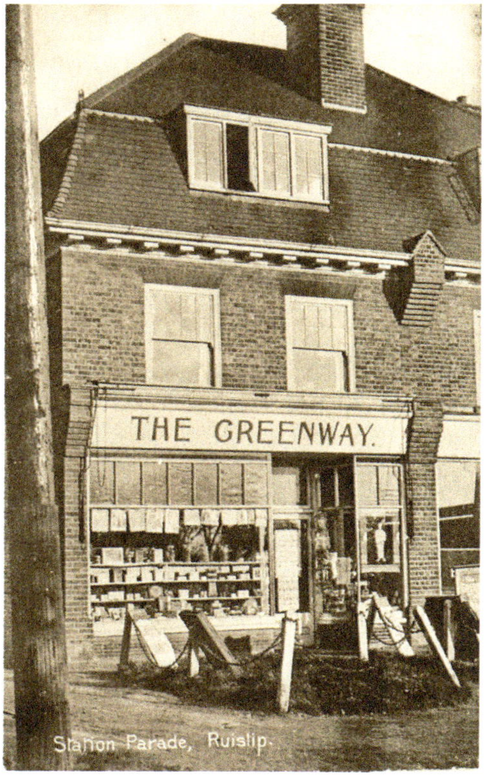

The Greenway Stores and Station Parade, c. 1920 and 2012

In the early twentieth century the name High Street only applied to the old village area near Manor Farm and St Martin's. Thereafter the road was known as West End Road and was still listed as such in the 1927 King's Gazette Directory. Plans for three pairs of shops were passed in 1911, to be built near the station. They were Nos 1–6 Station Parade. Cheyne Court, the adjoining shops with flats above, was not built until 1933/34. The Greenway Stores, seen left, was at No. 2. The Morris family sold sweets, newspapers and tobacco there, while in the room at the back men and boys could have their hair cut. The name was taken from the triangular patch of grass at the front. Oswald Morris, the distinguished cinematographer, was born here in 1915.

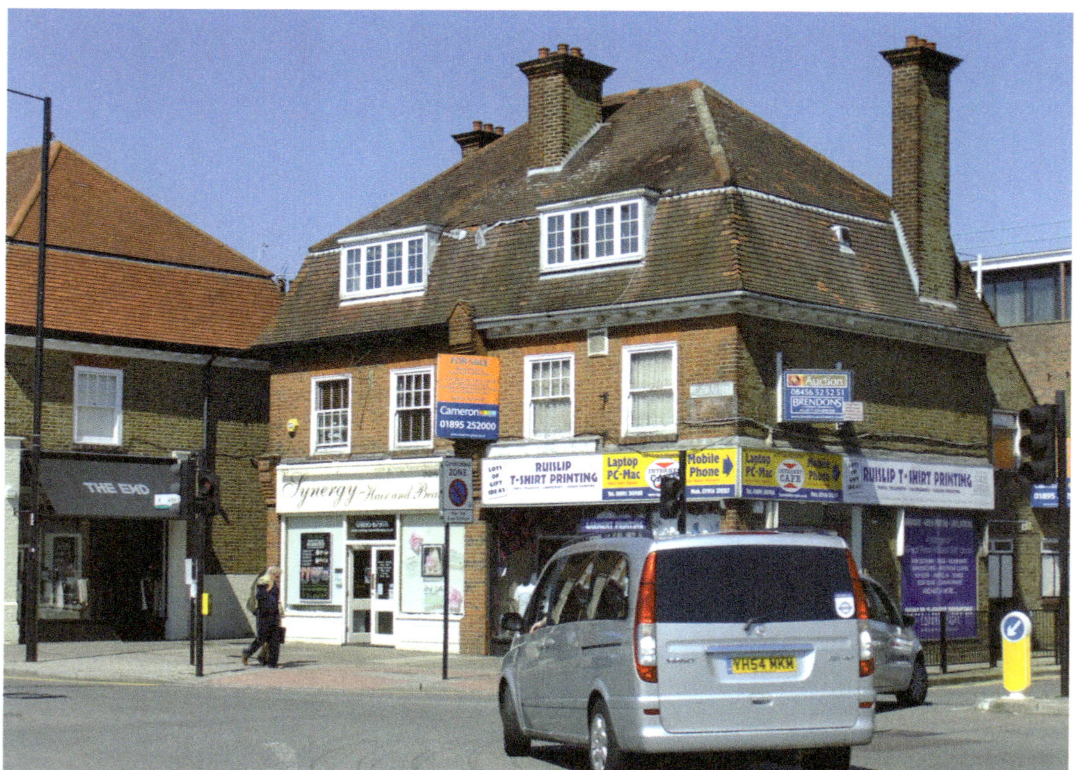

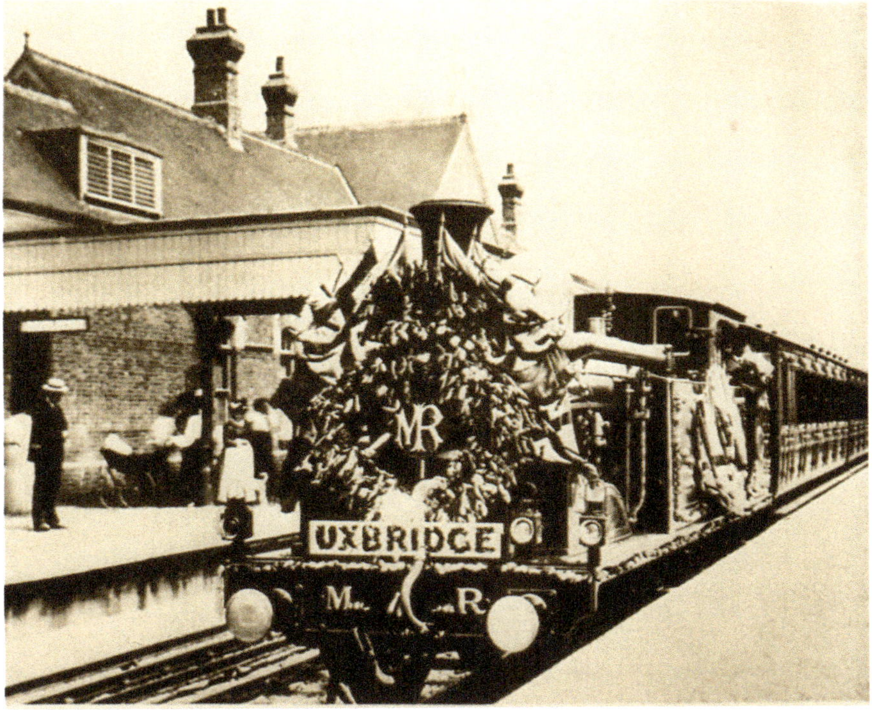

The Great Turning Point, the Coming of the Railway

Ruislip station opened in 1904, the only intermediate stop on the Metropolitan Railway's Harrow–Uxbridge extension. The official opening train is seen here at Ruislip on 30 June 1904. The station opened to the public on the 4 July and the line was electrified on 1 January the following year. Passengers travelling to Uxbridge had to buy their tickets, and then rush over the road bridge to reach the platform via a wooden gate. The station retains many of its original features.

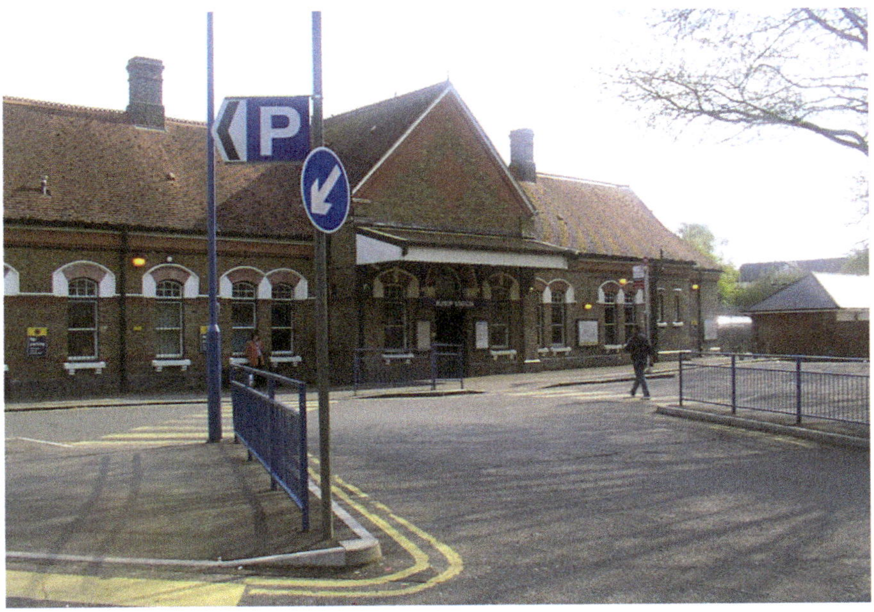

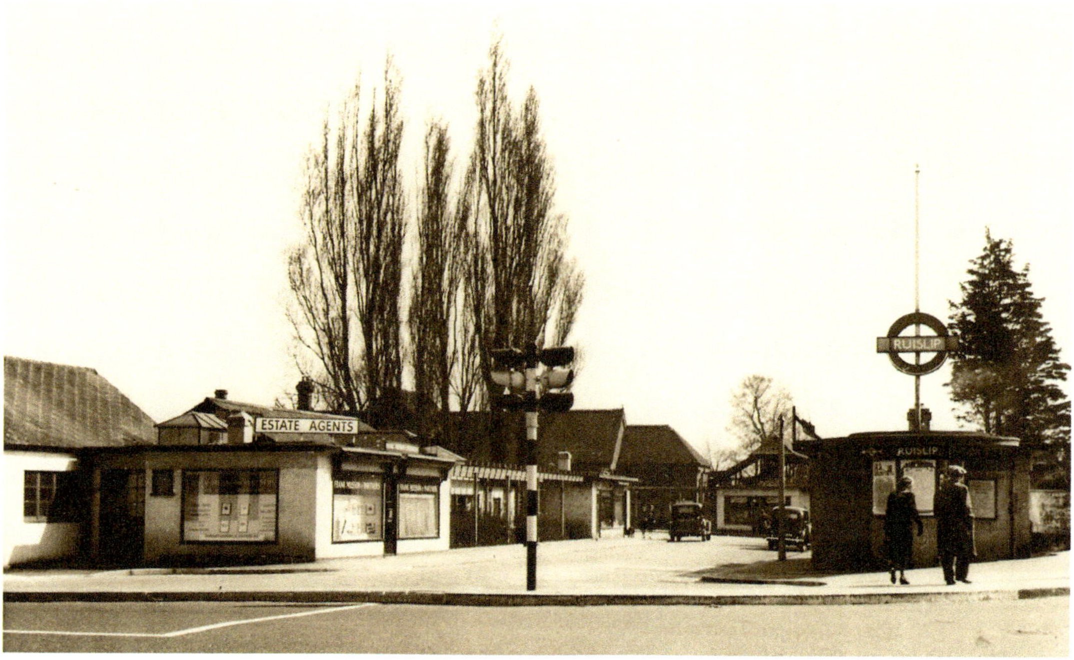

Ruislip Station Approach, 1957 and 2012

The building on the far left belonged to the Metro Tennis & Social Club, and there were two tennis courts beyond, out of the picture. Tennis was very popular in the new suburb and clubs abounded in the area. Coal merchants and estate agents occupied the offices and there were some small garden areas. Times House, an office block, was built on this site in 1960, its height completely out of scale with the rest of Ruislip's buildings.

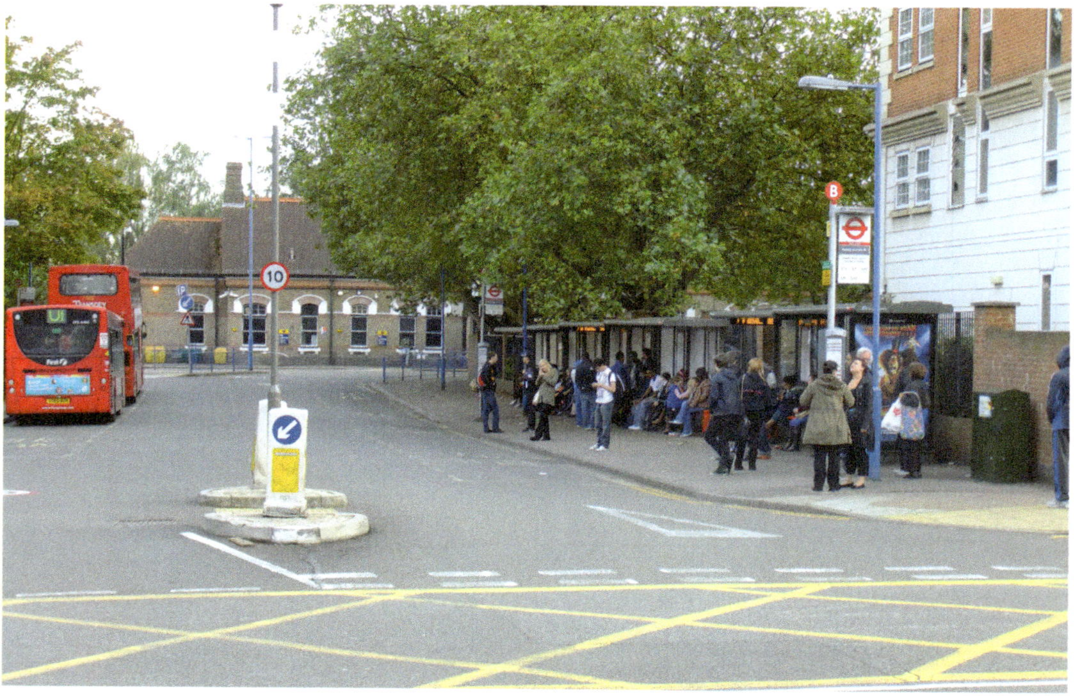

Times House to King's Lodge

In the 1960s the government was encouraging businesses to move their offices out of London to convenient positions served by public transport in suburban areas. By the 1990s the clamour for offices was on the wane and living accommodation was the order of the day. Times House was converted into flats in 1999 and renamed King's Lodge. The height was increased and the bulk of the building impedes the view from the High Street, but those within enjoy a panoramic outlook.

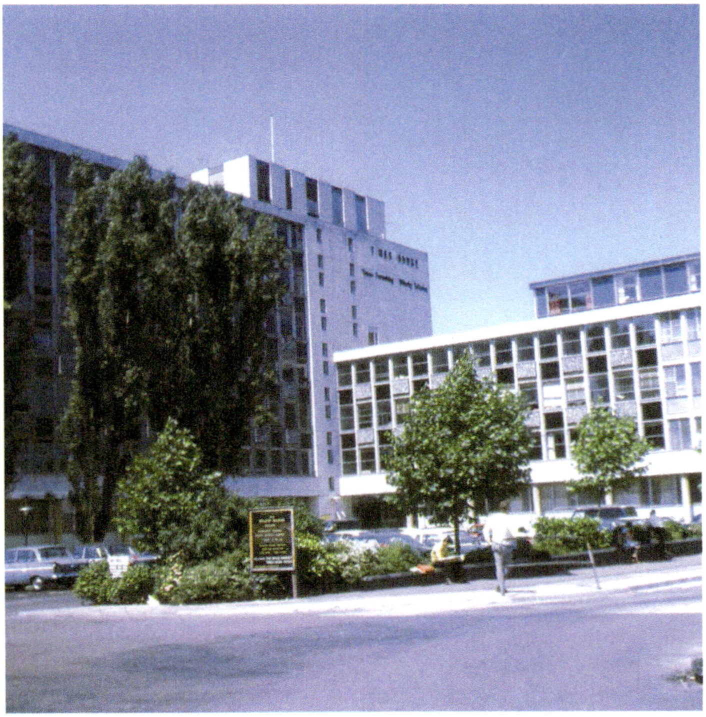

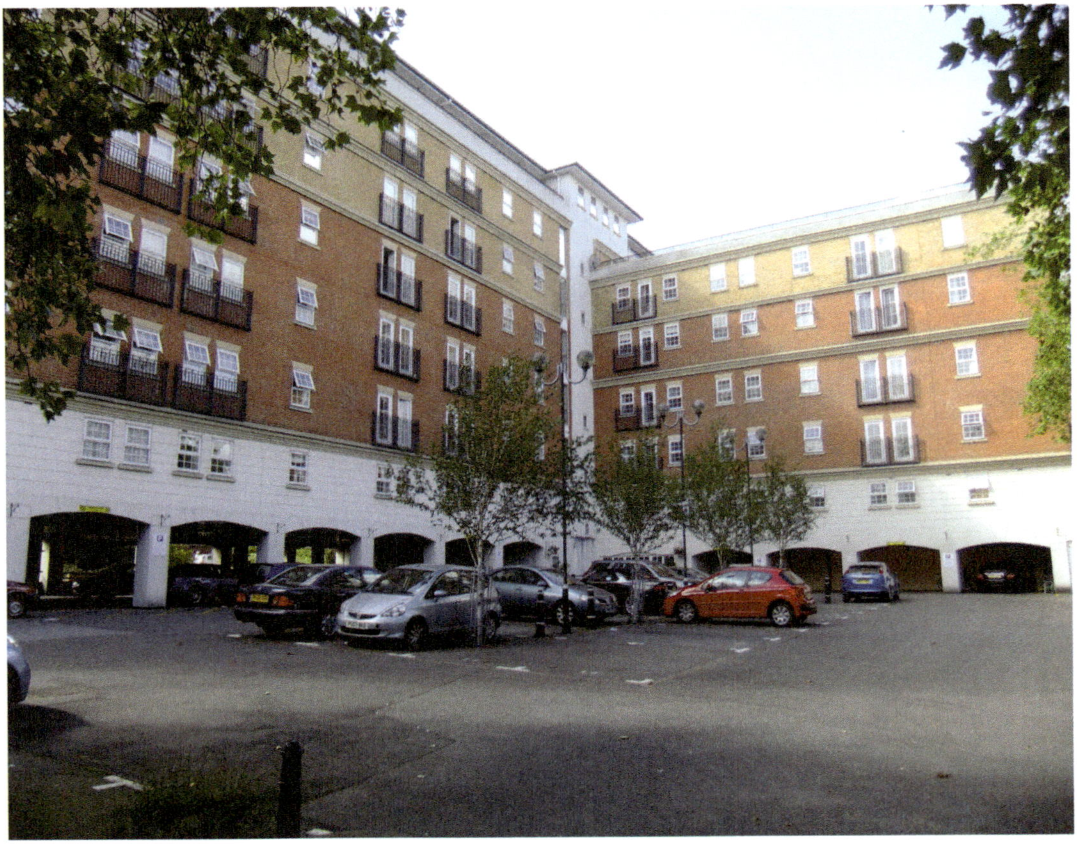

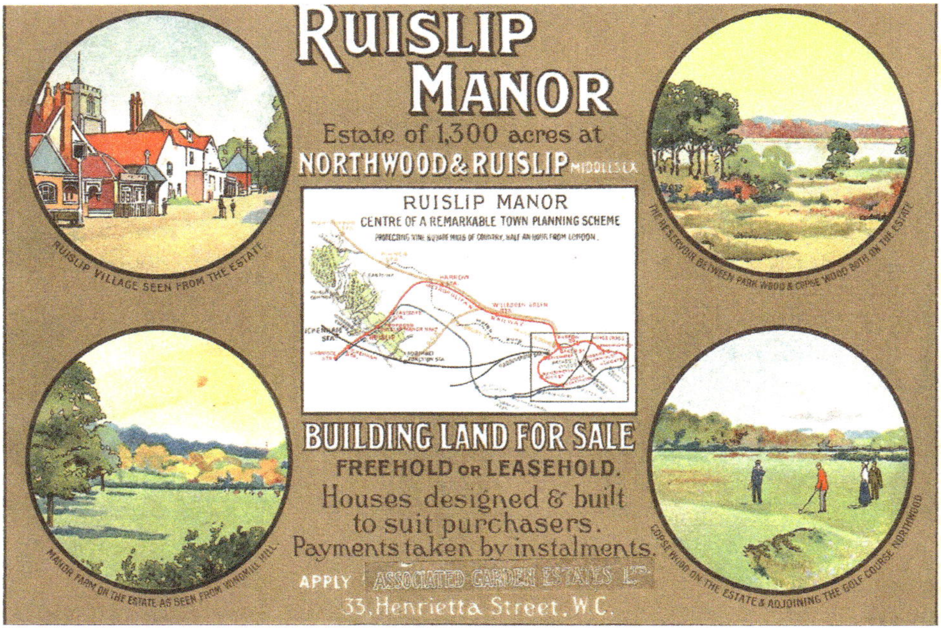

Ruislip Manor Ltd, Advertising Building Plots on King's College Land

Suburban development started soon after the opening of Ruislip station. The Ruislip-Northwood Town Plan of 1914 provided for low-density housing north of the railway line and higher density (twelve to the acre) to the south. The big rush to build came in the late 1920s and 1930s. H. A. L. Bowers built the Church Croft estate in 1929/30. The house in Croft Gardens seen in the lower picture sold for £985. The garage was added in 1937.

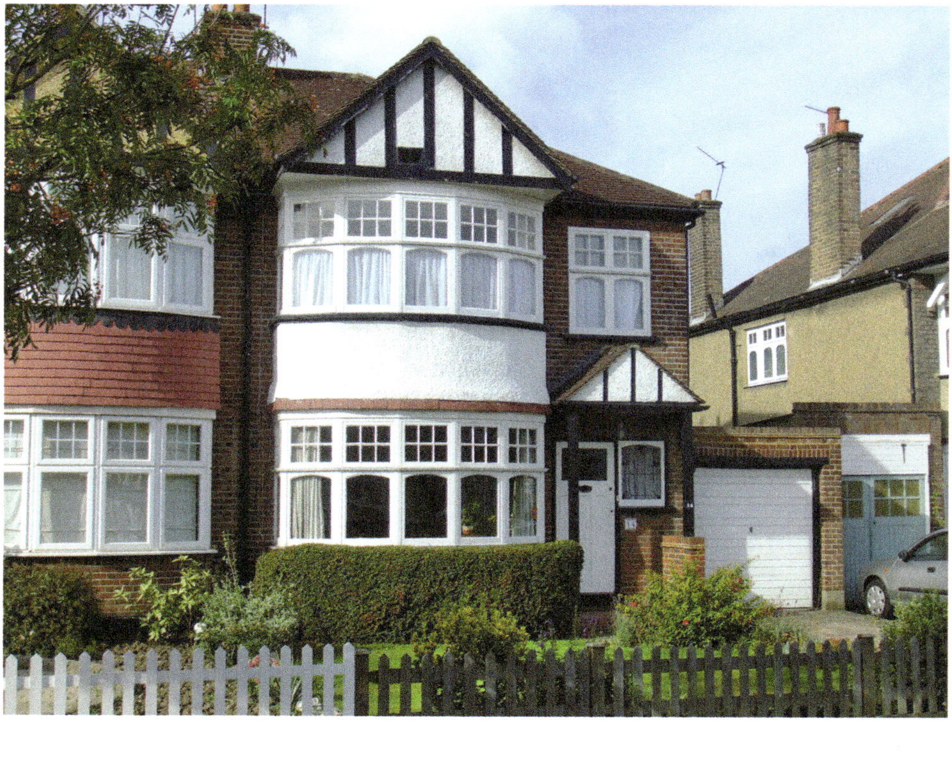

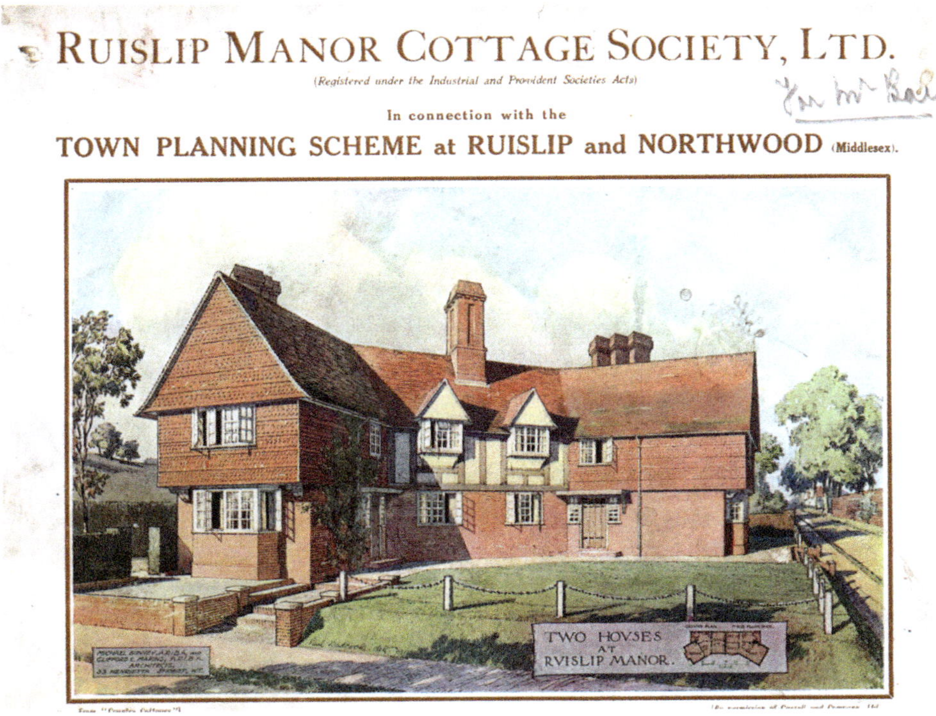

Ruislip Manor Cottage Society Brochure 1911 and Manor Way

The Ruislip Manor Cottage Society was established in 1911 to provide well-designed cottages for artisans. Tenants had to invest £25 in the society, paying £5 initially and the rest at a rate of not less than 5s per calendar month, entitling them to a share in surplus profits. The houses pictured, designed by Bunney & Makins, were occupied in 1912. They can be seen on the right at the bottom of Manor Way in the lower picture, taken in the 1920s.

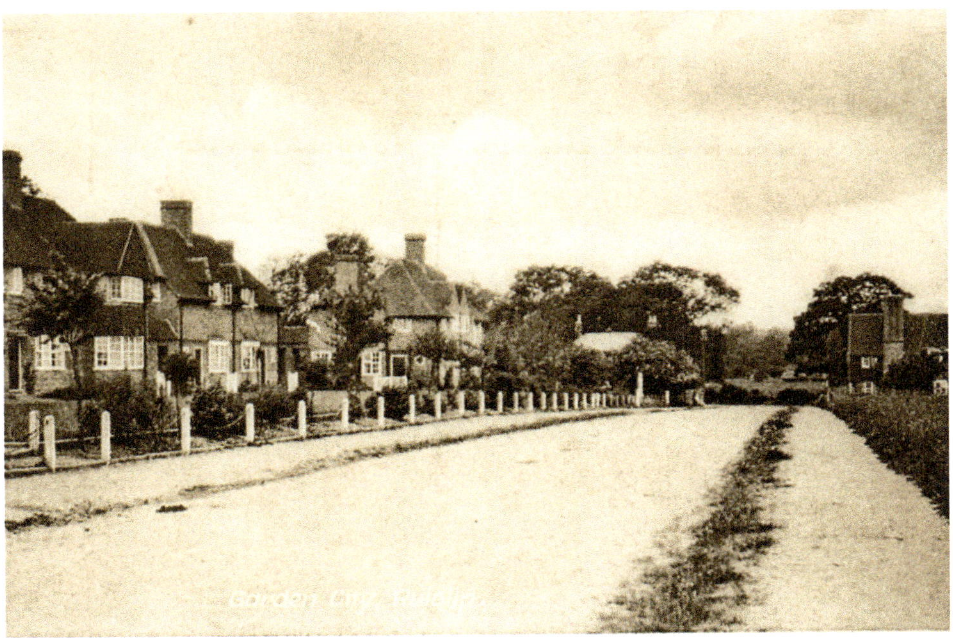

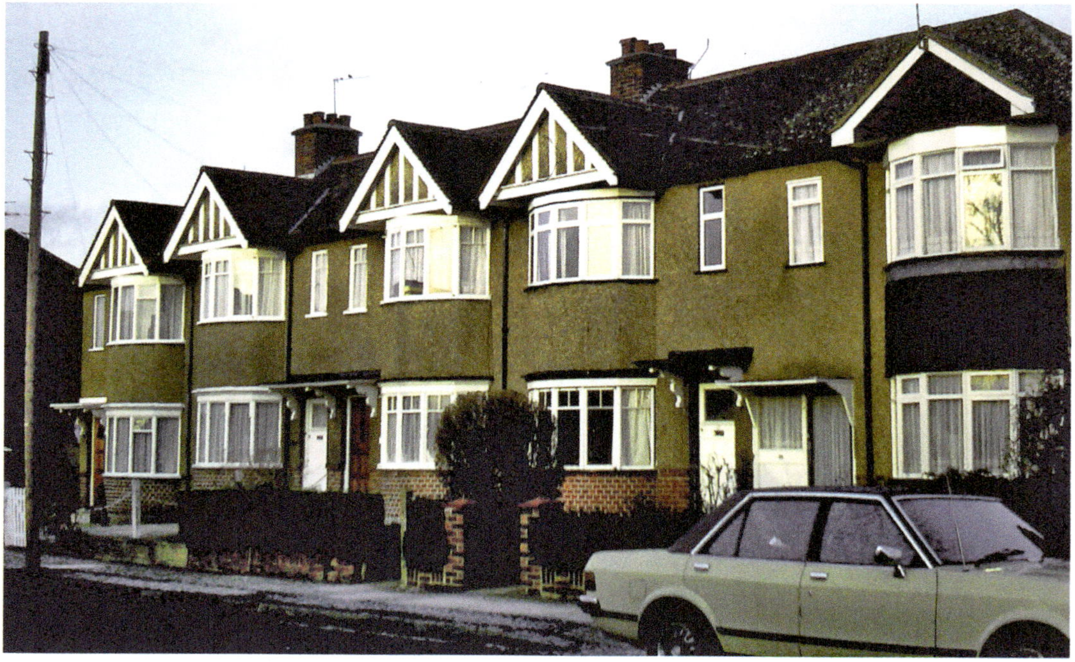

Traditional Manor Homes and Modernity in Park Avenue

George Ball built some 2,200 'Manor Homes', some examples of his work being Lady Bankes School, The Black Bull and St Paul's church, south of Ruislip Manor station, on what had been the fields of Manor Farm, between 1933–39. The building style, brick and tile with timbered gables, was typical of Metroland suburbs. By contrast Connell, Ward & Lucas designed these three houses in Park Avenue, close to Park Wood, in the modernist style in 1936. Labour-saving devices include revolving shelves between kitchen and dining area.

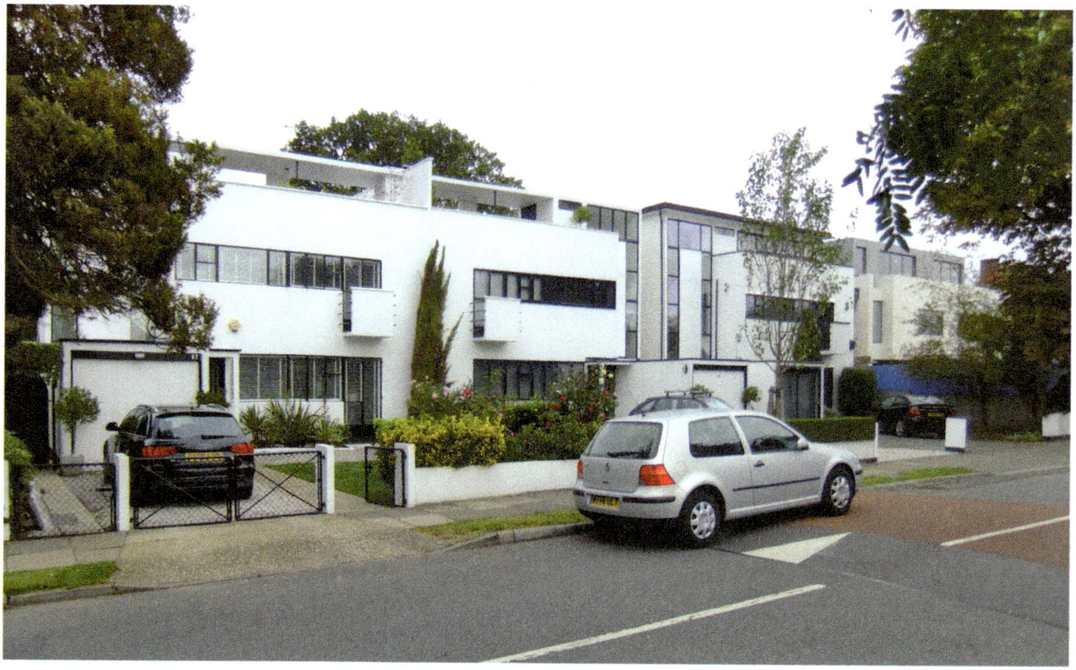

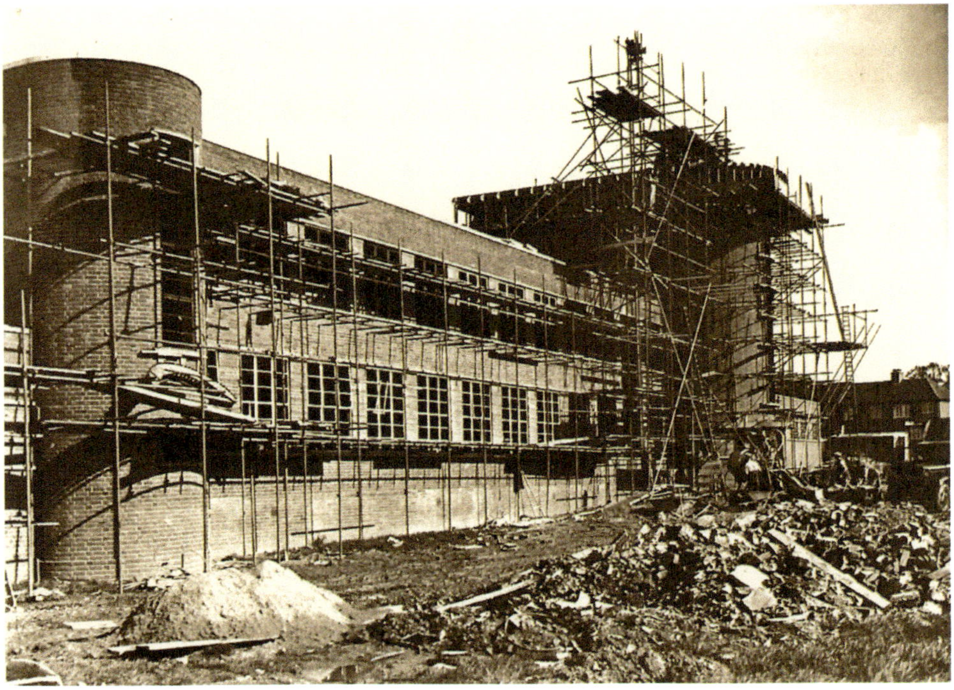

Lady Bankes School, 1935 and 1990

The school opened as Ruislip Manor Council School in temporary accommodation at Victoria Hall, Linden Avenue, on 17 October 1934. The splendid school seen under construction in the top photograph was built around a steel structure. It was designed by Curtis & Burchett in a modernist style much used by the Middlesex County Council and was ready for use in January 1936. It became a Grade II listed building in 1989. A baby clinic with library above, in the same style, was built alongside.

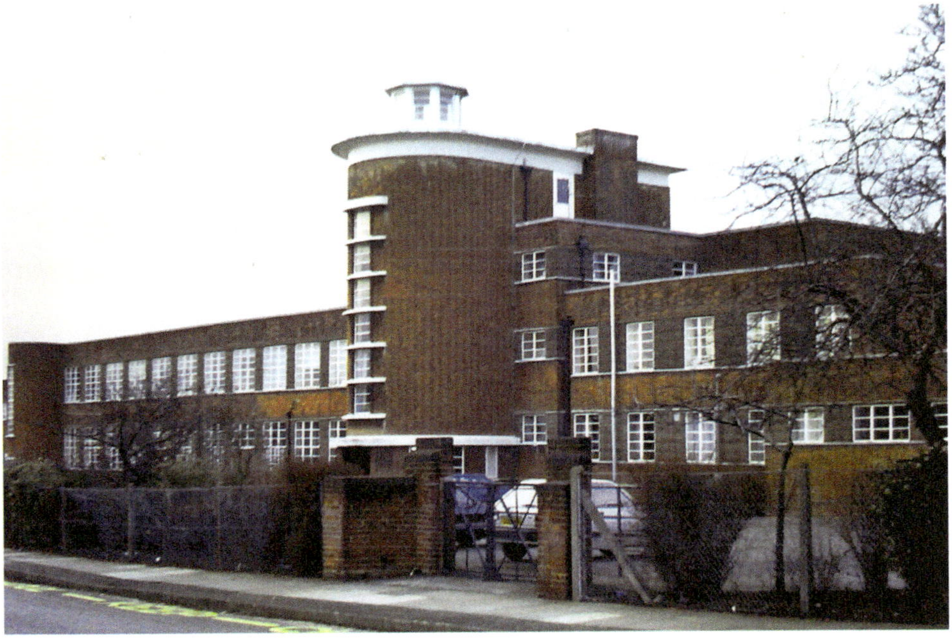

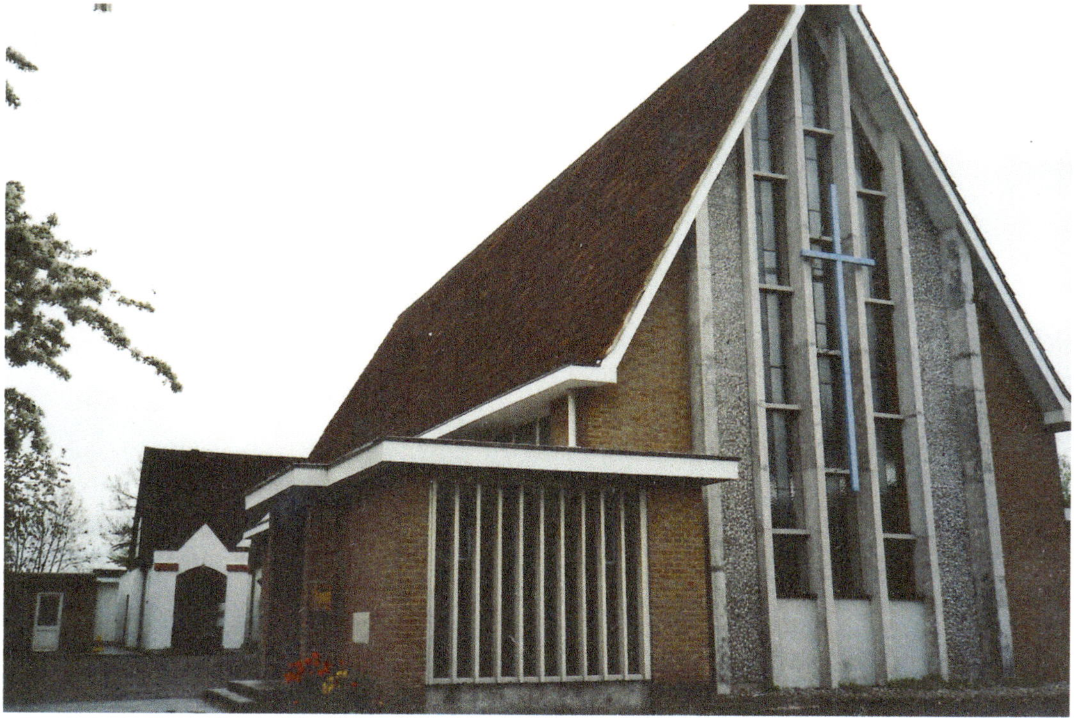

New Churches

These helped stabilise the new communities. Ruislip Methodists met at The Poplars from 1923 and soon built a church alongside, which is now the church hall. The building pictured was opened in 1962. The first Baptist church was the hut seen below, opened in 1937, a far cry from the large, modern building that now dominates West Way, Ruislip Manor, which has recently celebrated its seventy-fifth anniversary.

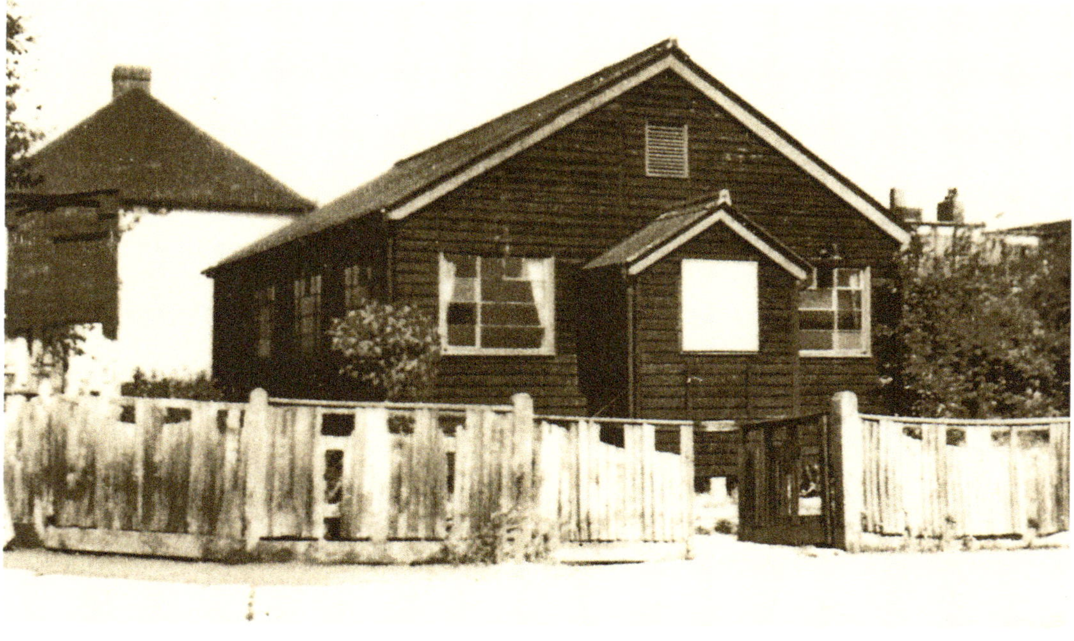

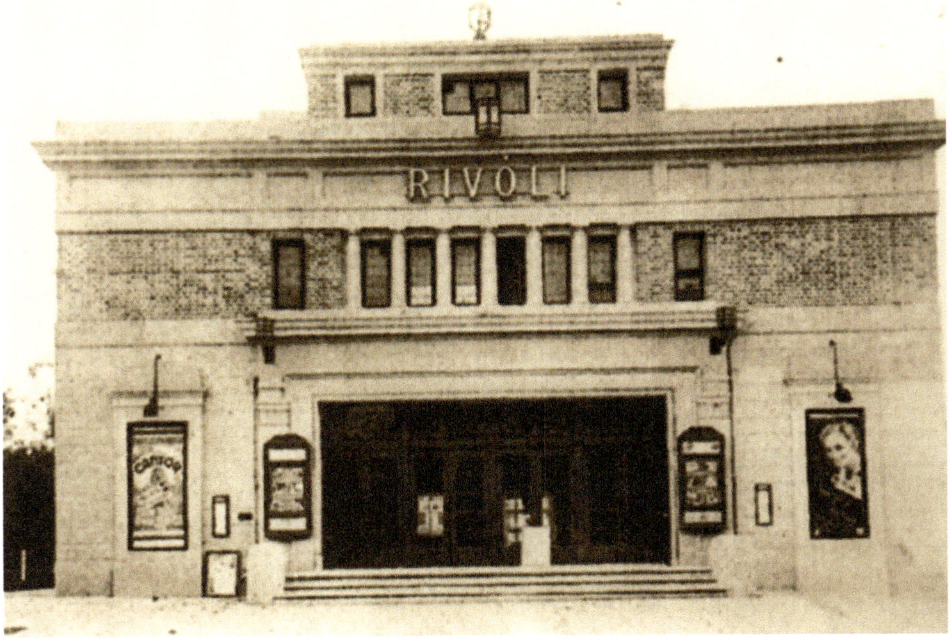

Cinemas Provided Entertainment for the Masses

Ruislip acquired cinemas: the Rivoli cinema in 1929, situated at the bottom of Ickenham Road, and the Astoria on the High Street five years later. The Rivoli was replaced by Sainsbury's supermarket in 1966 and a block of flats now stands on the site. Ruislip Operatic Society used the Astoria for its shows. The cinema had a makeover in 1967, acquiring a rather futuristic façade and being renamed the Embassy. It lasted until 1981.

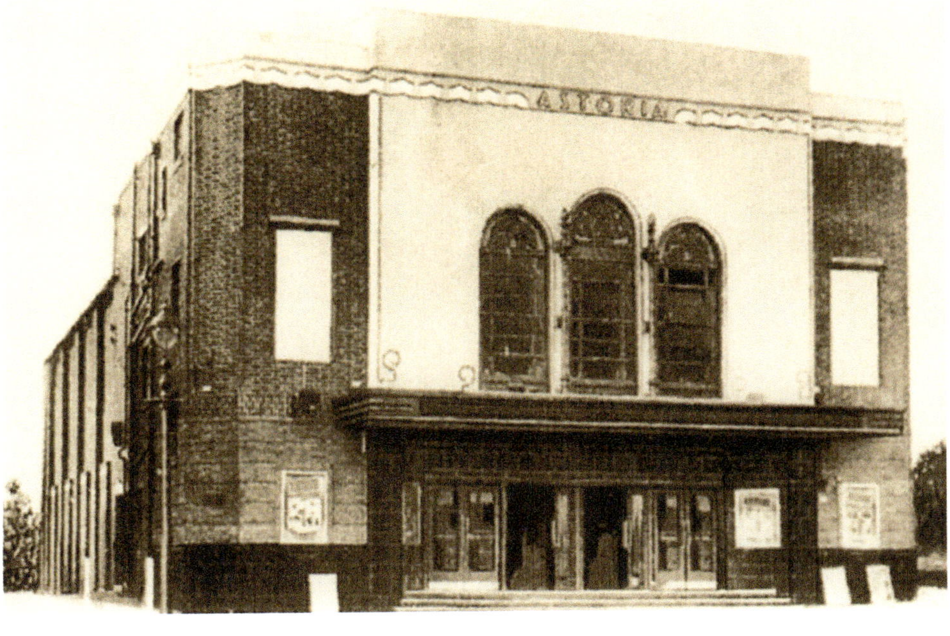

The Manor, Centre of the Community

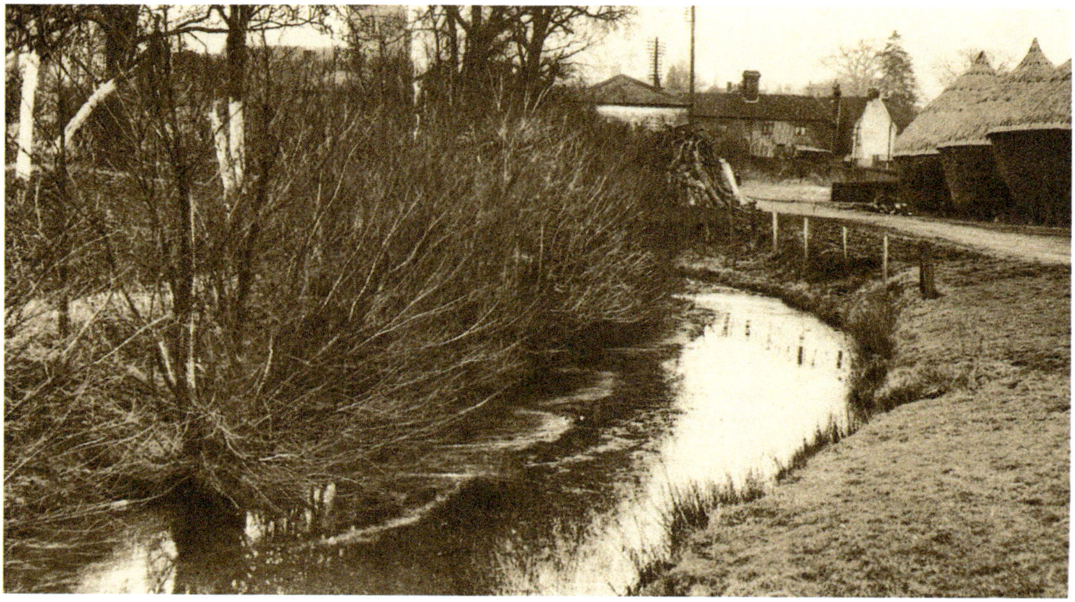

Motte-and-Bailey Site

The earthworks at Manor Farm suggest that there was a motte-and-bailey castle here in the late eleventh century. This 1932 picture shows the water-filled moat surrounding the motte. St Martin's church can be discerned in the distance. The hayricks stand on what is now a bowling green. The Abbey of Bec's priory stood in the bailey. The buildings were replaced in 1506 by the present Manor Farm House, viewed here from across the motte.

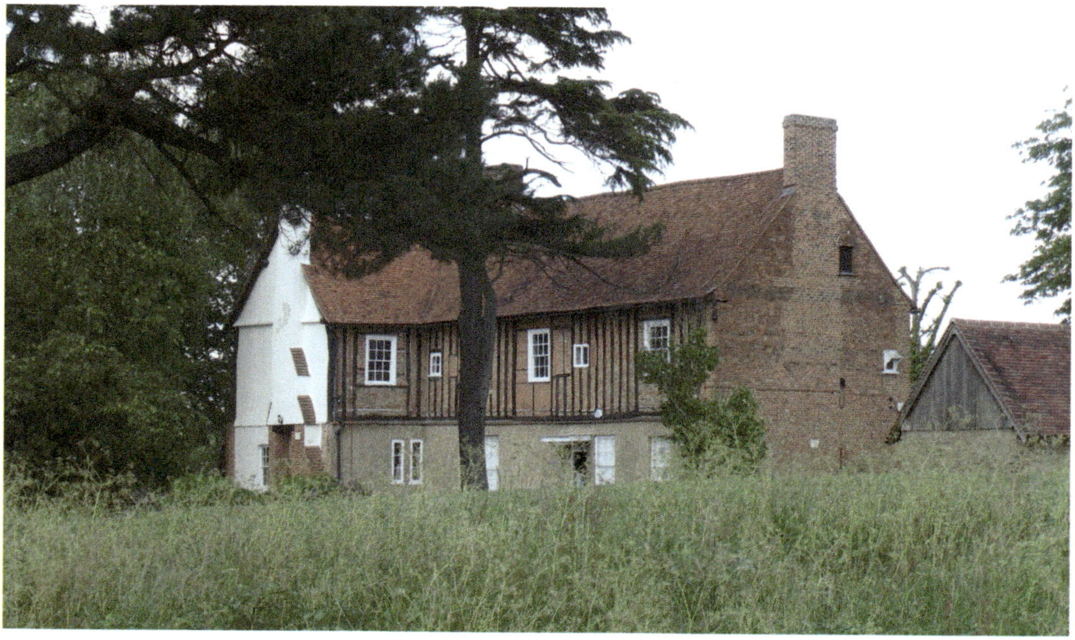

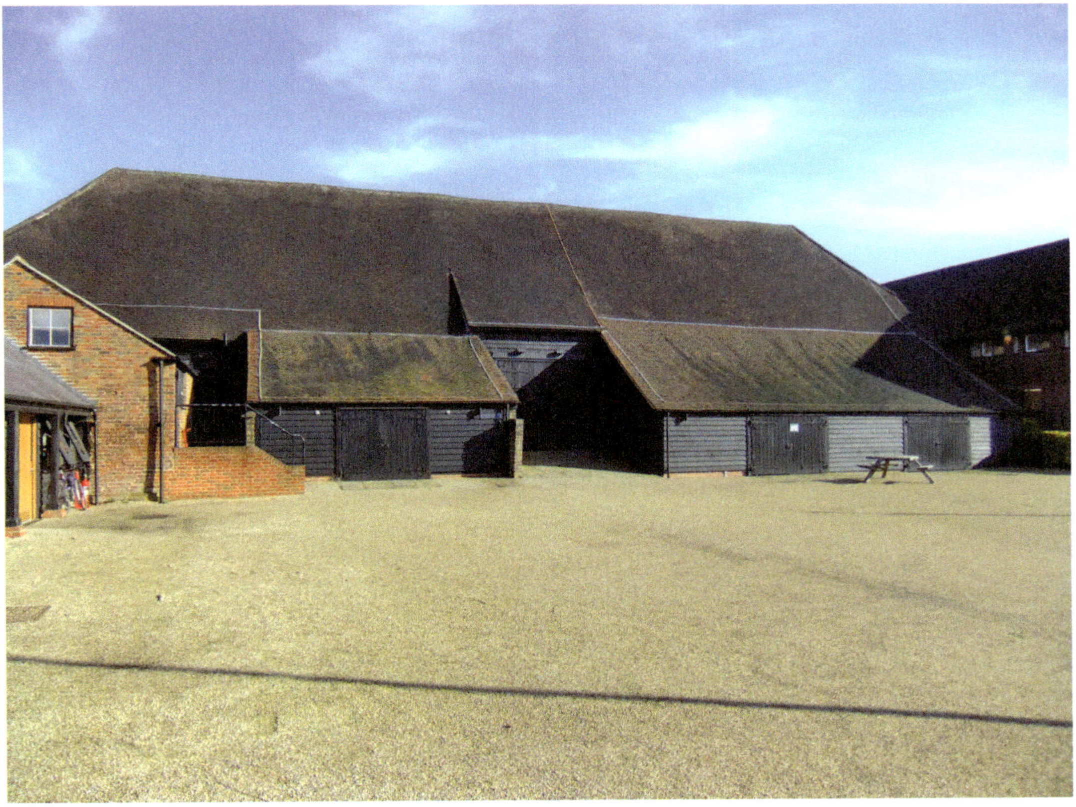

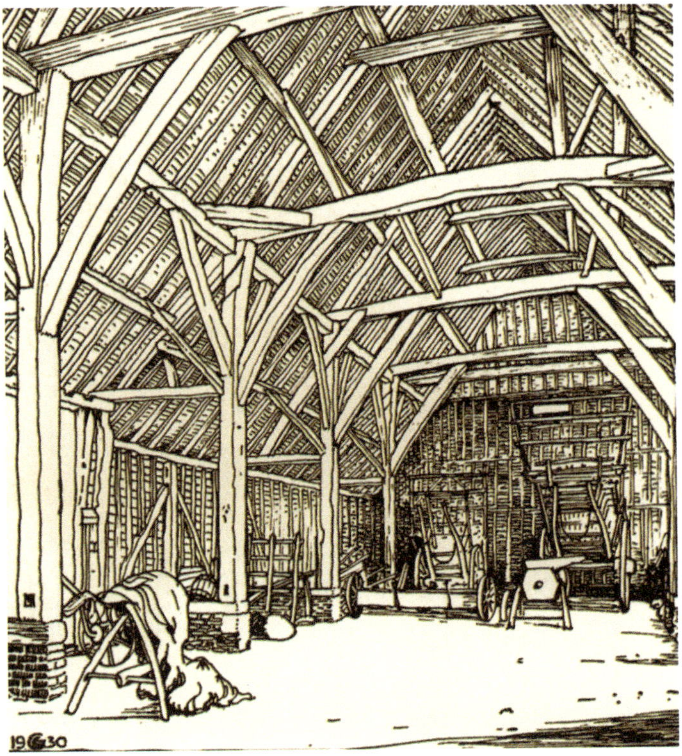

The Great Barn

Two views of the late thirteenth-century Great Barn, the only building to survive from the time of the Abbey of Bec's overlordship. The modern picture shows the west front with modern additions on either side of the wagon doors.

The drawing depicts the Great Barn in its latter days as an agricultural building. It has an aisle on either side of the central nave, giving it a church-like appearance. It is the oldest timber-framed barn in the Greater London area and contains interesting features of early carpentry such as passing braces and lap joints.

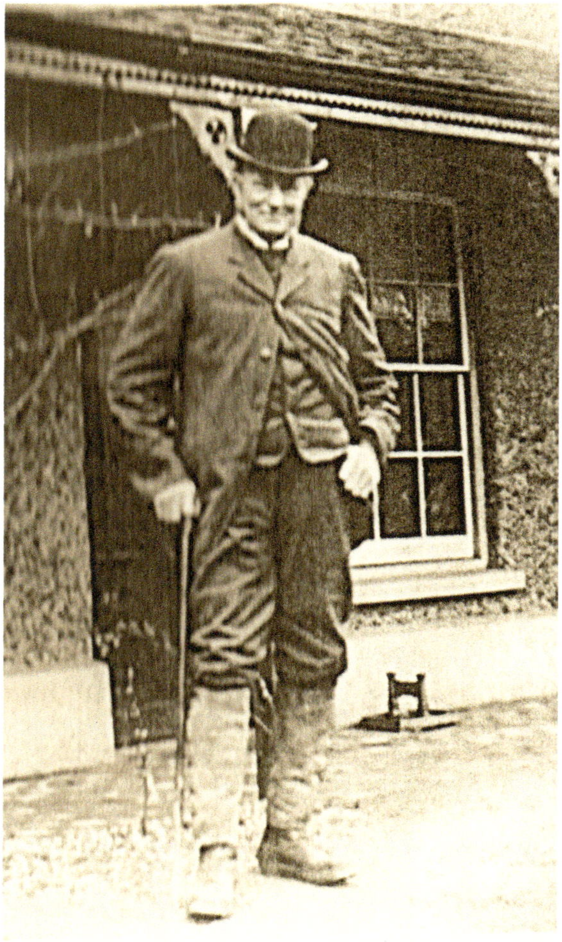

Henry James Ewer and the Manor House in Late Victorian Times

The house served as lodgings for the provost and other college officials on their occasional visits to Ruislip, as a venue for Manor Courts, and as home for the man who farmed the demesne. It was known as Ruislip Court until the mid-nineteenth century, when it became Manor Farm. When it was built in 1506 there was a hall, where the courts were held, a parlour, kitchen, buttery, and entry on the ground floor. The provost's chamber above his parlour had a gardrobe (privy) discharging into the moat. These self-contained facilities were probably used by the farmer and his family when no officials were in residence.

From 1872 Manor Farm was let direct to tenant farmers. Henry James Ewer (1846–1916) came in 1886 and his son, Richard Ewer, was the last farmer, leaving in 1932 when much of the farmland had already been sold for suburban development.

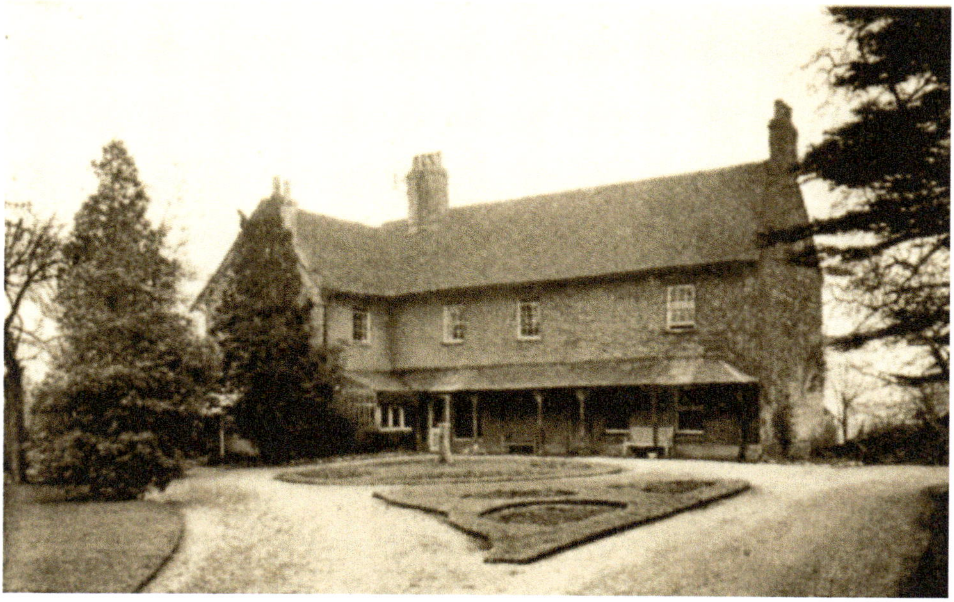

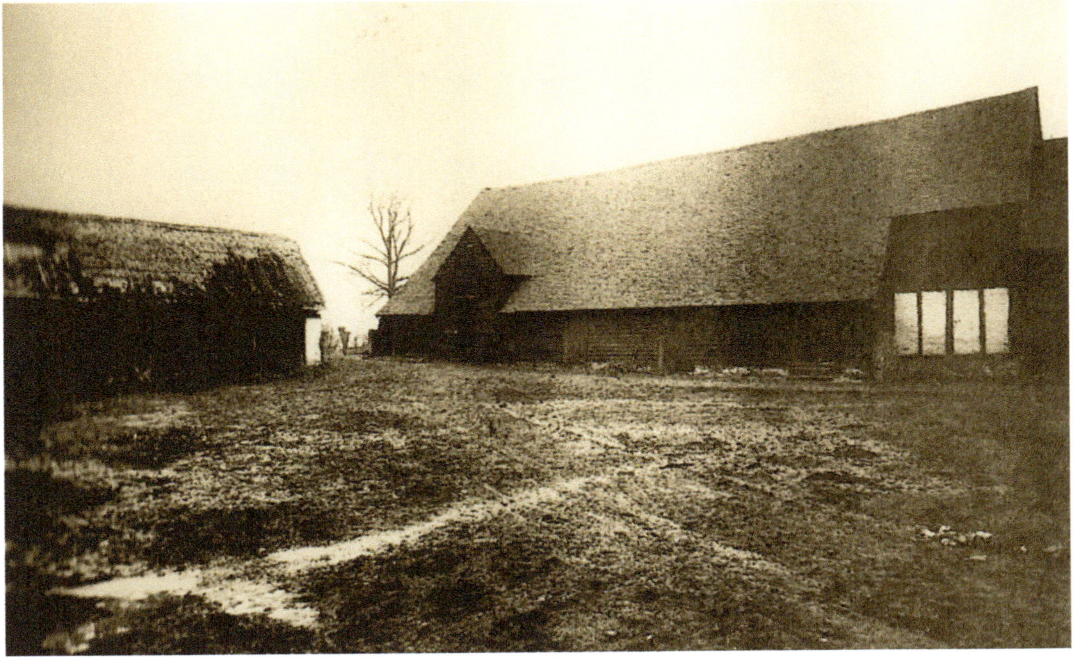

Sixteenth-Century Little Barn and Nineteenth-Century Cowbyre

The farm buildings, seen above, standing in a muddy courtyard, were eventually brought into public use after Manor Farm was given to RNUDC for the people of Ruislip in 1932. The lower picture shows the same scene shortly after the Little Barn had been converted into a magnificent library in 1937. The Cowbyre, unusual in being the only thatched building there, was used by Ruislip Horticultural Society.

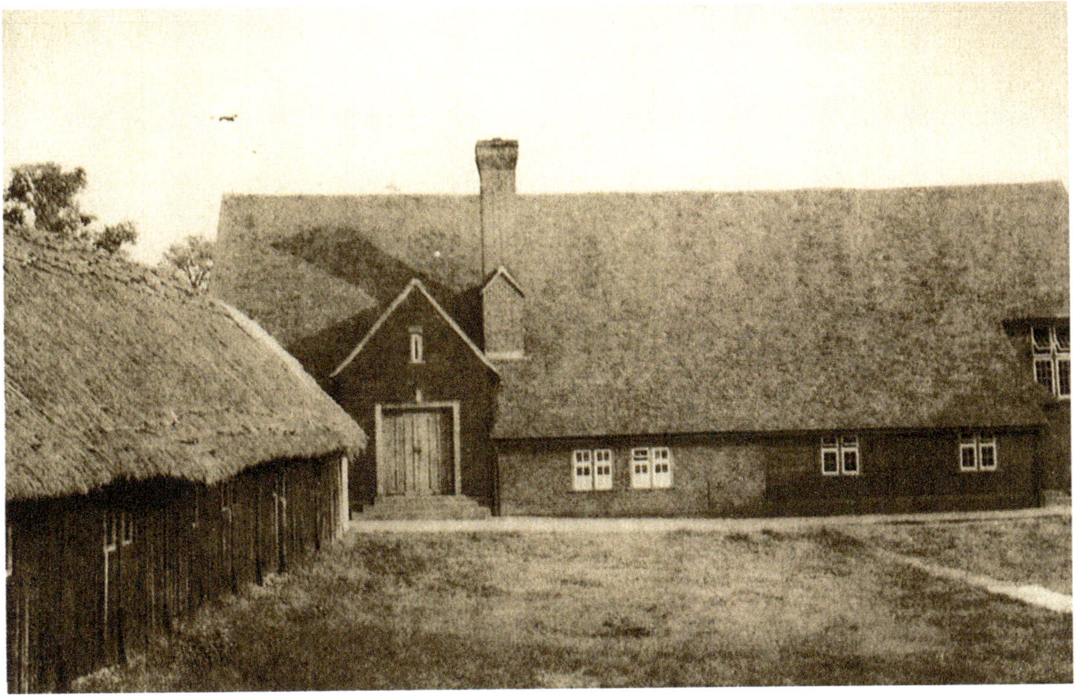

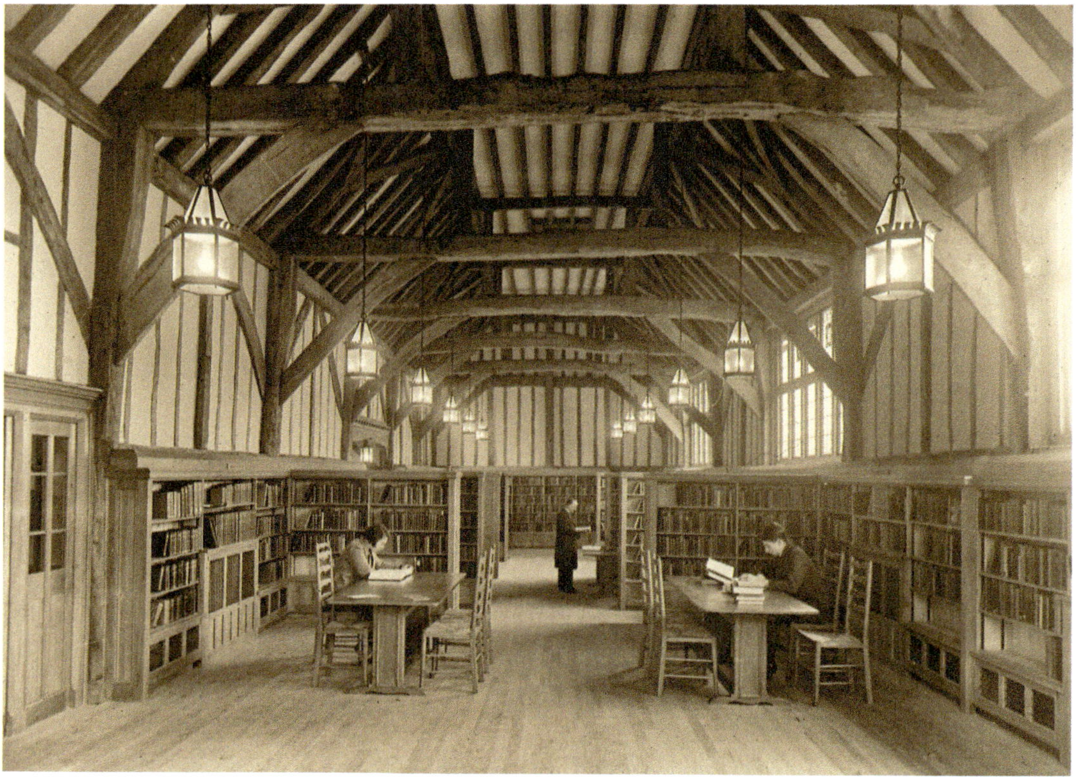

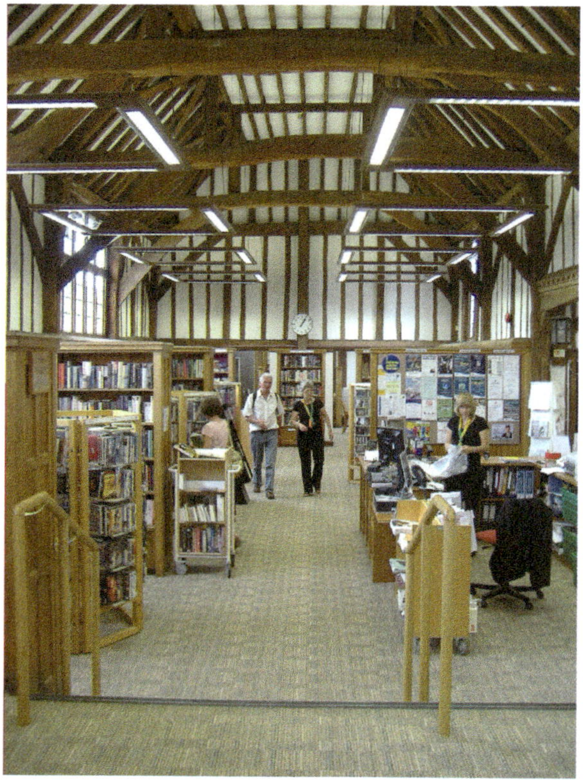

Manor Farm Library, 1937 and 2008
The new library was given oak shelving, oak-veneered tables, and ladder-backed and rush-bottomed chairs, to be in keeping with the ancient timbers. The windows have stained-glass inserts with motifs relating to the history and purpose of the building. They include the arms of King's College and the County of Middlesex.

Modern furniture and lighting have transformed the library, shown here at its reopening after refurbishment in 2008.

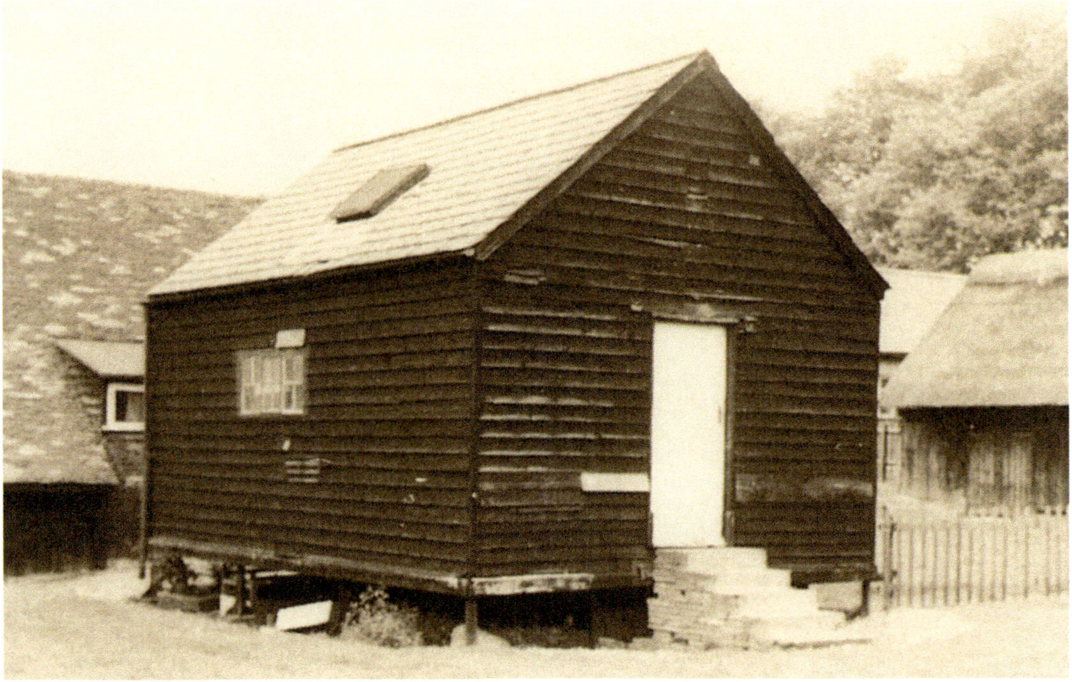

The Inner Courtyard

The granary, built on cast-iron staddles rather than the traditional stone mushrooms, was built in Edwardian times and was unfortunately destroyed following a lightning strike in 1980. It was being used by Ruislip Operatic Society to store scenery at the time. The eighteenth-century cow shed and dairy behind has been used as a guide hut since the 1930s. The Cowbyre, which had already been burnt down in 1979, was replaced with a popular exhibition centre and café.

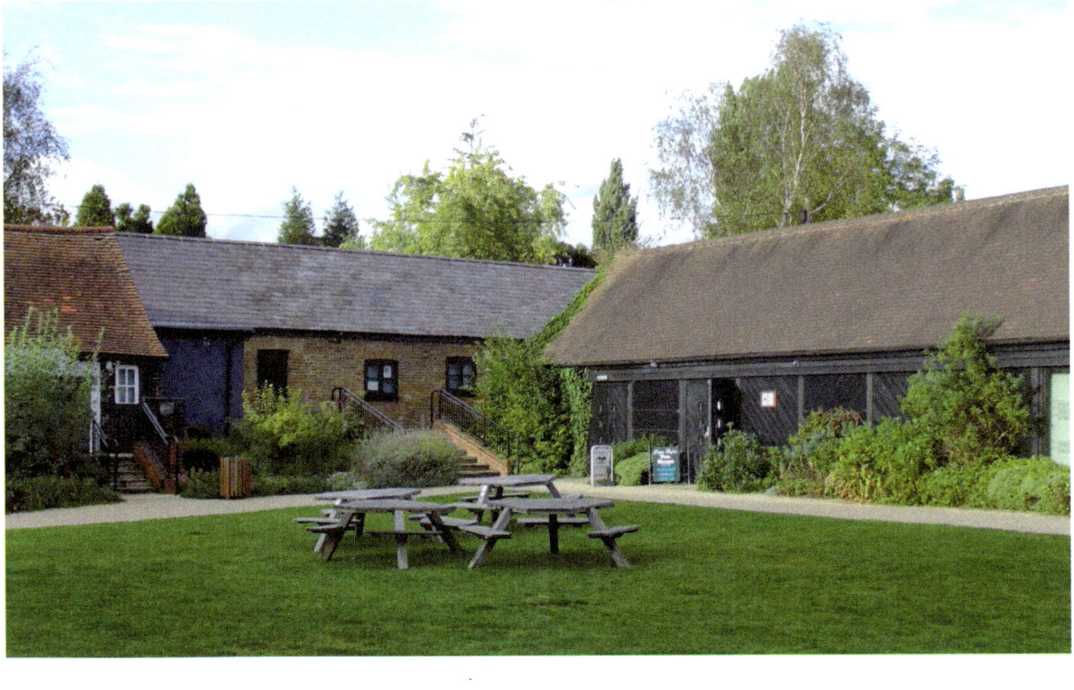

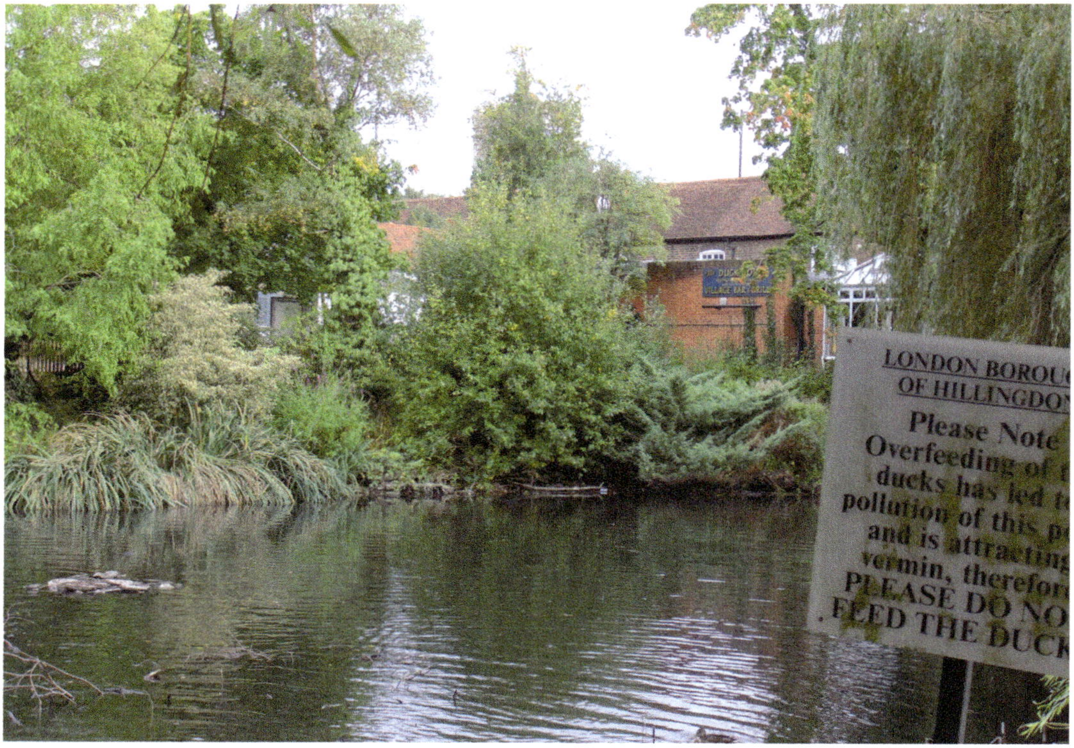

Duck Pond

Now the haunt of wild fowl, the pond was known as the Horse Pool in the sixteenth century, presumably because the farm horses slaked their thirst there at the end of the day. The lower picture shows a unit of the Territorial Army swimming in it during the First World War. The haystacks in the rickyard and the Little Barn can be seen across the pond.

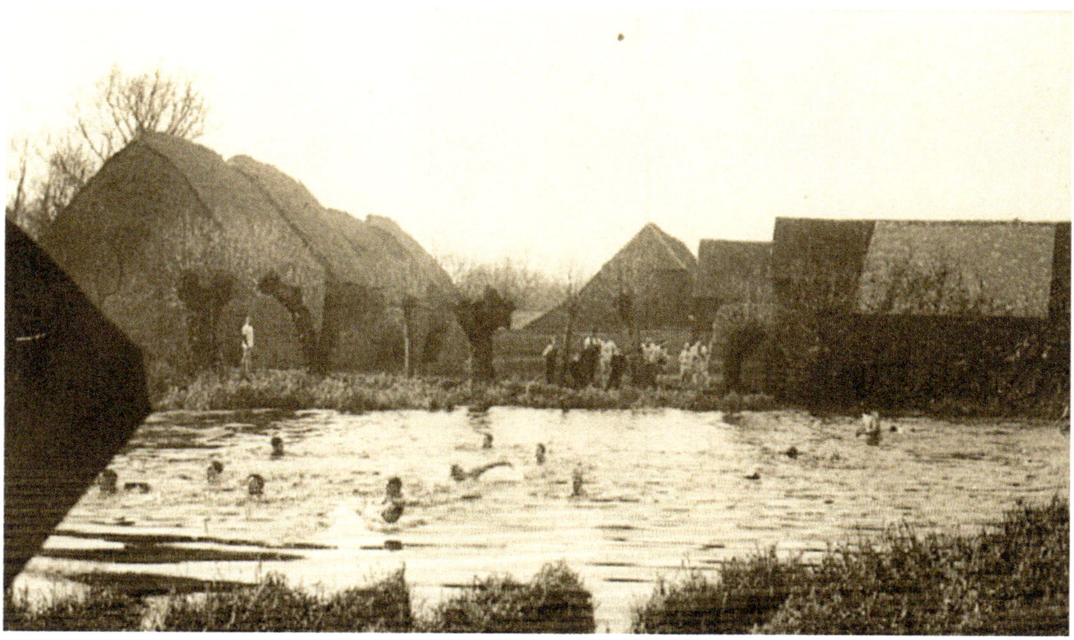

Archaeology
Members of the Ruislip, Northwood & Eastcote Local History Society excavating a trench across the ditch at the northern end of the Manor Farm site in 1976. The ditch was once considered to be part of a village earthwork that surrounded an early settlement, but is now believed more likely to have originated as an extension of the enigmatic earthwork called Grim's Dyke, which was probably dug in the pagan Saxon period. Finds of Roman potsherds – one being a piece of a mortarium from the Roman kilns at Brockley Hill, Stanmore – and burnt daub with grooves for wattles, confirm that the ditch itself is post-Roman in date.

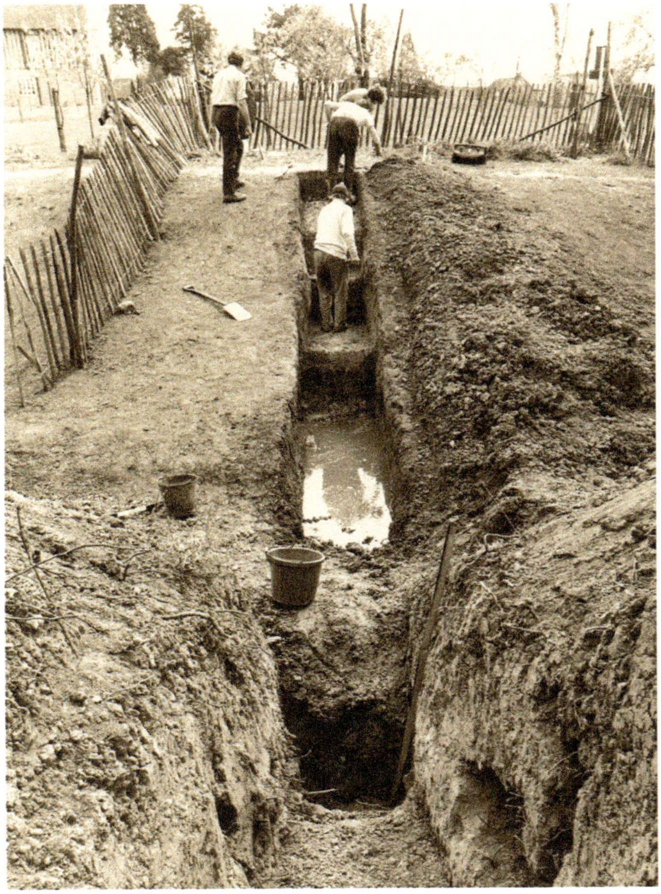

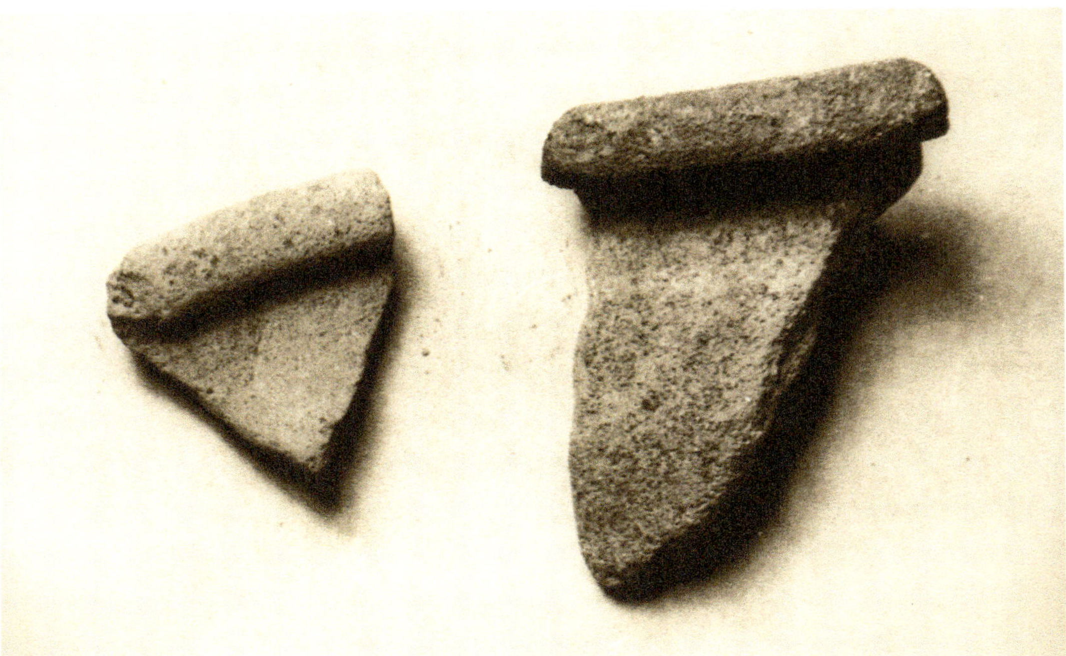

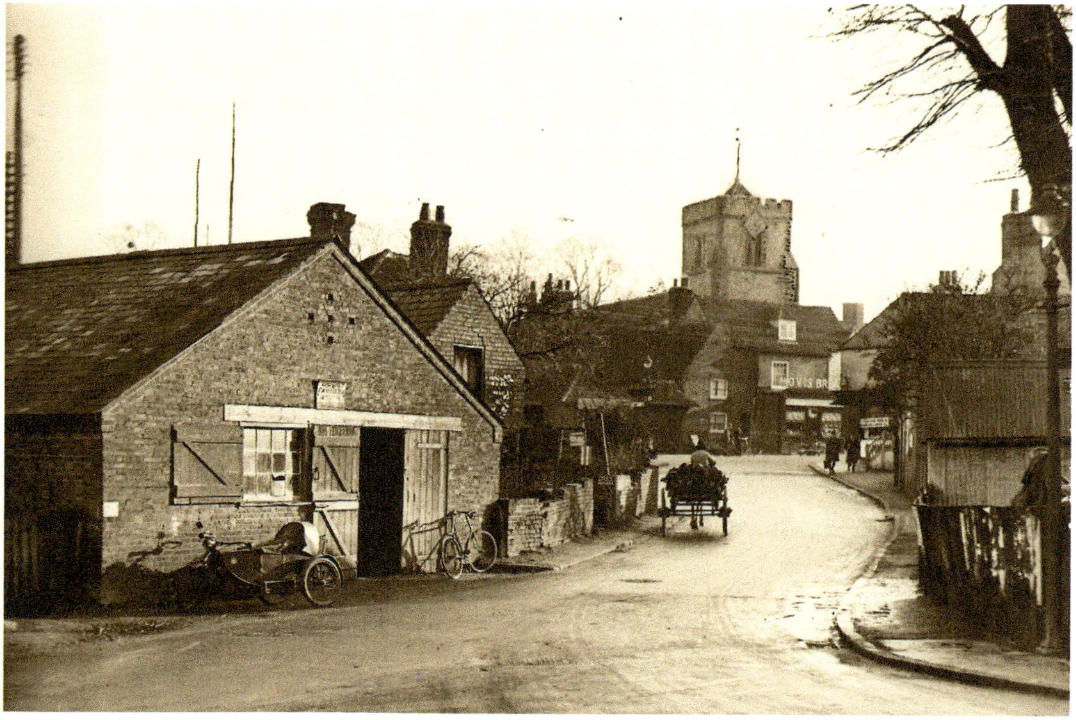

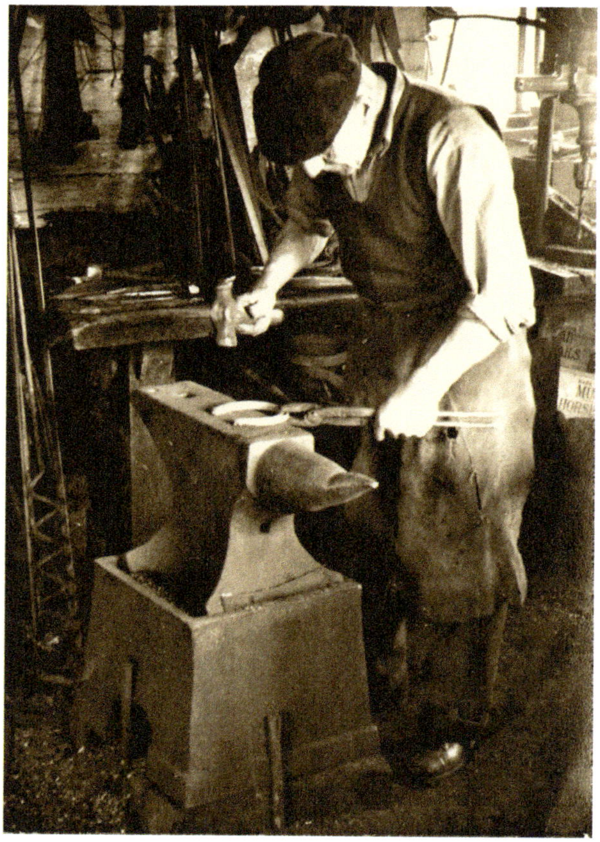

The Smithy

As early as 1435 there are references to a smithy at the Court Gate, when Emma Smith, who was probably a widow, was there. Thomas Smith was enlarging his forge near the church at the same time. Around 1910, when this picture was taken, Ted Doe's smithy was just around the corner in Bury Street, backing onto the pond. Road widening in 1930 removed this smithy, but it was replaced by a smaller one further down the street. Mr G. Hyan is seen working there in 1953. A peripatetic farrier was still visiting in the late 1960s to shoe horses from local riding stables, but the building has since been demolished.

St Martin's Church and Churchyard

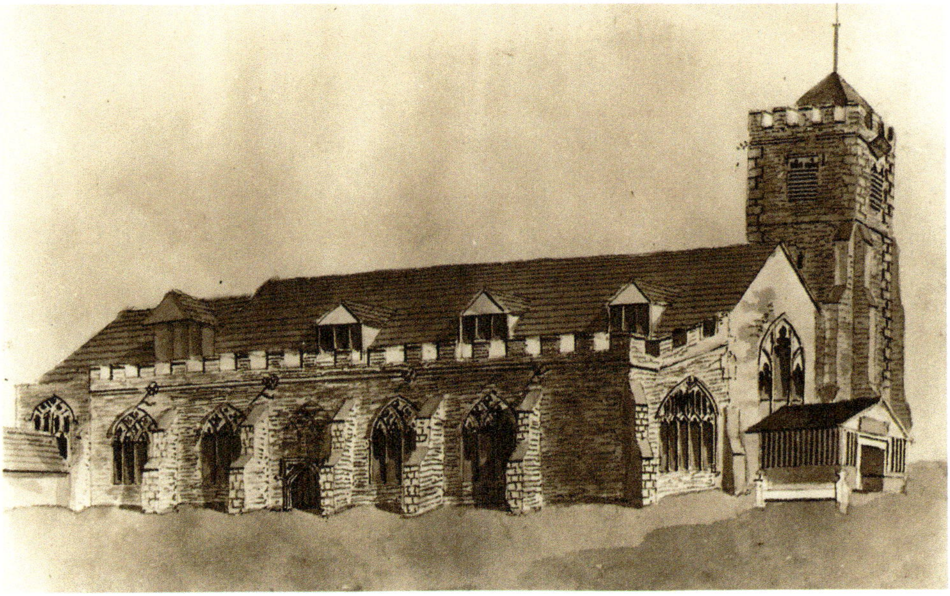

St Martin's Church, 1795 and 1970

The priest mentioned in the Domesday Book presumably served a church on this site, but the present St Martin's dates mainly from the mid-thirteenth century. It was not only an ecclesiastical centre, but by the early seventeenth century the group of leading parishioners known as the Vestry, after the place where meetings were held, administered the Poor Law and set local rates. The 1795 picture shows the vicar's vestry sticking out from the chancel and dormer windows lighting the nave.

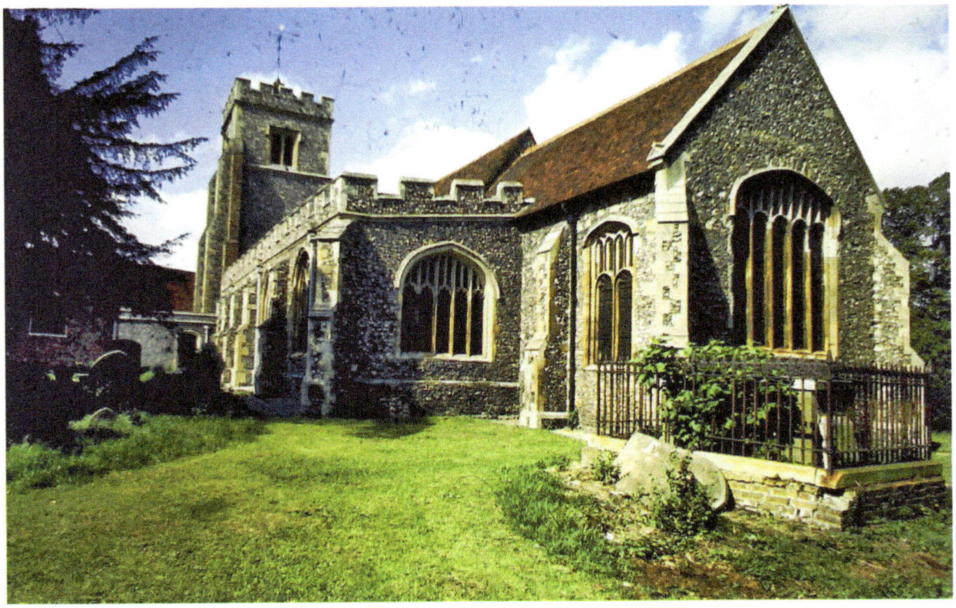

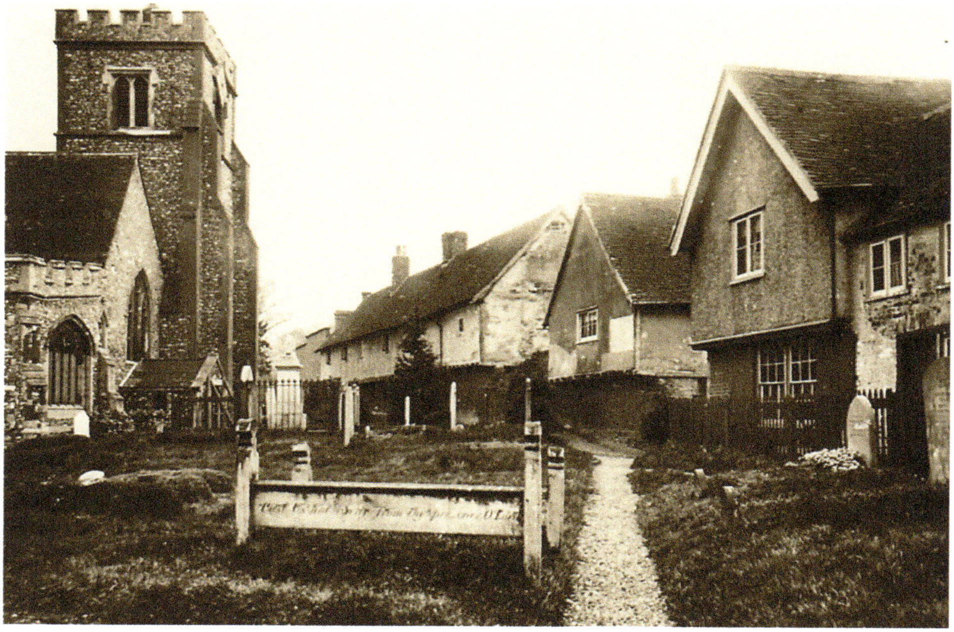

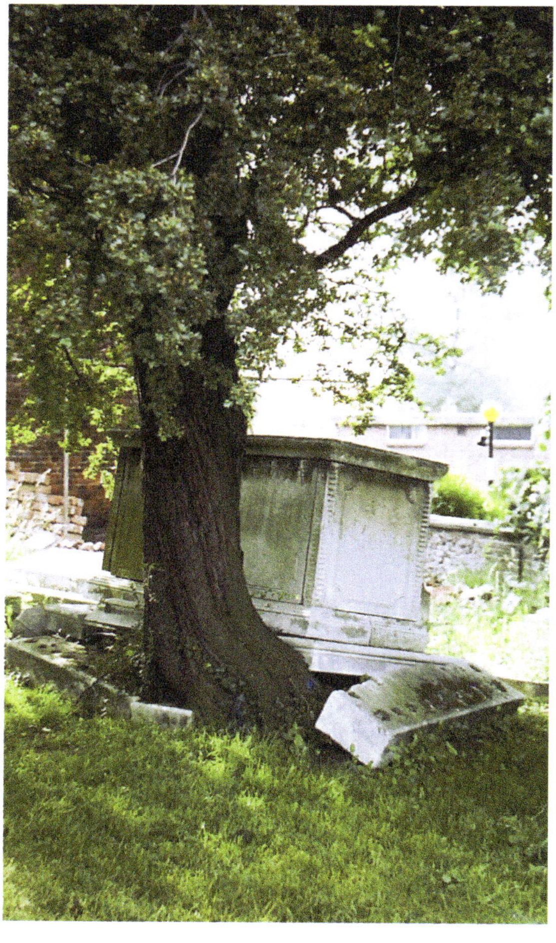

Church and Churchyard, c. 1860
The churchyard had many wooden grave-boards which ran lengthwise along the graves. 'Cast us not away from thy presence O Lord' is written on the one in the centre of the picture. The porch is in a bad way and supported by wooden buttresses. The building on the right is the Old Bell, to which Vestry meetings sometimes adjourned in the eighteenth century.

The chest tomb of John Davis of 'Berry Street', who died in 1790, is in a restrained Classical style. The grave has been stabilised since this photograph was taken in 1979.

About 7 per cent of the people buried at St Martin's between 1700–1900 were strangers, the largest proportion coming from London, Westminster, Lambeth, Paddington and Chelsea. It may be that as the city and urban churchyards became overcrowded and insanitary, those who could afford the expense buried their dead in the less populous areas surrounding the capital. Very few seem to have had local connections.

St Martin's Bells

The earliest reference to bells at St Martin's is in a will of 1463, when Thomas Bettz left money for their repair. There were six bells by the eighteenth century. James Ewer noted in his diary 'Ruislip bells was new run in March 1802 and com home the 6th and the Tenner was filled with Strong Bear and hild 300 quarts'. It must have been an occasion of general rejoicing. Several bells were recast in 1878, some at the expense of Lady Hume-Campbell of Highgrove. The chime bell seen here was recast again a century later, when the vicar was Kenneth Toovey, and Denis Hills and Alan Seymour were churchwardens.

The bells hang in the tower that was added to the church in stages in the fifteenth century. A new porch was built in 1896. It still stands with a statue of St Martin dressed in his robes as Bishop of Tours in a niche above the door. Stained-glass windows, designed by C. E. Kemp, showing St Martin cutting his cloak in half to give to a beggar, and the saint's subsequent vision, were placed in the chancel in September 1901 in memory of the Revd Thomas Marsh Everett, vicar 1878–1900.

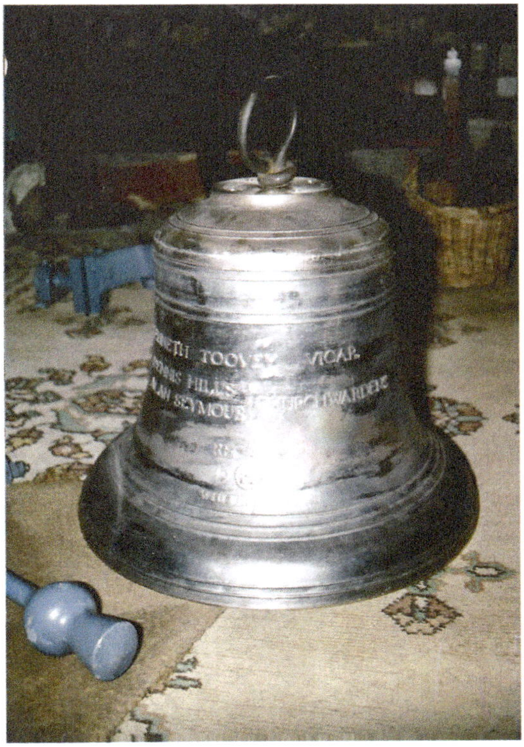

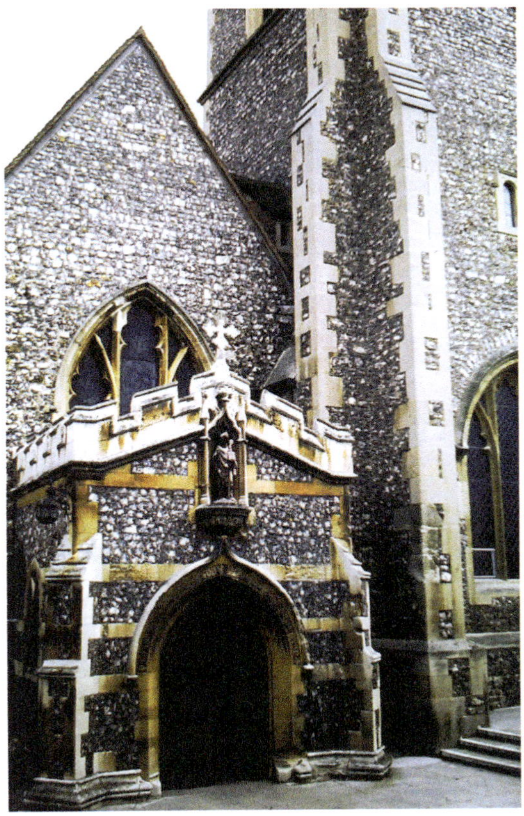

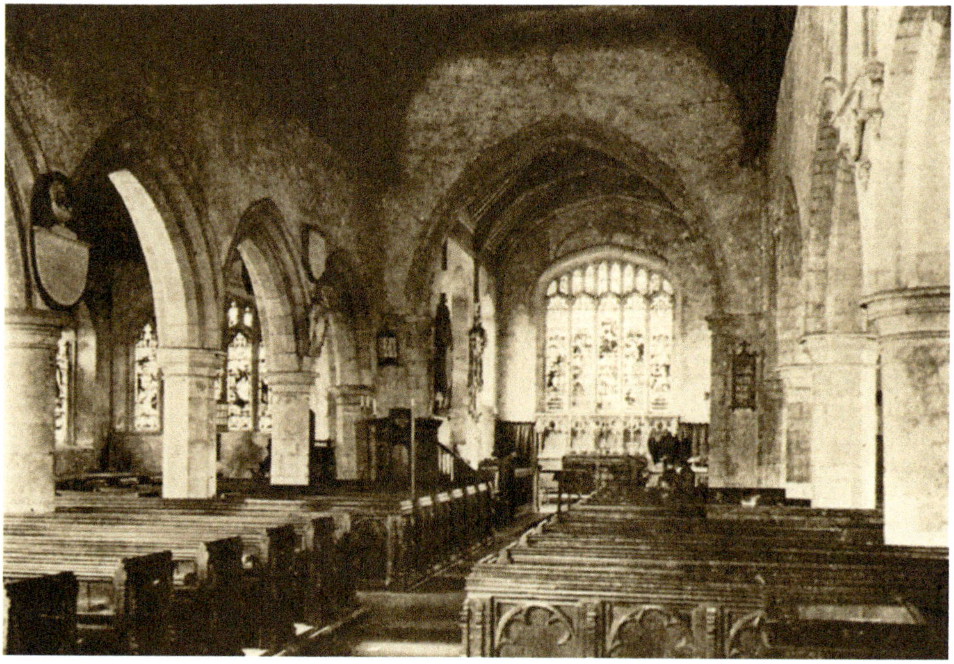

The Church, 1932 and 2012
The Victorian reredos was designed in 1872 by Robert Lewis Roumieu, uncle of the curate, J. J. Roumieu, who published a history of the parish in 1870. Several parts of the church have been reordered in recent years, especially at the west end where the font has been moved to create more space. The modern rood was erected in 1957 in memory of Mrs Gower. Some medieval wall paintings can be seen above the arcading.

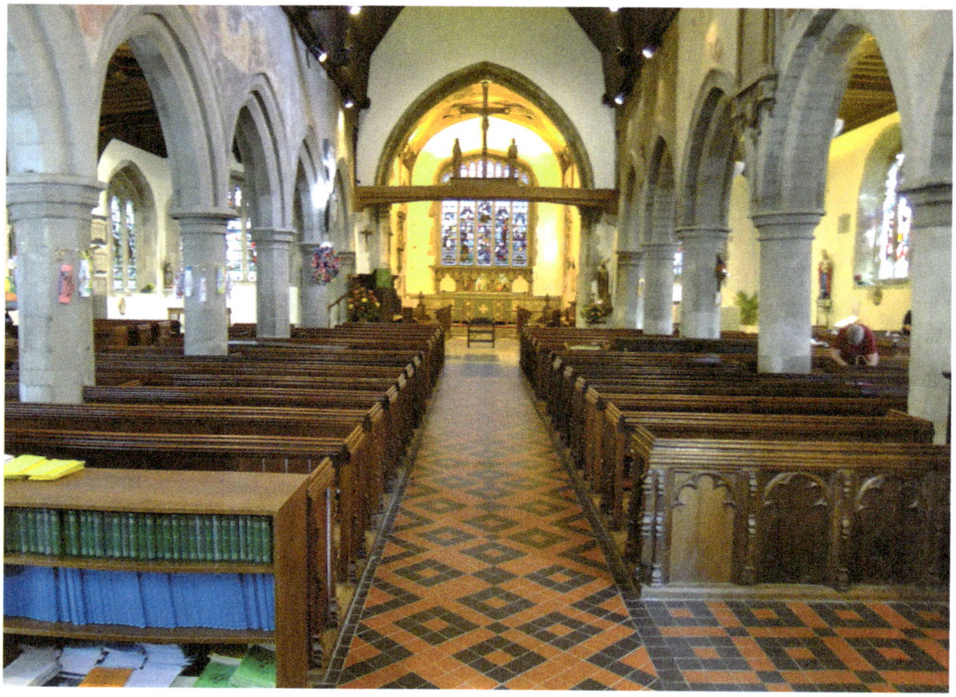

Fine Woodwork

A handsome livery cupboard hangs in the north aisle. It is dated 1697 and is the gift of Jeremiah Bright, son of a former vicar. Twelve loaves of bread were to be placed on the shelves each Sunday 'for ever'. The custom continued until 1955. There were other benefactions made over the years to assist poorer members of the parish. Richard Cogges left two closes of land in Fore Street in 1717 to the churchwardens, who were to let them and distribute the income to the needy. When Elizabeth Rogers of Eastcote House died in 1803, she directed her executors to place £380 in 3 per cent consols. From the proceeds the vicar was to receive two guineas on the first Sunday after Easter, provided that he had preached a sermon on Good Friday. The residue was to go to those poor families who had most regularly attended divine service. The charities are now part of the Ruislip Combined Charity and gifts are made to individuals and suitable organisations at Christmas time.

The chest below, one of two at St Martin's, was originally used for the storage of valuables, liturgical books and, from 1538 onwards, parish registers. This one in the nave is almost certainly made of elm. It has iron bonds and there are locks for both sides of the double lid. It possibly dates from the early fifteenth century.

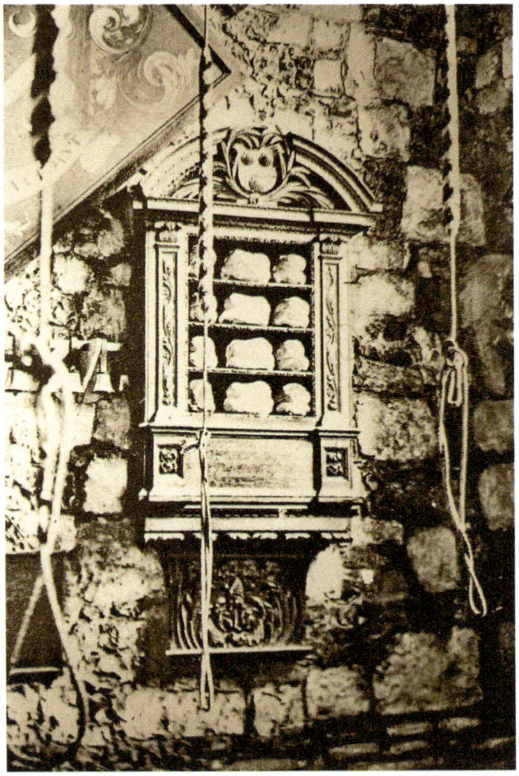

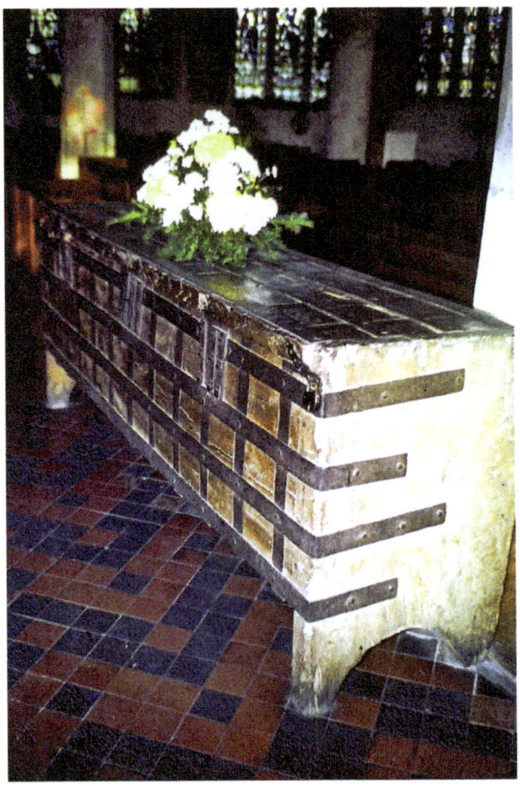

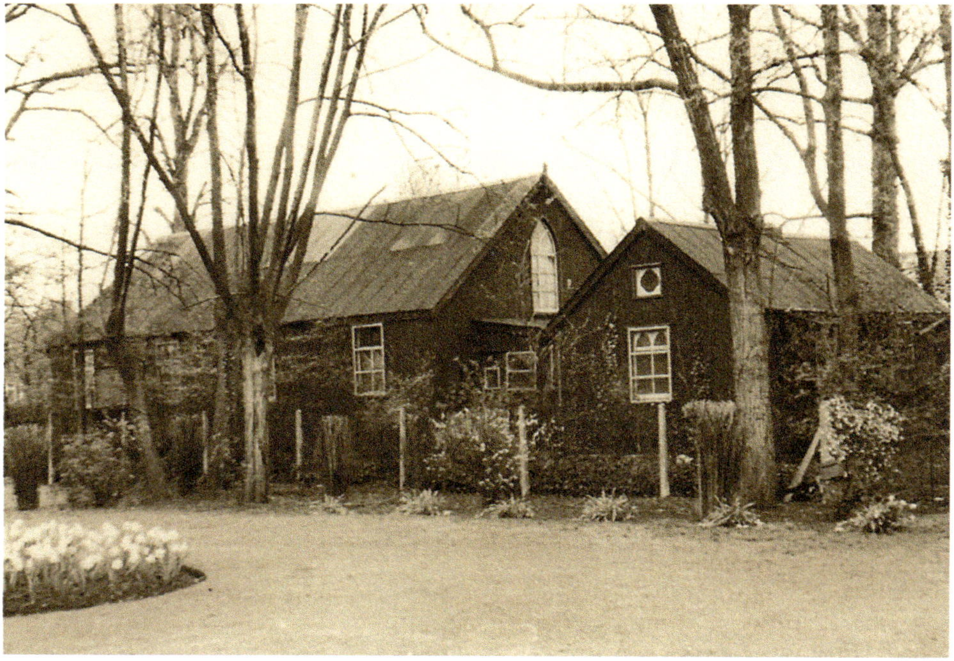

Church Rooms

The Church Rooms in Bury Street were the gift of Eleanor Warrender of Highgrove in 1911. They served as a hall for social activities, lantern-slide lectures, drama and exhibitions until 1969 when the new hall, shown below, was built in the graveyard near the south-east end of the church. A number of old gravestones had to be removed. Several were eighteenth-century headstones. The one commemorating 'Tho Prest late balef to Ralph Hawtrey Esq' is decorated with a simple classically carved pattern of an hour glass, a *memento mori.*

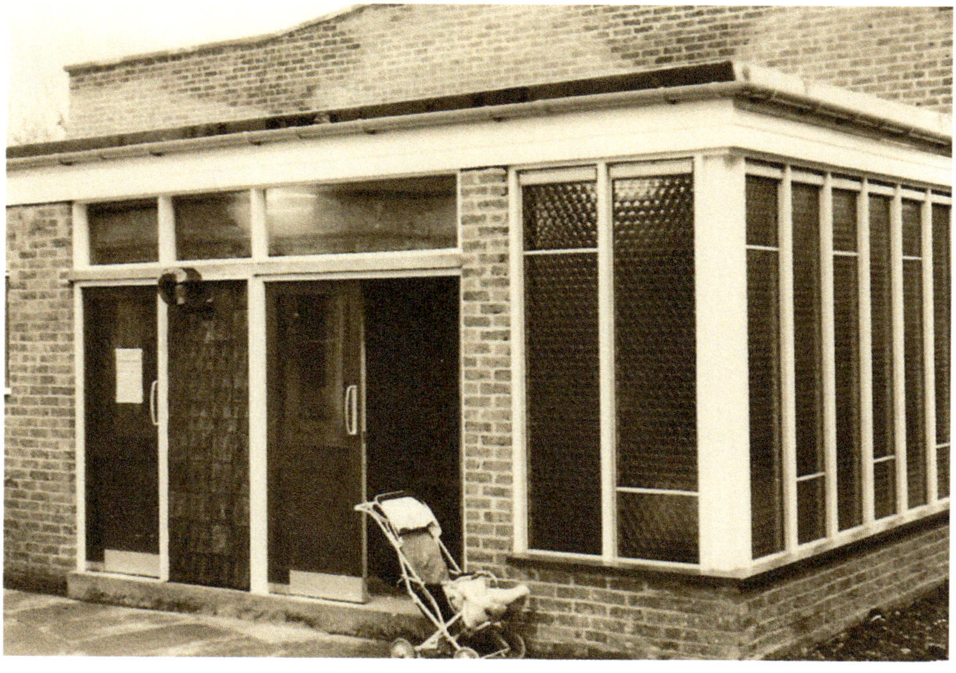

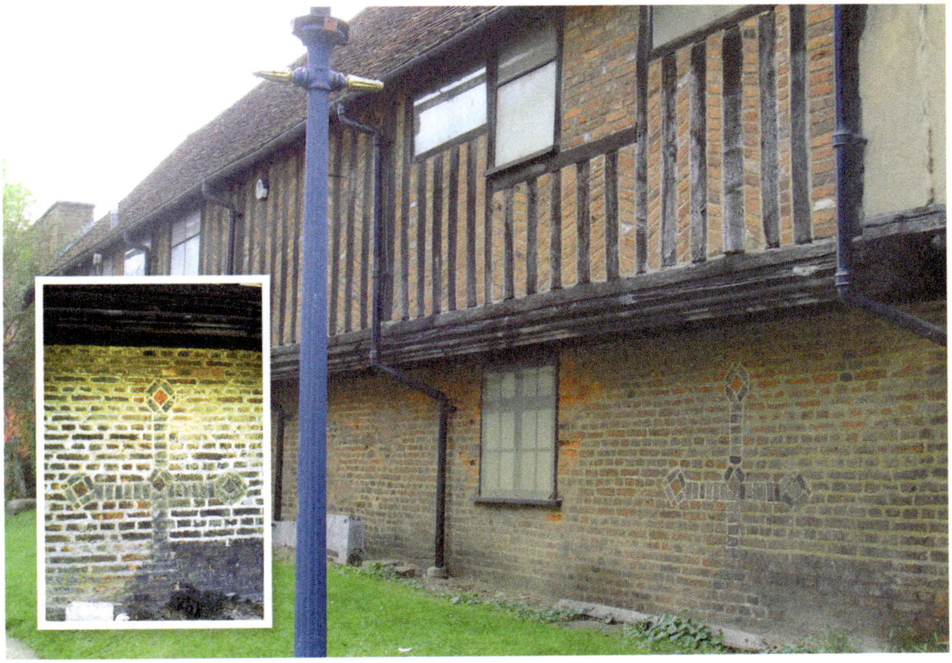

Church Cottages

The back of Church Cottages shows their most prestigious face to the church. The upper storey, which is closely studded with brick nogging, has a jetty supported by a moulded bressumer. Directly opposite the west door there is a cross set in blue headers, and in most of the bays diaper work and other patterns can be traced. The Church Cottages belong to the Ruislip Village Trust, which was set up at the instigation of Mr Tait of King Edwards Road in 1931 to protect this ancient building. The jetty at the back of the Old Bell has a carved brace with a floral decoration.

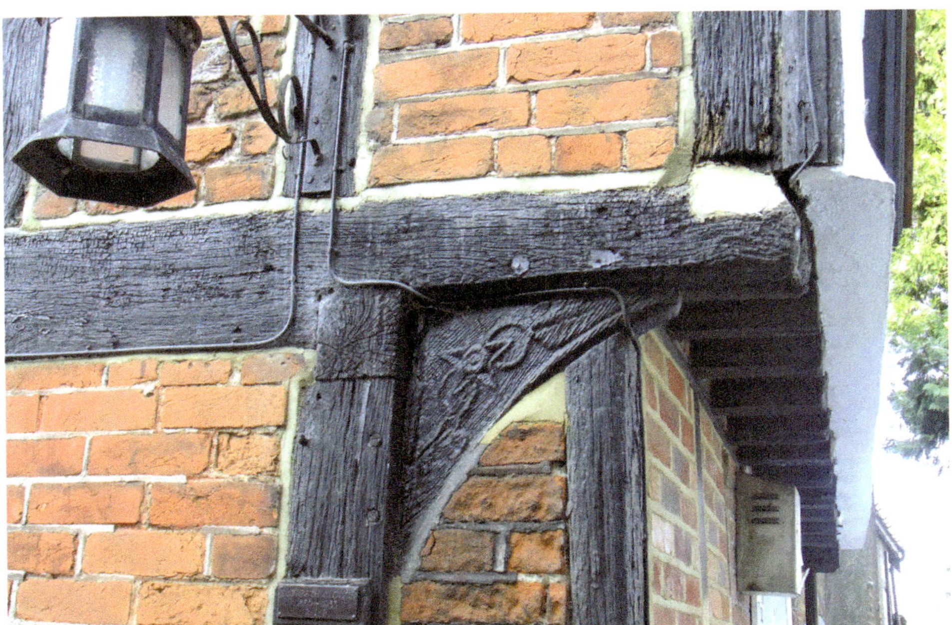

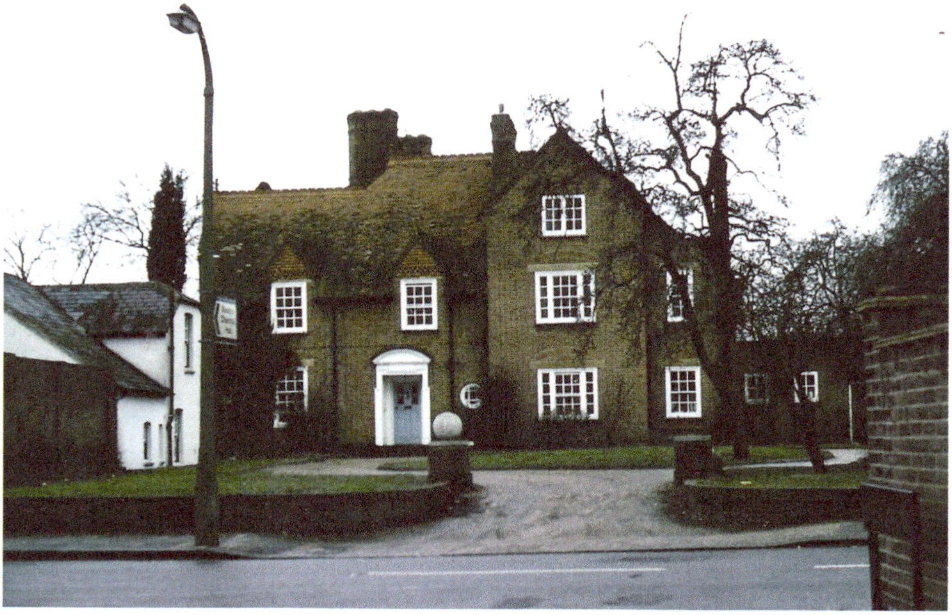

Vicarages Old and New

Ruislip vicarage stood on the north bank of the River Pinn in Bury Street from 1391, oddly distant from the church. The Revd Thomas Marsh-Everett had this new vicarage built in 1881/82, in readiness for his marriage. It was built to the side of the old vicarage, which was demolished, except for what was then a new wing and is now the Vicarage Cottage, a separate building, seen on the left. The house below, opposite the church, became the vicarage in 1983.

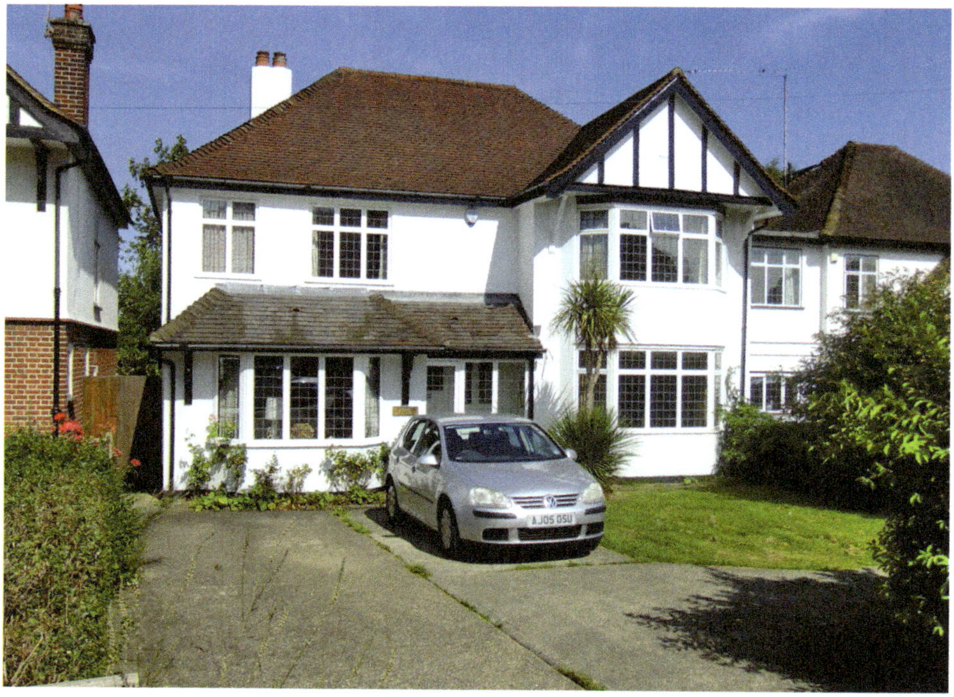

North from the Village Centre, Bury Street to Ruislip Common

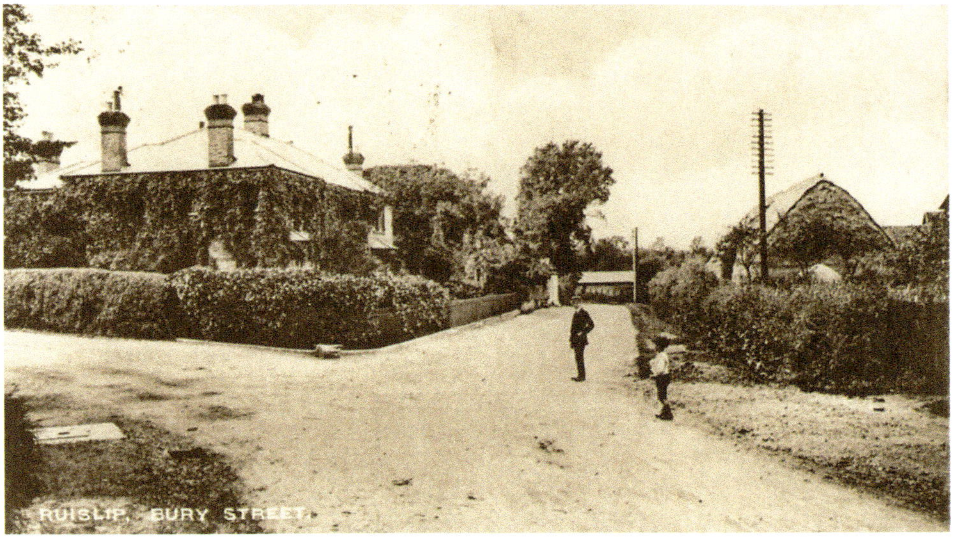

Junction of Bury Street and Sharps Lane, *c.* 1905 and 2012
Rosebank Villas in the foreground were built in 1895 on ground belonging to the Old House next door. One of the sheds at Manor Farm can be seen in the middle distance and the haystacks in the rickyard are on the right. Now the villas and Old House still stand, stripped of their creepers. The sheds can still be seen. Well-dressed gentlemen and small boys would be foolhardy to pose for the camera on this spot today.

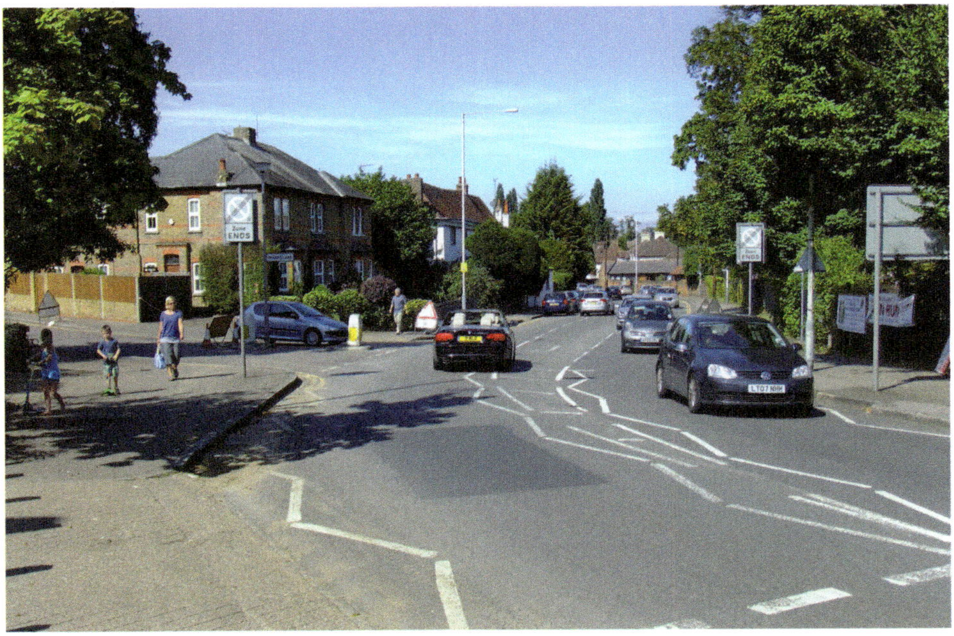

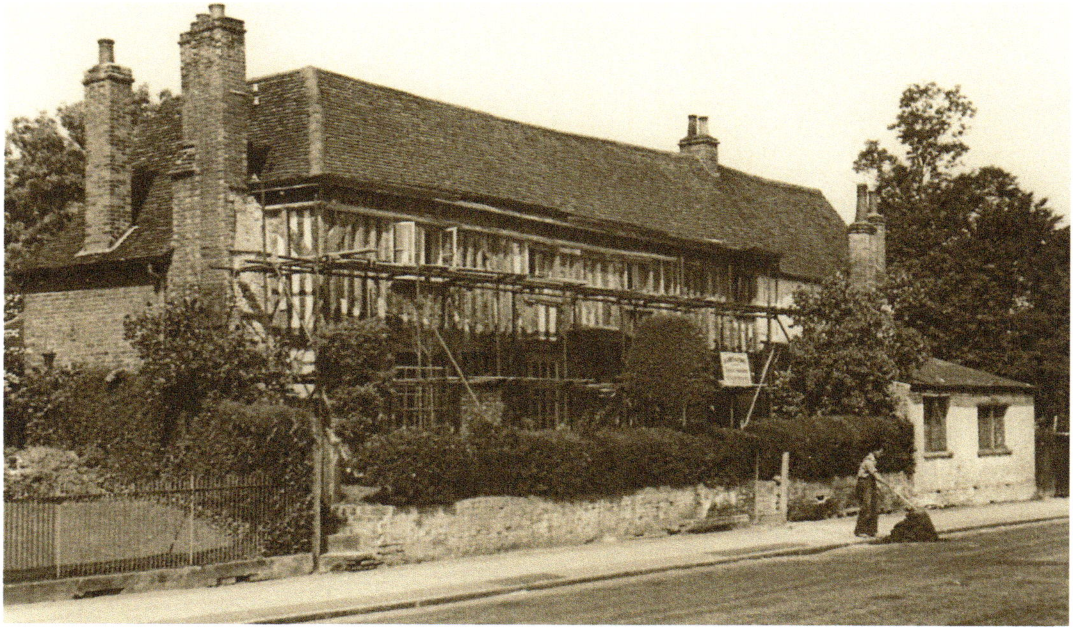

The Old House

The house was built before 1557, and was given a new fashionable façade around 1720. A later addition, seen on the right, was used as a bakery and became Green Cottage. John Ewer married the baker's daughter and his children built the villas next door. The upper picture shows the original timber frame, revealed in 1936 during restoration. The house as it appears today can be seen below.

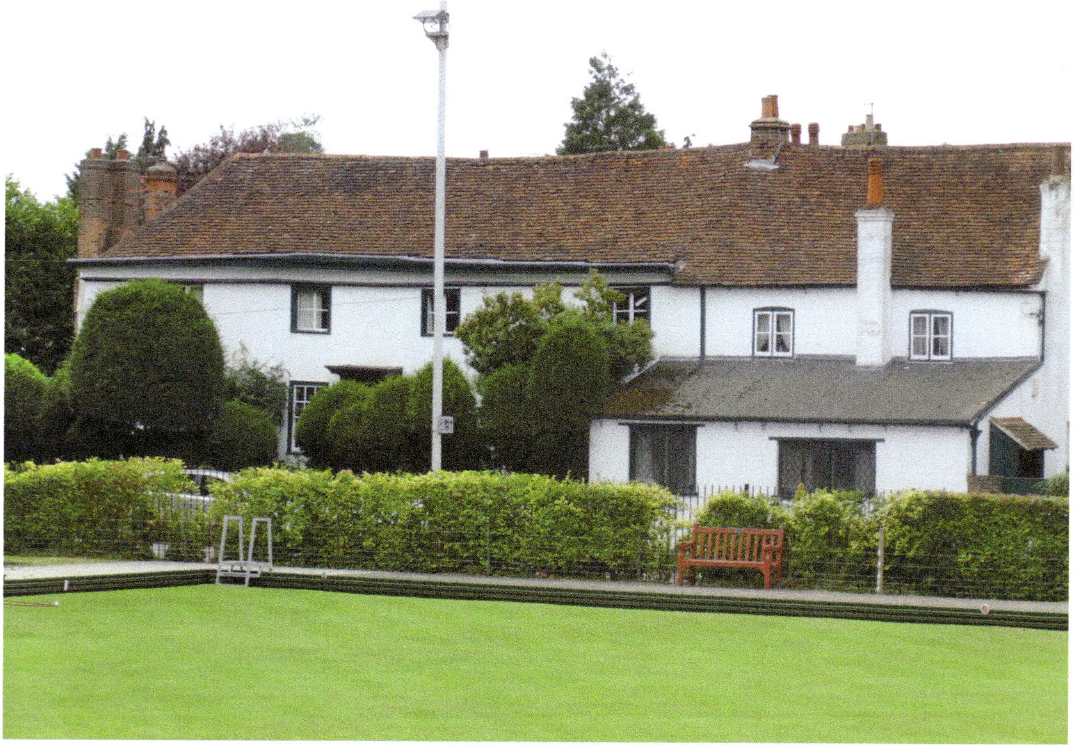

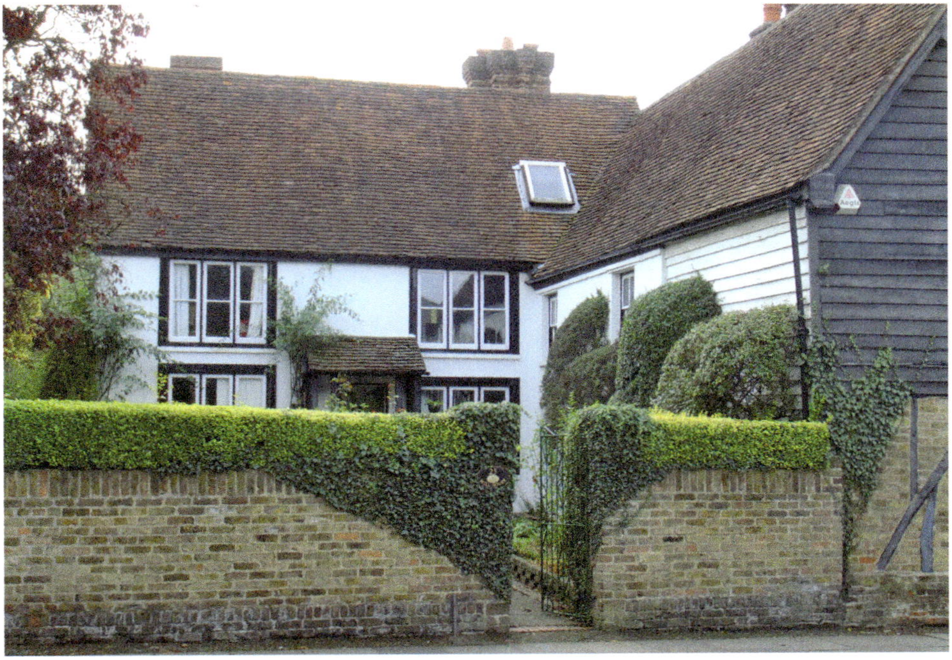

Mill House and the Ewers

Richard Ewer was admitted to this cottage at a Manor Court in 1598. The L-shaped house has a wooden addition end-on to the street, seen particularly well in the lower picture. The family remained in possession until 1948, apart from a break in Victorian times. Nelson Ewer (1878–1947) became an engineer and started an engineering business, Gurney & Ewer, in a large adjoining barn. There were motor repair, body-building workshops and petrol pumps.

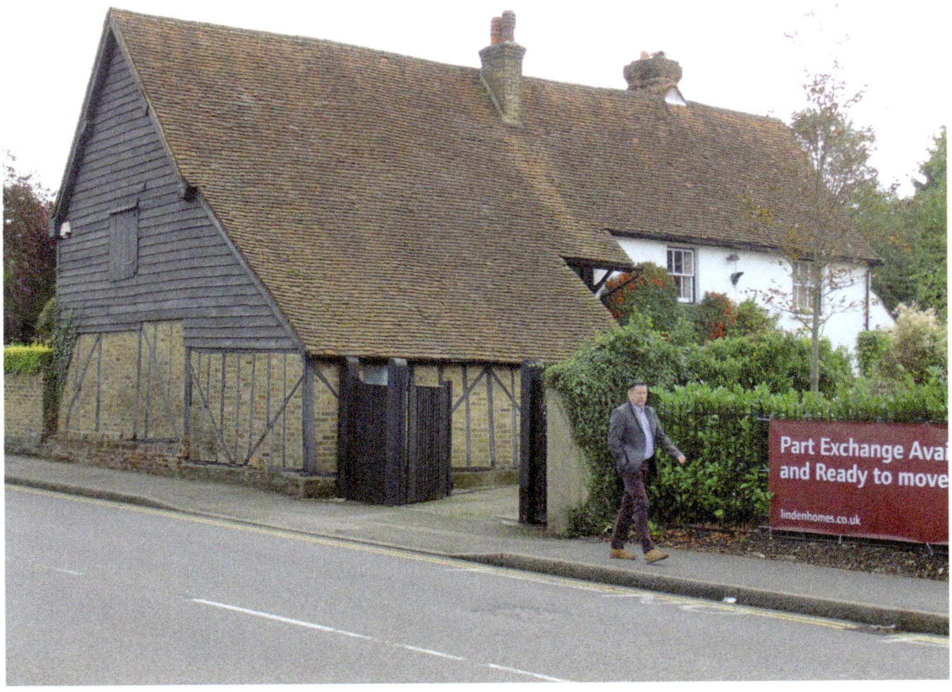

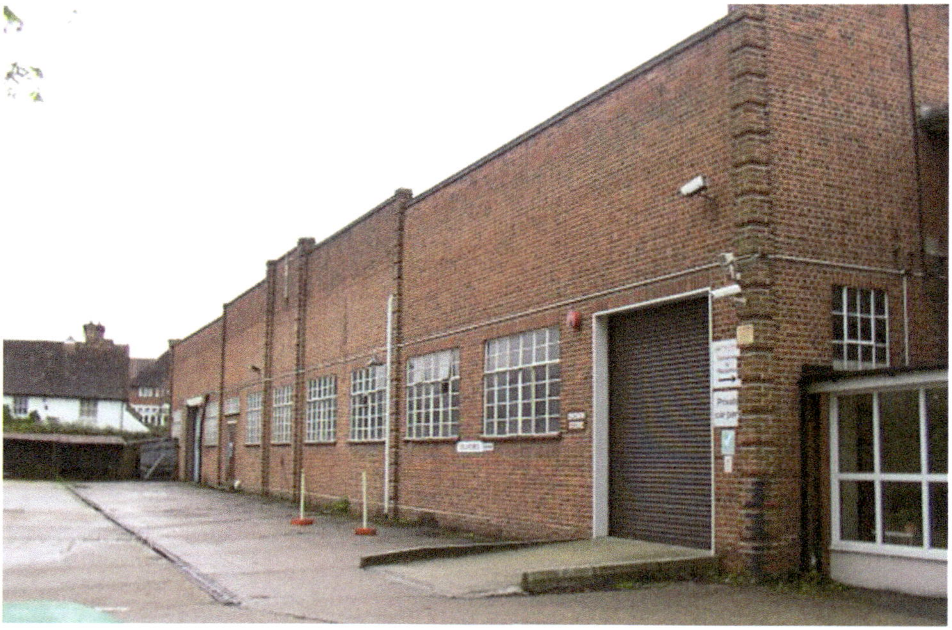

EMI and a Housing Estate

Gurney & Ewer demolished the barn to build this new workshop in 1936. They made munitions during the Second World War. Young Nelson, born in 1905, designed a new way of producing Sten Gun breechblocks on an automated process. The business was sold and EMI occupied the site from 1952, making a variety of valves here. After takeovers the firm closed in 2009 and the houses and flats seen below have been built on the site.

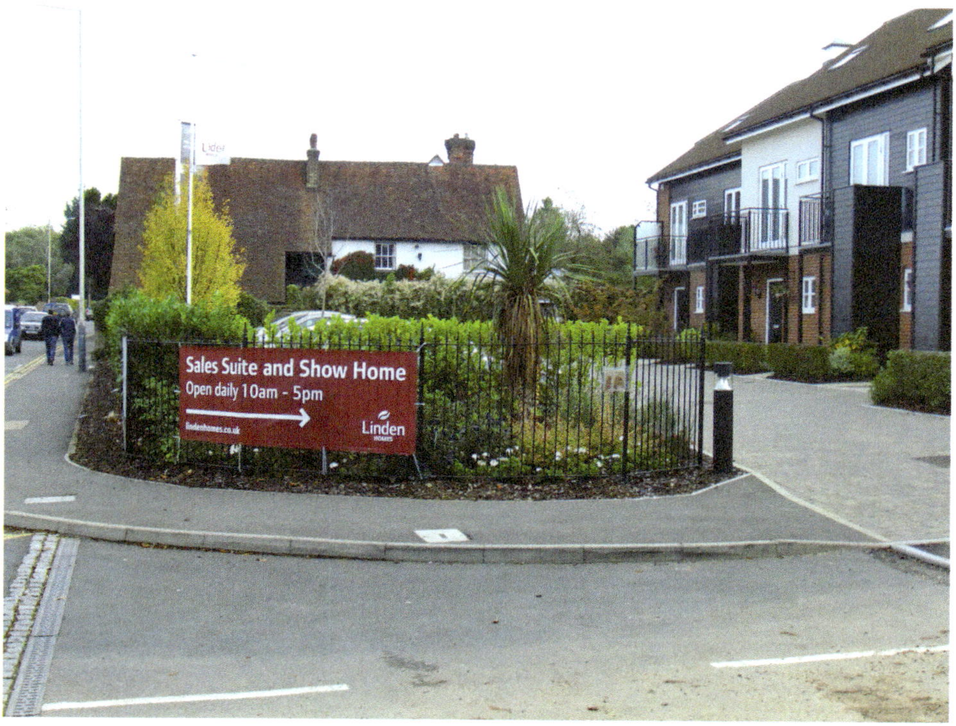

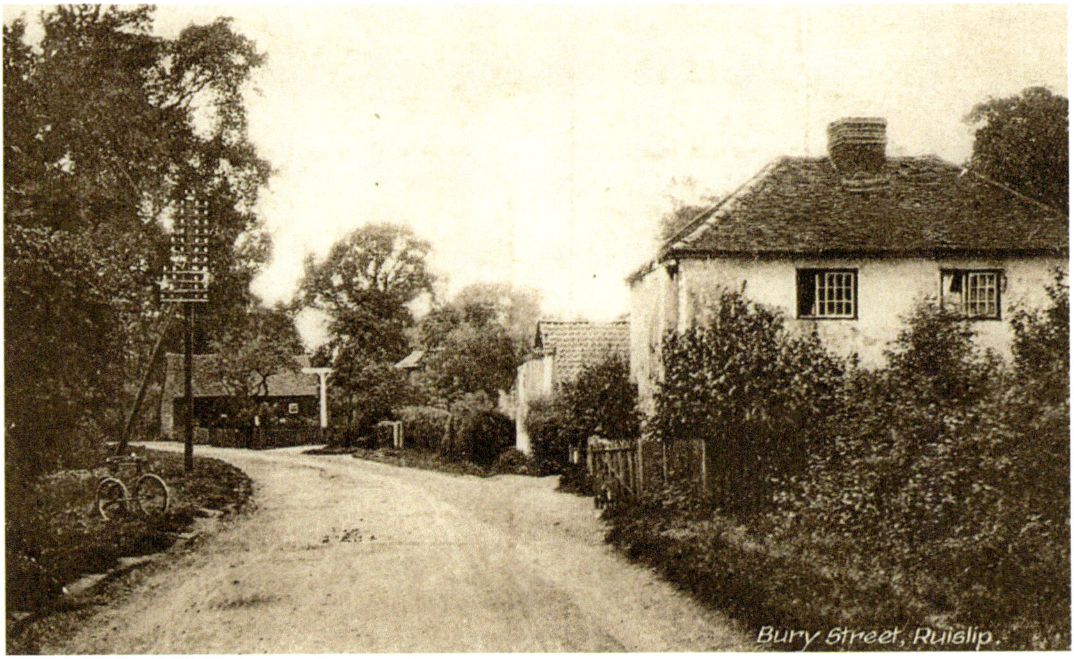

Silver Street Green in the Middle of Bury Street

This hamlet of seven houses set back from the road around a green was known as Silver Street Green in the sixteenth century. The sign in the picture above is outside the Plough. The barn of Bury Street Farm lies beyond. Barter's Cottages on the right are near the Berries, which still stands. The scene in 2012 is leafy, but houses have replaced the barn and the cottages have gone.

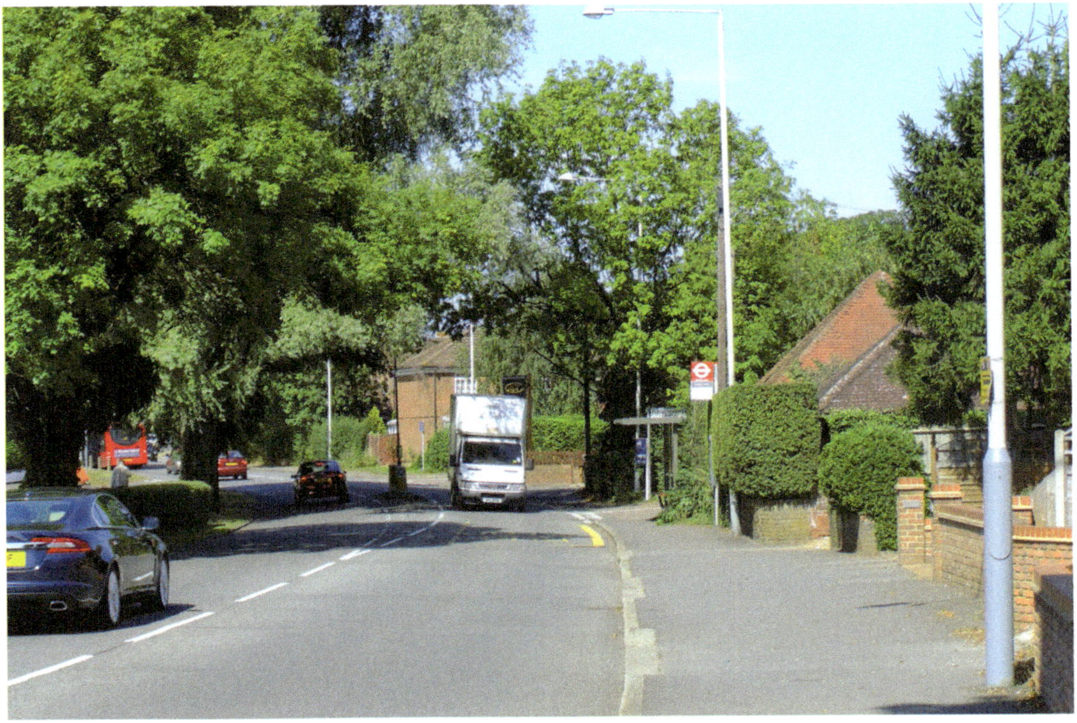

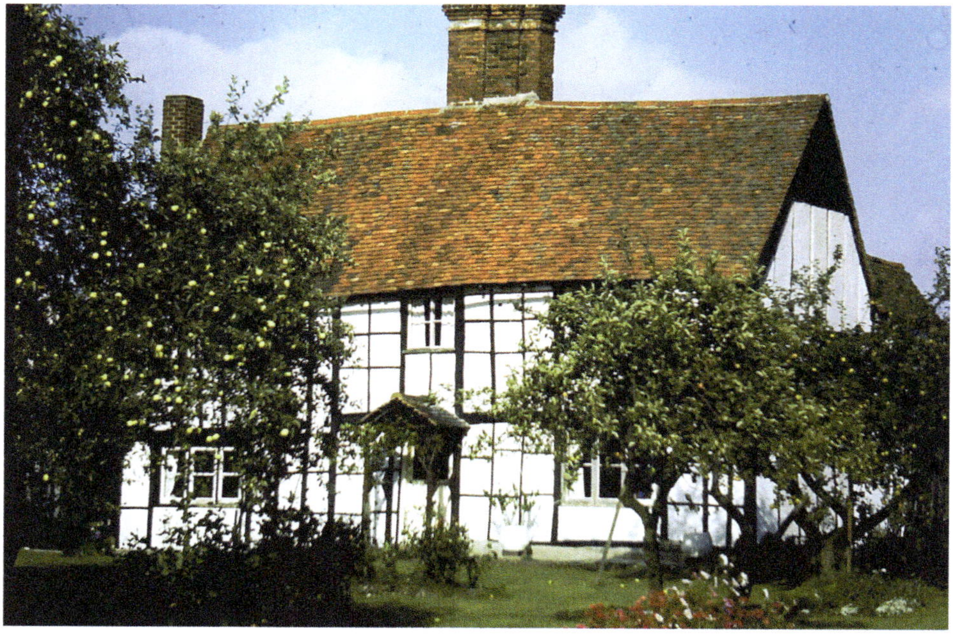

Woodman Farm

The name comes from the appropriately named Woodman family, who lived here from 1855. They employed kindle-wood makers: women, children and elderly people who made up the bundles of firewood. The kindling came from coppice cut in the woods behind Bury Street. The barn was demolished in 1983 and Plough Farm Close, the houses of which can be seen dwarfing the old house in the lower picture, was built on the orchard. The house has several intriguing structural features, including the stair turret seen here.

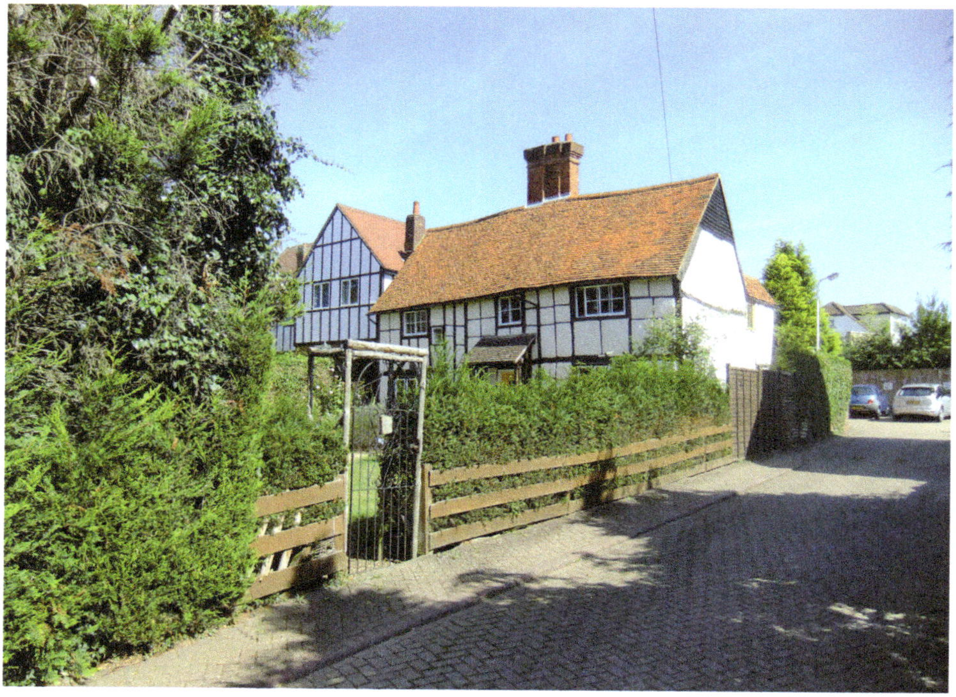

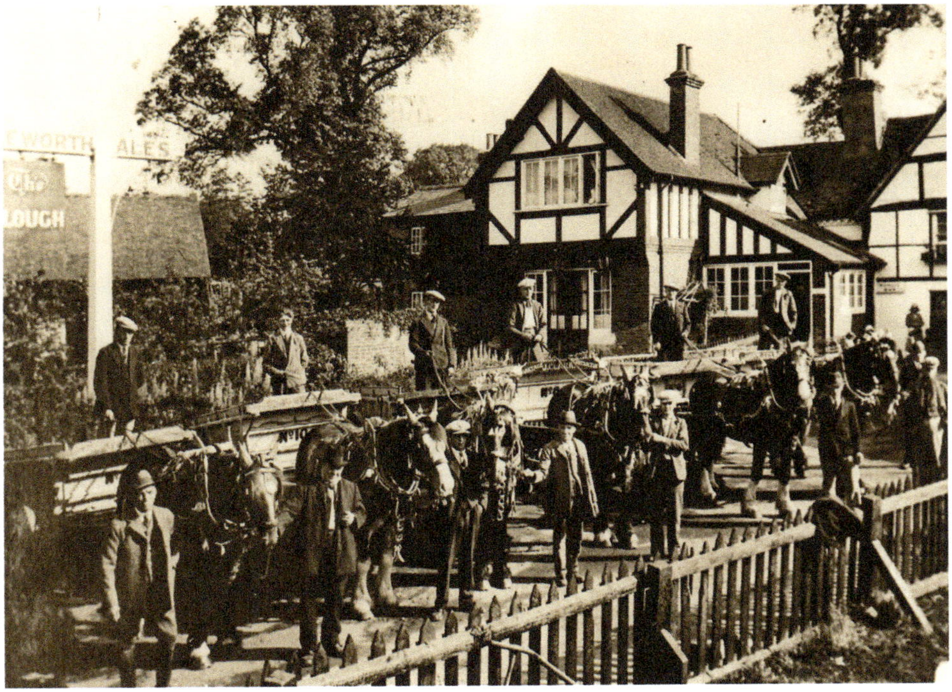

The Plough, *c.* 1929 and 2012

This old house became a beerhouse in 1847, and remained a public house until 2012, when it became a restaurant. The top picture shows a child called Joan Heron, who was ill with measles, peering through the upstairs window at the teams of horses and carts lined up and ready to go to Uxbridge Show. They belonged to her grandfather, seen on the left, who had a carriage business. Her grandmother and mother ran the pub.

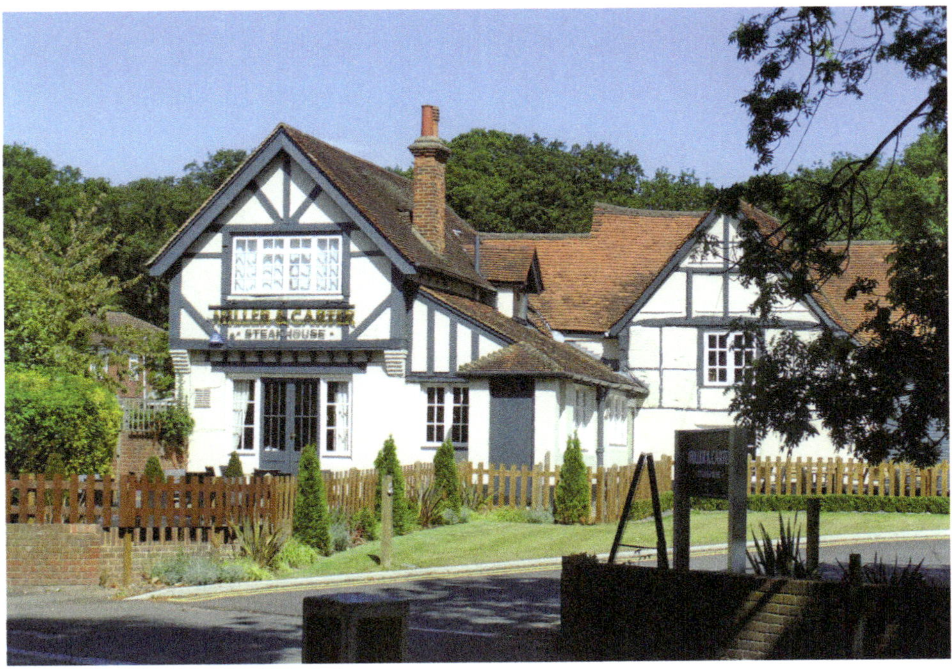

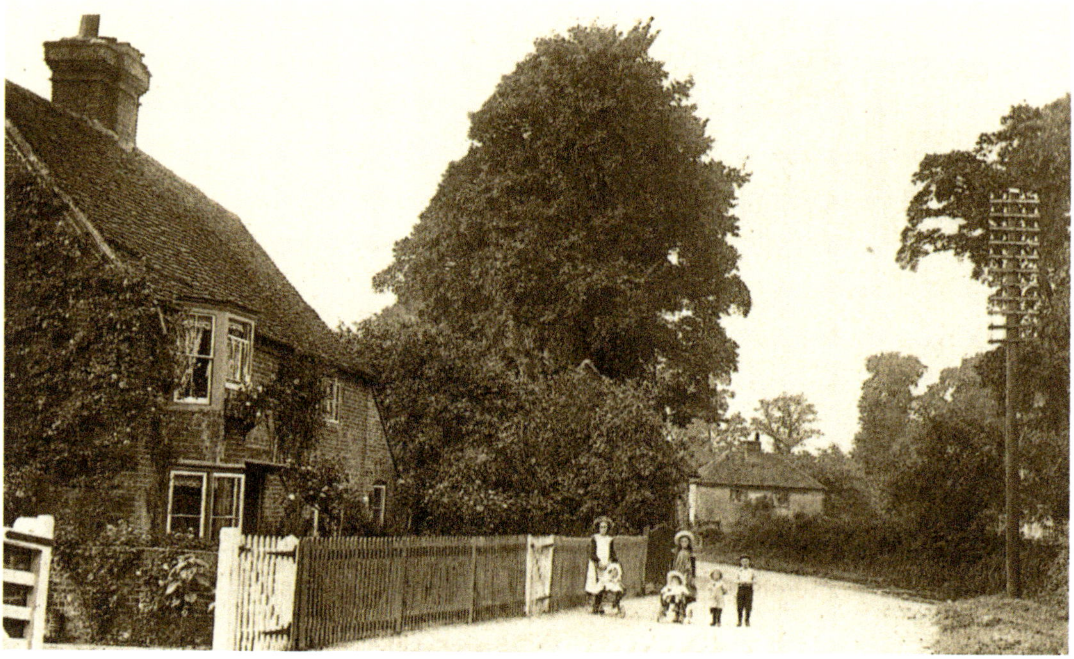

Bury Farm

On the opposite side of Bury Street stands Bury Farm. The main house dates from around 1600 and is on the site of a medieval hall and crosswing house. The central hearth of the medieval hall has been found underneath the floorboards. A Victorian kitchen on the right of the picture finally replaced the crosswing. The façade was rebuilt in the eighteenth century.

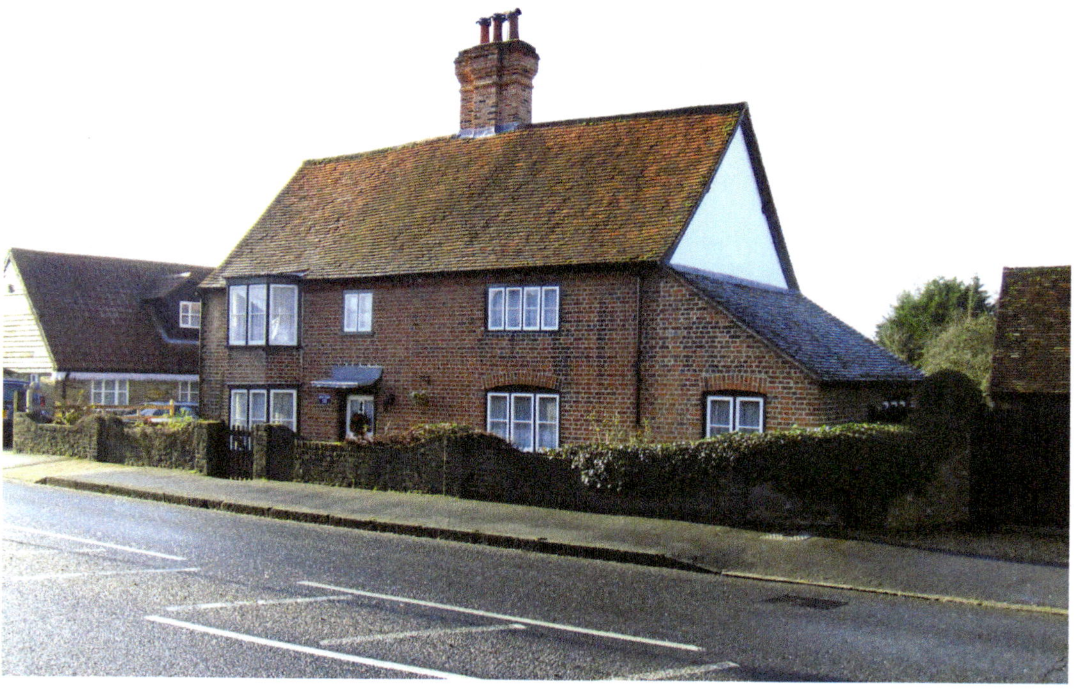

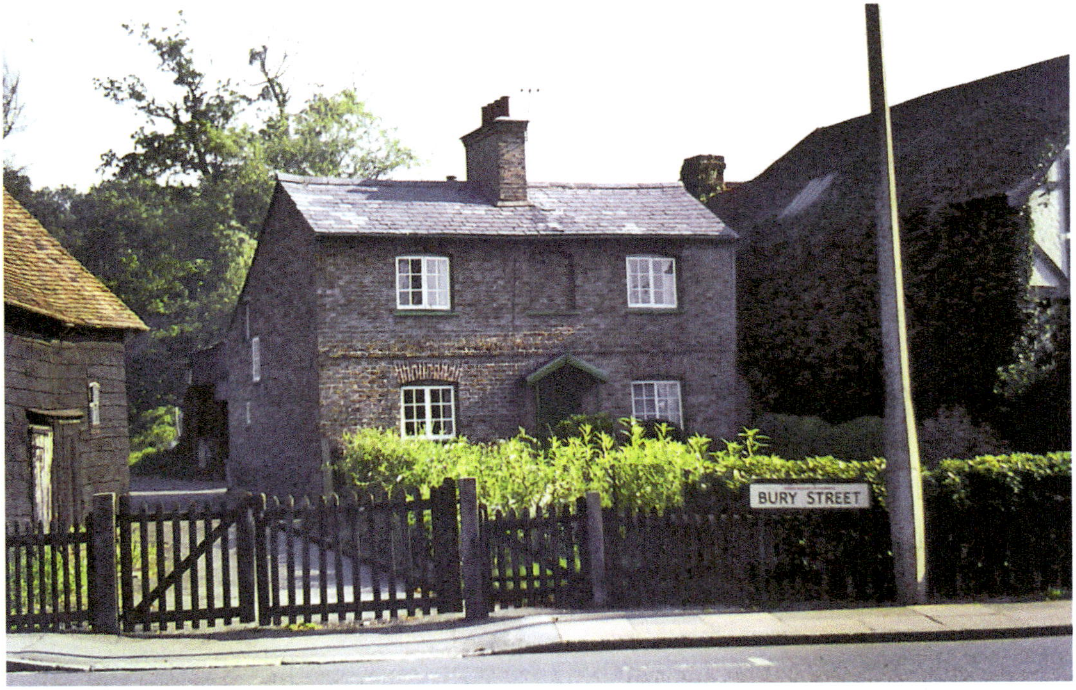

Bury Street Farm in 1974 and Laburnum Grove in 2012
This small slate-roofed cottage was built beside the woodway, an entrance to Park Wood, *c.* 1840. It was mainly occupied by hay dealers and the last one to do so was James George Collins, who moved in about 1912. He died in 1955, but his widow, Mrs Florence Collins (the former Miss Boyle of Priors Farm), lived there until her death in 1978 at the age of ninety-five. The house and barn were then demolished and Laburnum Grove was built on the ground.

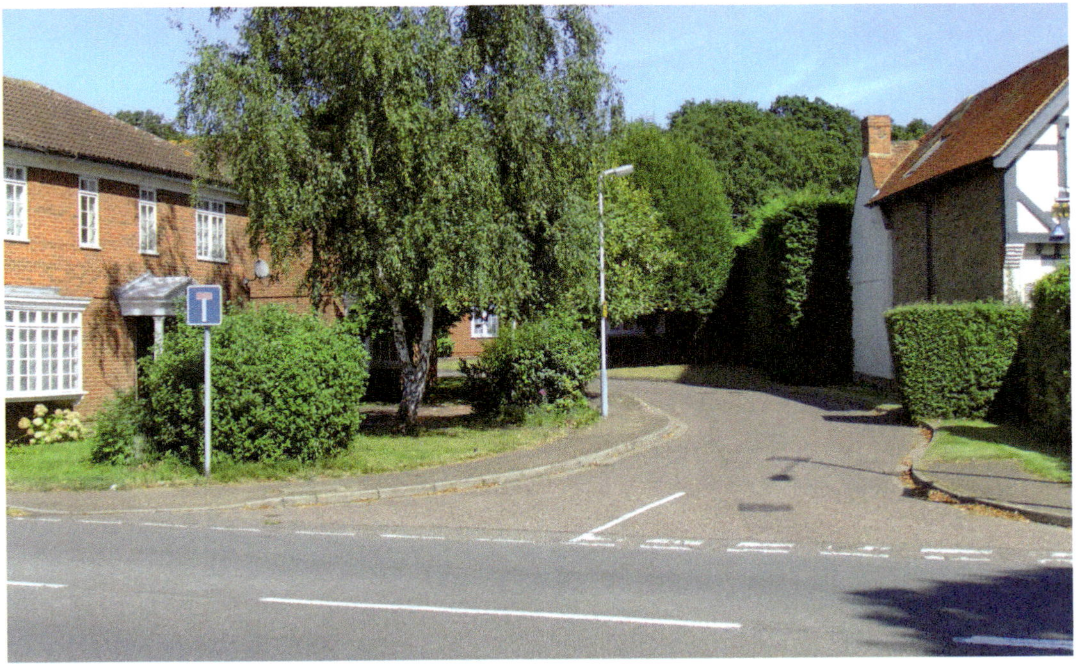

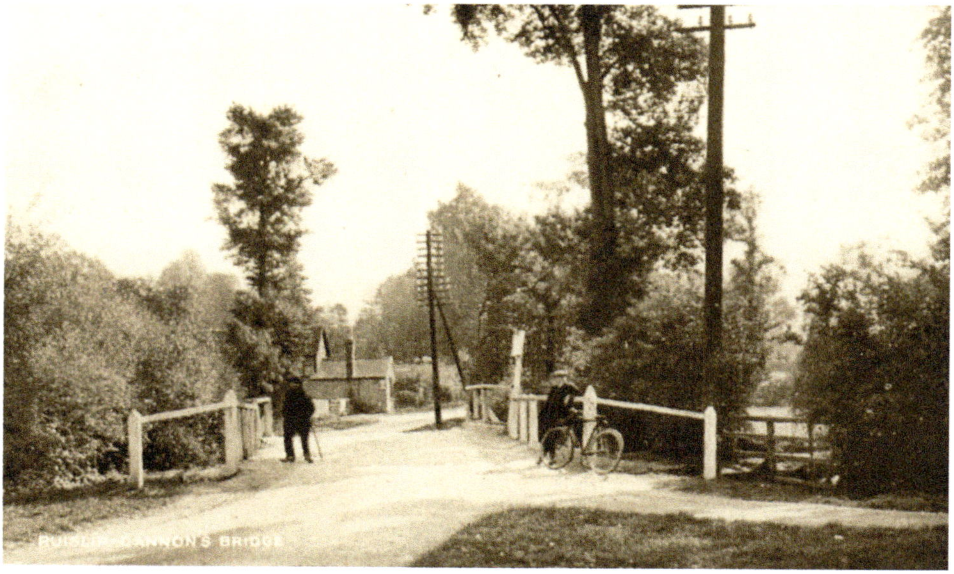

Cannons Bridge, at the Top of Bury Street

A stream called the Cannon Brook and the canal feeder run from Ruislip Reservoir underneath Bury Street, close to the junction with Breakspear Road. Beyond the narrow bridge, Cannons Bridge Farm can be seen. It had been rented to Brills, Lavenders & Tobutts, who were wood and hay dealers or agricultural labourers. Mr Brown, an architect, removed the ugly addition from the front, renovated the timber frame and brickwork, and added a large extension to the side in 1958.

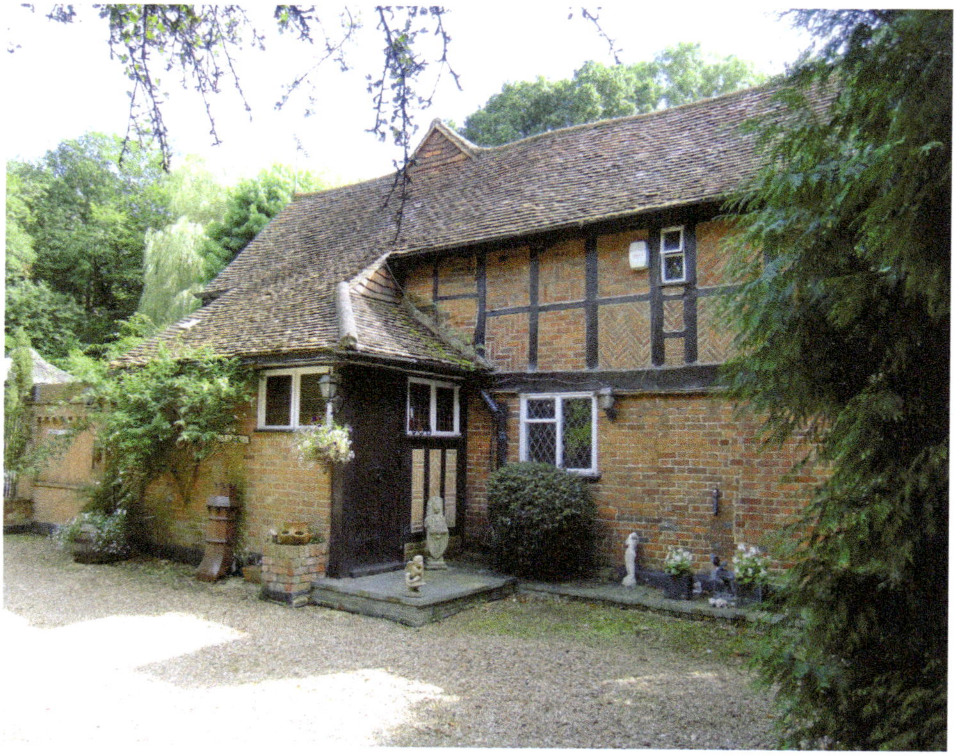

Ruislip Common

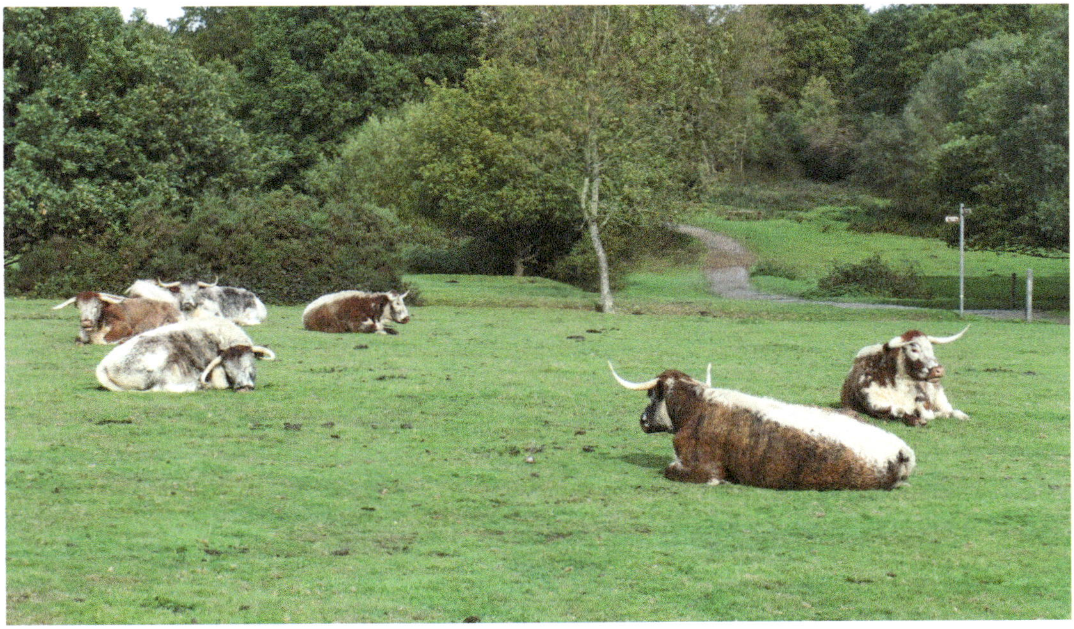

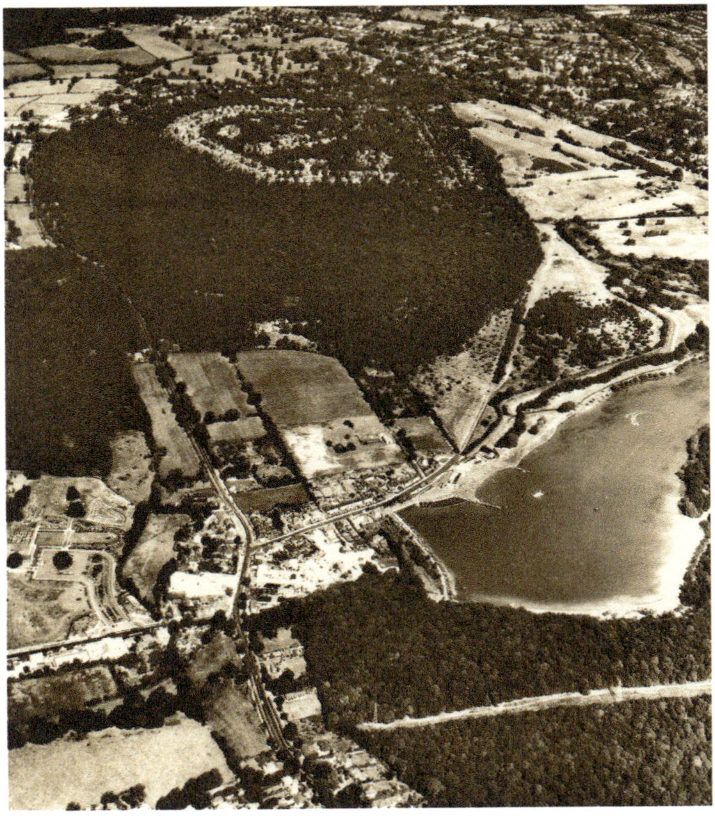

Cattle on Ruislip Common and an Aerial View of the Reservoir

Ruislip Common is a general name given to the hamlets near the common or waste, where inhabitants could graze their animals and collect fuel. Much was enclosed 1804–14, but the Enclosure Commissioners set aside 39 acres here to compensate poor cottagers.

The Grand Junction Canal Company purchased the former common for the reservoir, which was built by the Grand Junction Waterworks Company in 1811. A feeder was constructed in 1816 to convey water directly to the canal near Hayes.

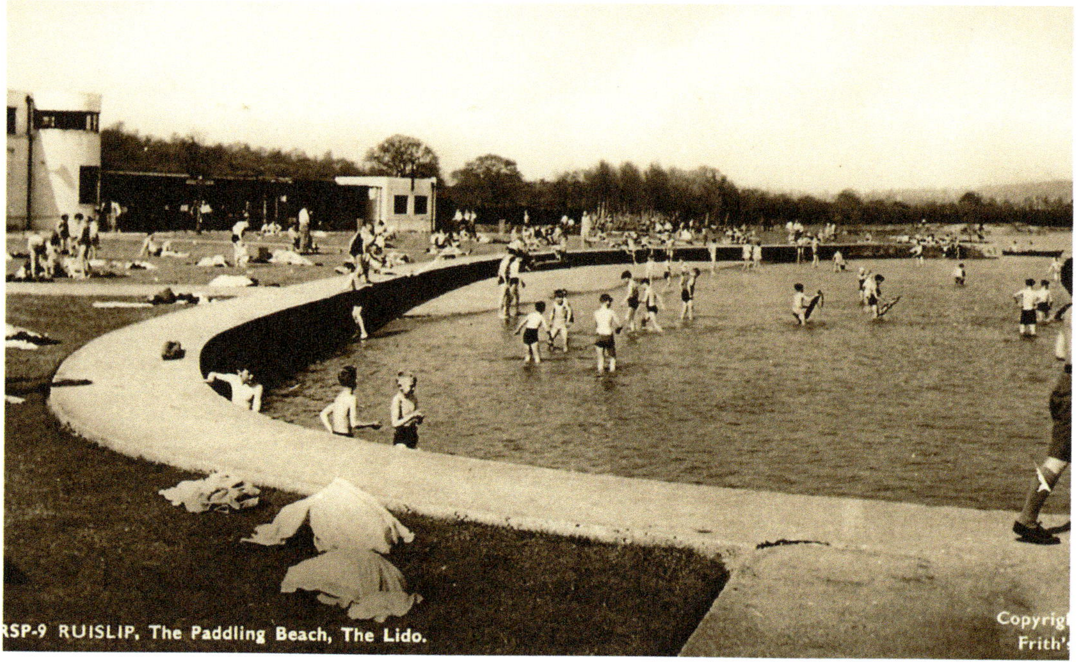

The Early Lido and the Lido in 1998

The reservoir became a lido in 1936 and enjoyed immense popularity, with swimming, boating and a children's beach available in summer, and there was skating in the winter months. The modern-style buildings were designed by George W. Smith. The present lido buildings, seen here in 1998, were erected in 1994. Copse Wood can be seen in the background. It is the remnant of the Common Wood that once covered the whole area that became Northwood Hills.

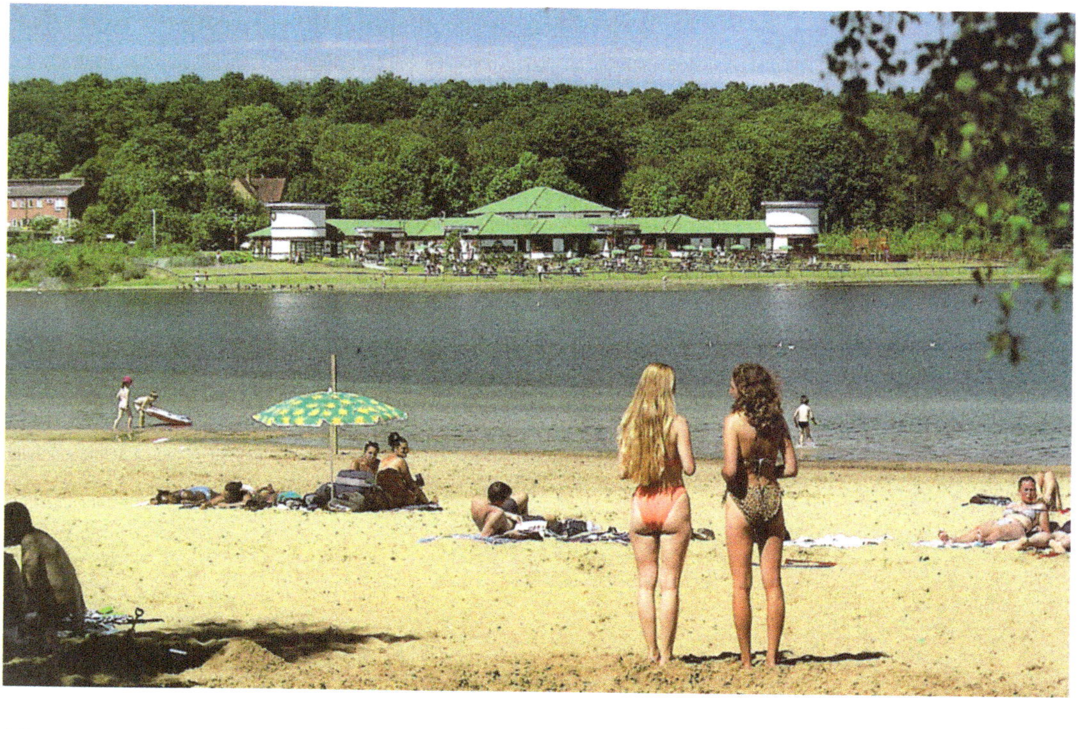

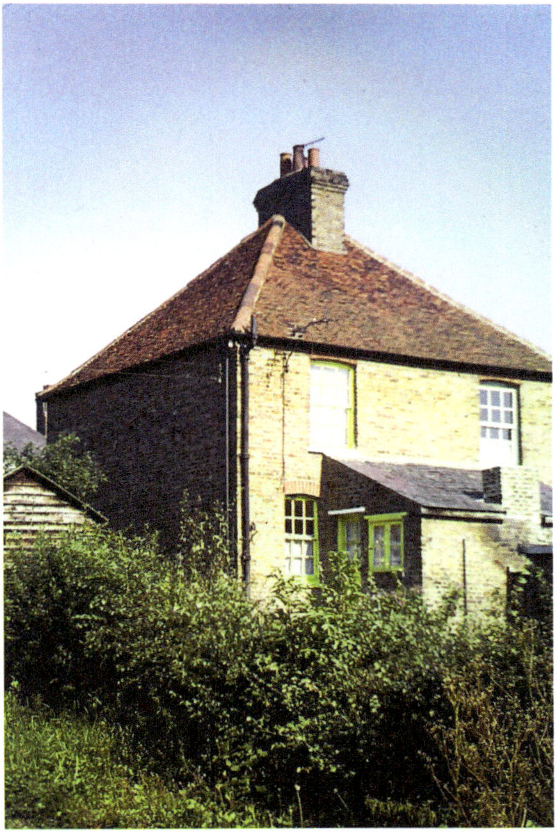

Cottages and Council Houses on Reservoir Road

Ruislip Common tended to be home to relatively poor people, and the nineteenth-century cottages seen above were usually overcrowded and lacked sanitary facilities. The area was struck by a cholera epidemic in 1848, leaving many dead, despite Hannah Lavender's devoted nursing of her neighbours. The first council houses in Ruislip were built there in 1921. In accordance with the council's desire for a garden suburb, the architect was A. S. Soutar, who designed in cottage style with some Art Nouveau features.

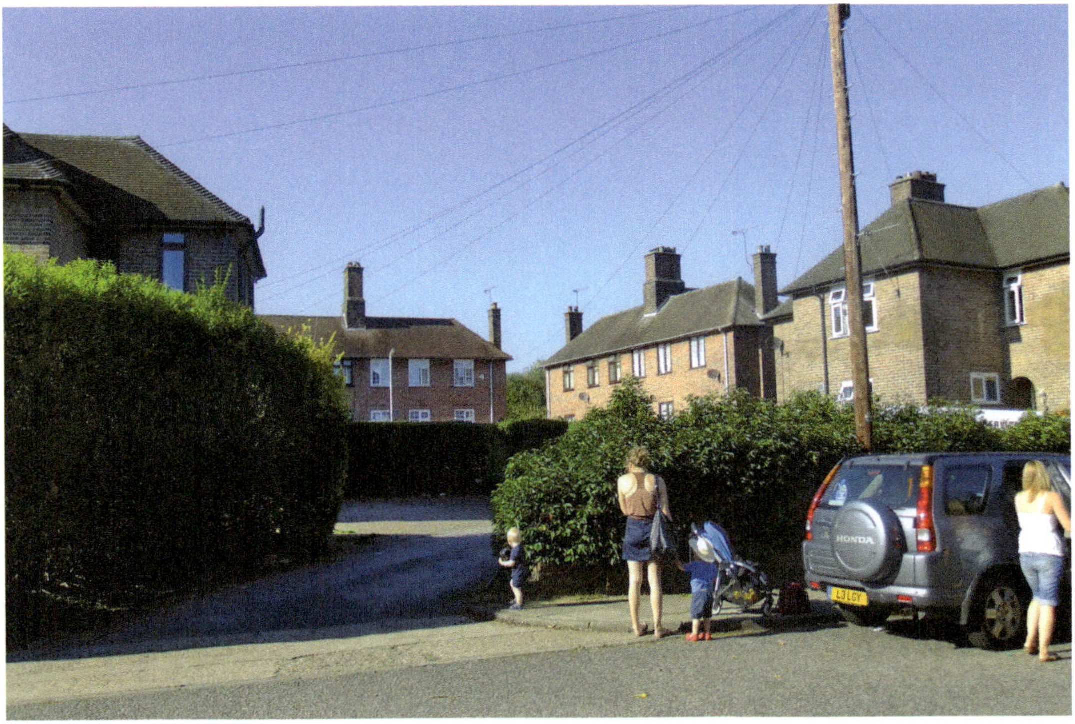

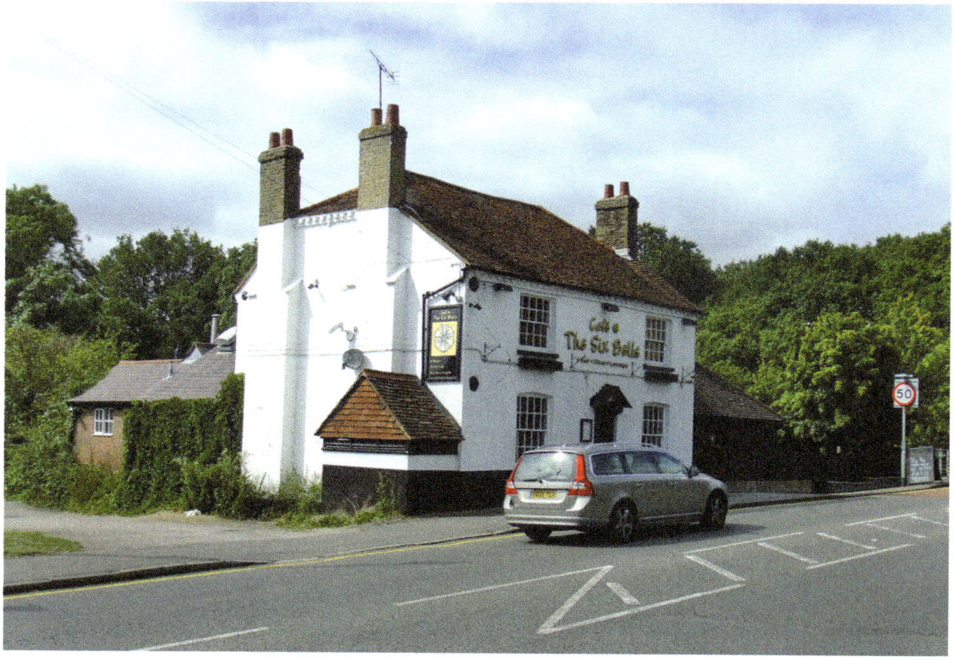

Pub and Chapel

The community was served by the Six Bells, owned by the Rickmansworth brewer Samuel Salter. Two inquests were held here in 1844 and 1845; in both cases the deceased was found to have died from starvation and lack of medical care.

A free chapel opened in 1852, later becoming attached to the Watford Methodist Circuit. It provided a much-needed social centre for local women and encouraged thrift, with savings and coal clubs and a Sunday school for children. Temperance meetings were very popular.

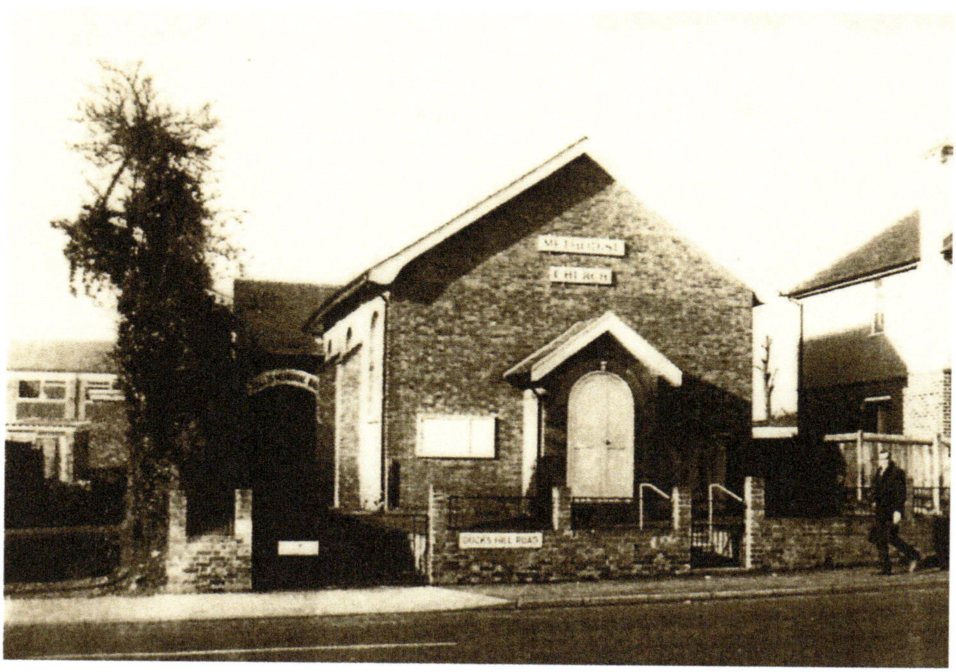

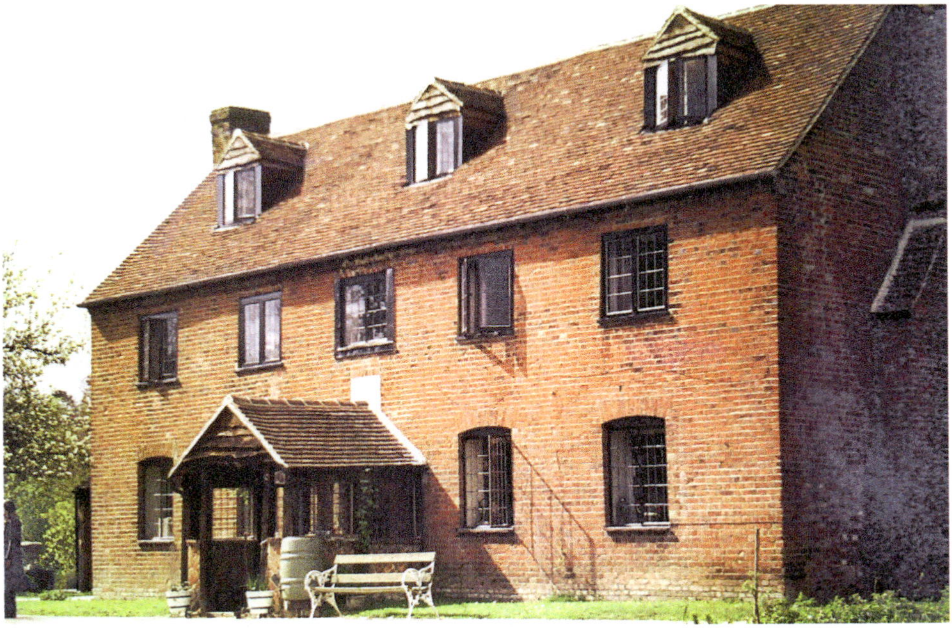

The Old Workhouse: the Front in 1982 and the Back in 1974
Built in 1789, the workhouse was run by a governor, who contracted to maintain the poor for an annual sum of £286 in 1795. The house was converted into cheap tenements in 1838, when the Uxbridge Union workhouse opened. Around 1914 the families living in them were employed spasmodically on such jobs as hay binding, wood dealing and tree felling. It was sold to William Page, the Northwood builder, in 1921, and Waldo Emerson Guy, an architect, restored and extended it to make a very desirable residence.

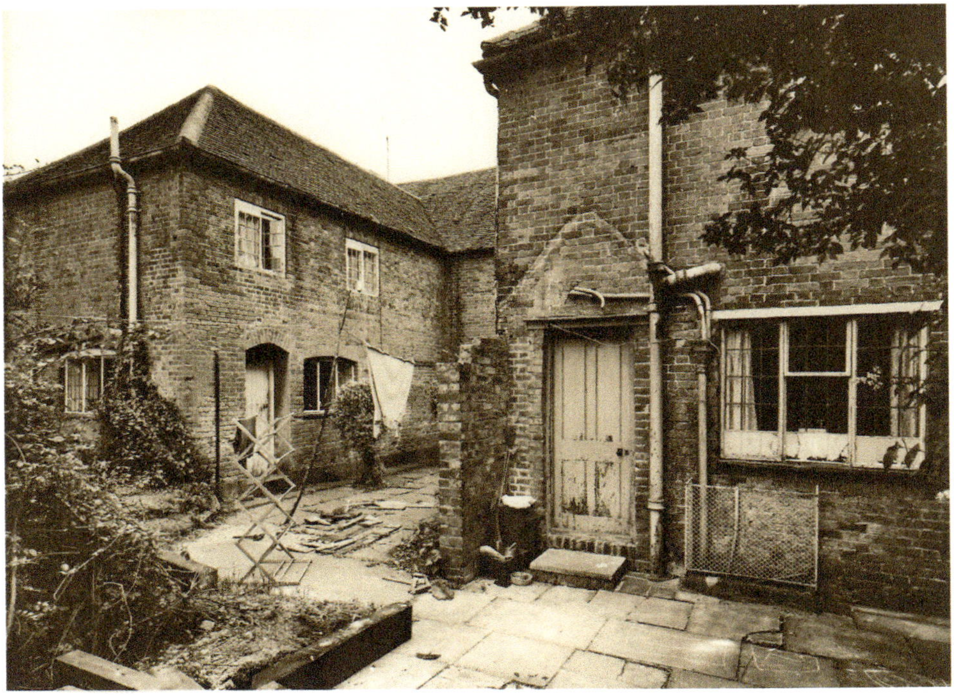

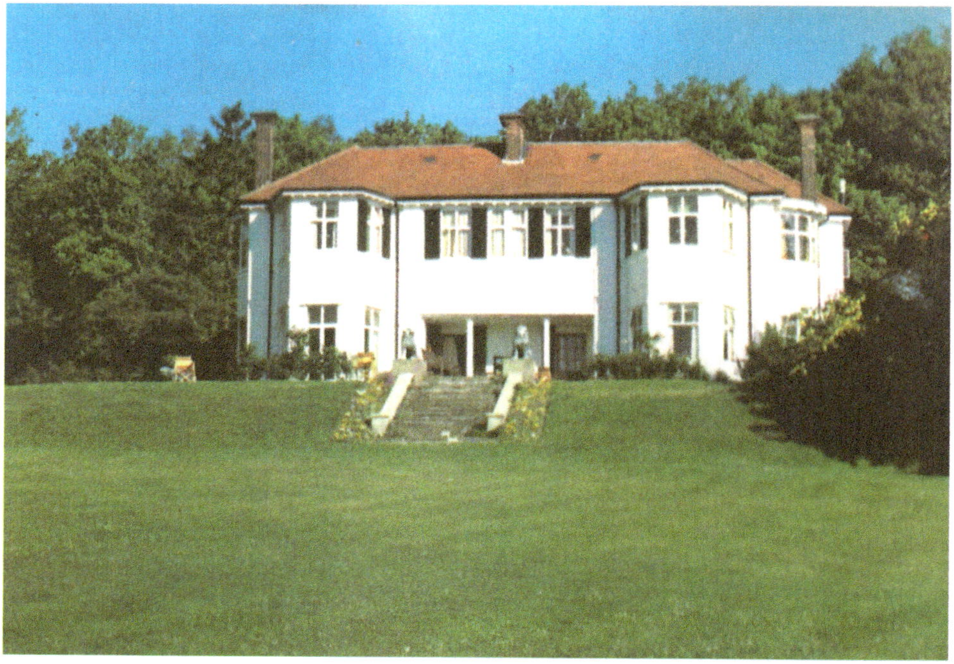

Battle of Britain House (Horsens) and Wartime Shooting Range (Below)
Josef Conn, whose wife was a physiotherapist, had this house built on part of Copse Wood in 1908 as a health hydro. It was requisitioned during the Second World War and allocated to the United States Forces as HQ for a 'Clandestine Operations' Division. Agents were trained there for sabotage operations in occupied Europe. Later, it became a short-term residential college, with courses for schoolchildren and adults. It burnt down in August 1984 and was returned to the woodland from which it sprang.

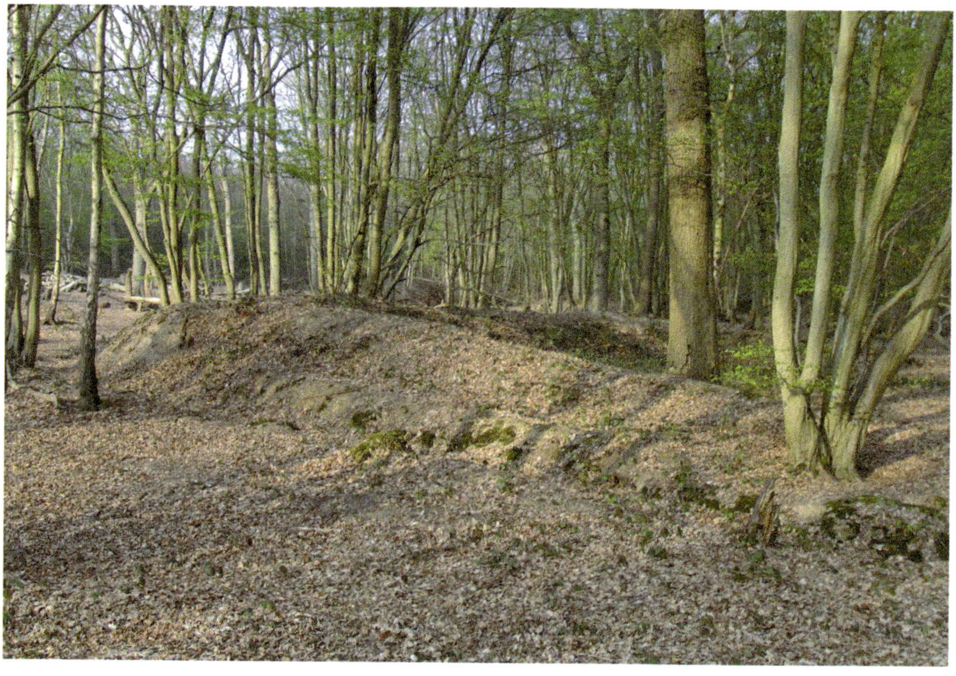

St Catherine's Manor

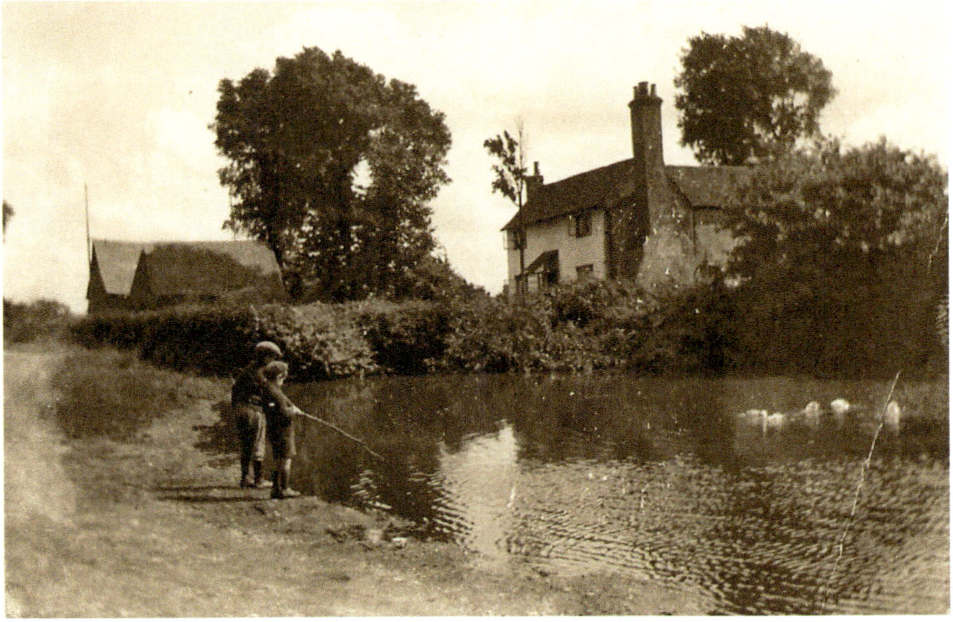

Southcote Farm

Southcote Manor House, surrounded by a moat, stood on the north side of Ladygate Lane. It disappeared in the nineteenth century, but the moat remained until 1935, when the last vestiges were obliterated while suburban houses were being built. The estate belonged to the forester of Harmondsworth in medieval times. Southcote Farm, in the picture above, stood on the site of Whiteheath Junior School, and the farm buildings were on the opposite side of the lane. Charles Martin was the last farmer.

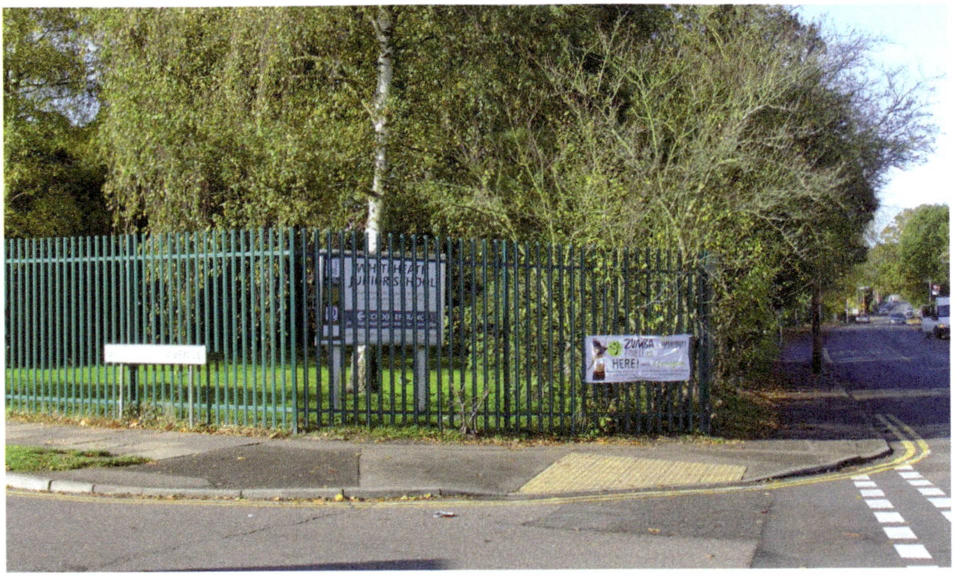

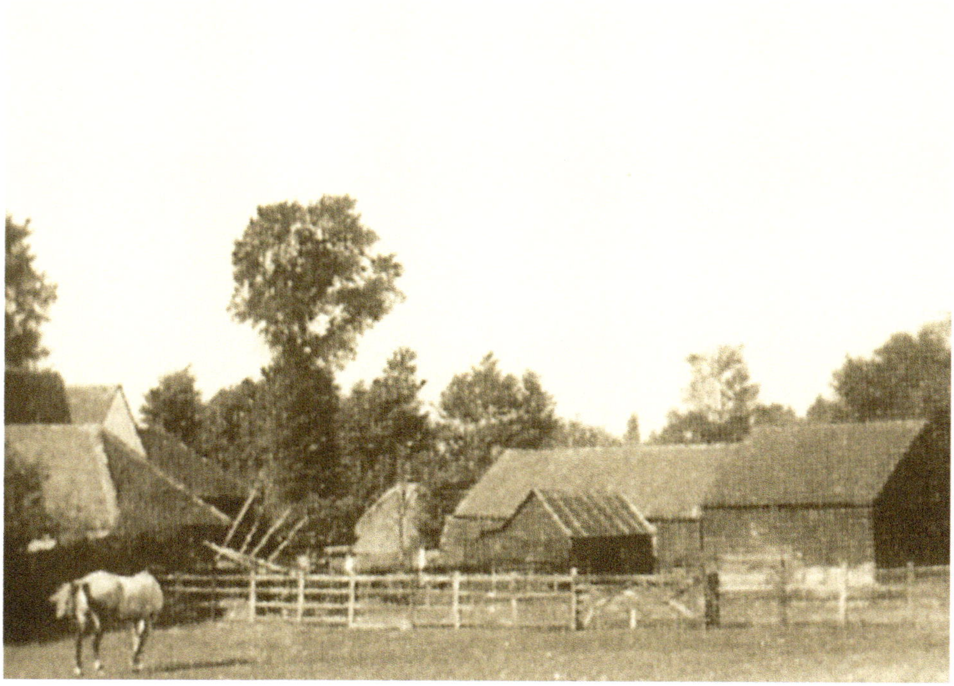

Little Manor Farm

This house has smoke-blackened timbers in the roof, suggestive of a medieval hall. When it became part of the vicar's glebe in 1878, the land that went with it included the old moated site of Southcote. The picture above shows the house with its farm buildings. The house and 27 acres were sold to English Houses Ltd in 1935. The land was developed, but the house survives at the top of Arlington Drive, as seen in the lower picture.

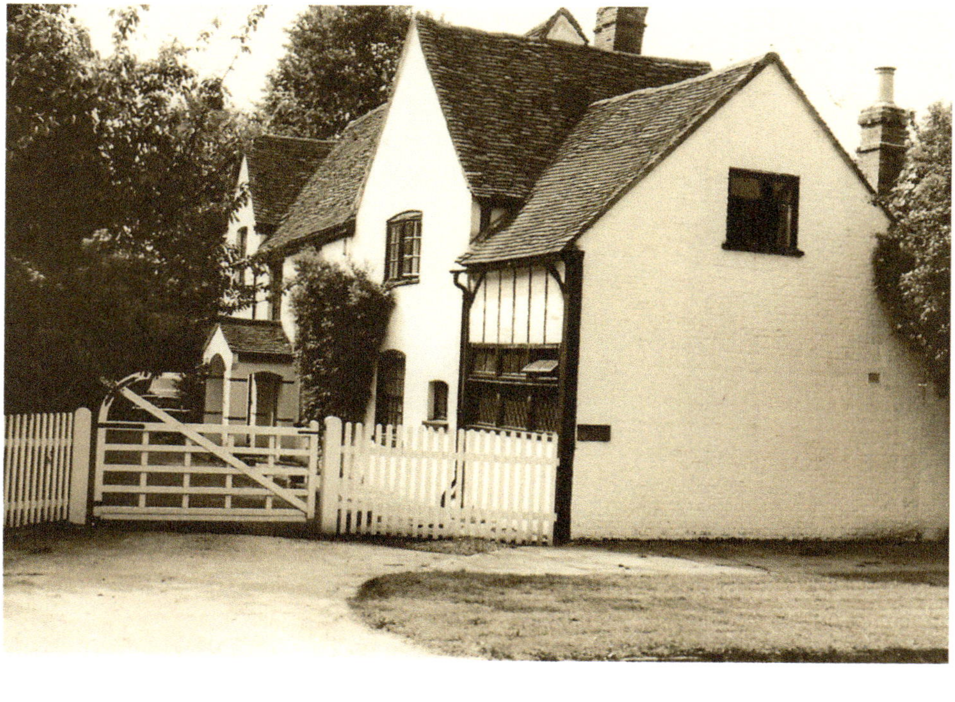

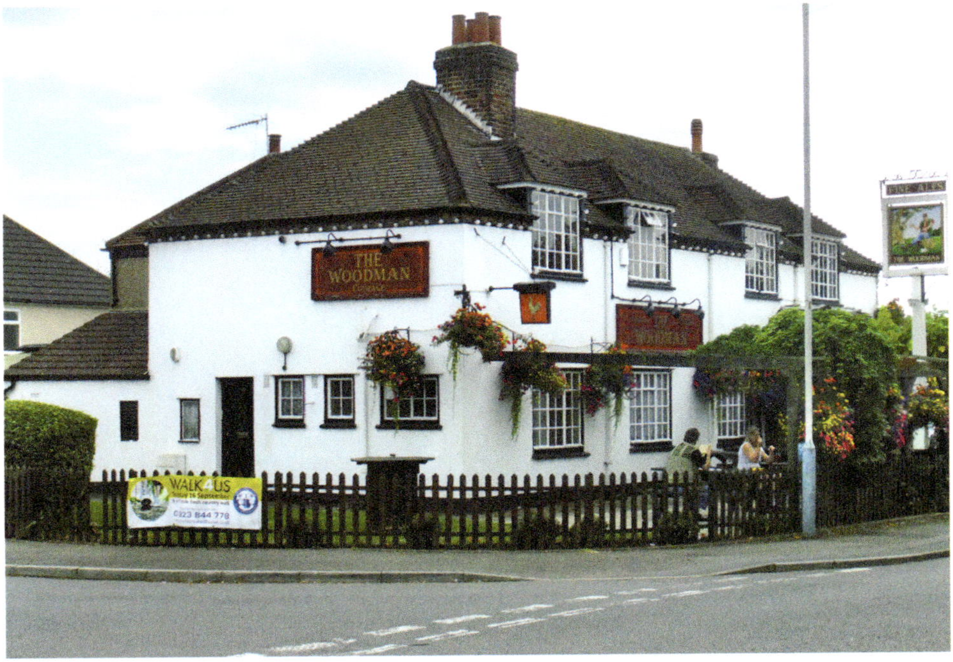

The Woodman and Oak Cottage

The Woodman has been modernised so much that it is barely recognisable as a Victorian cottage. It was built on the same plot of ground as Oak Cottage, which may have been the first beerhouse. The Woodman was owned by Harman's Brewery at Uxbridge from 1847. The houses beside Oak Cottage in the lower picture are in Stowe Crescent, a new road built by Wimpey in 1972, close to the canal feeder. Oak Cottage was replaced by houses some years later.

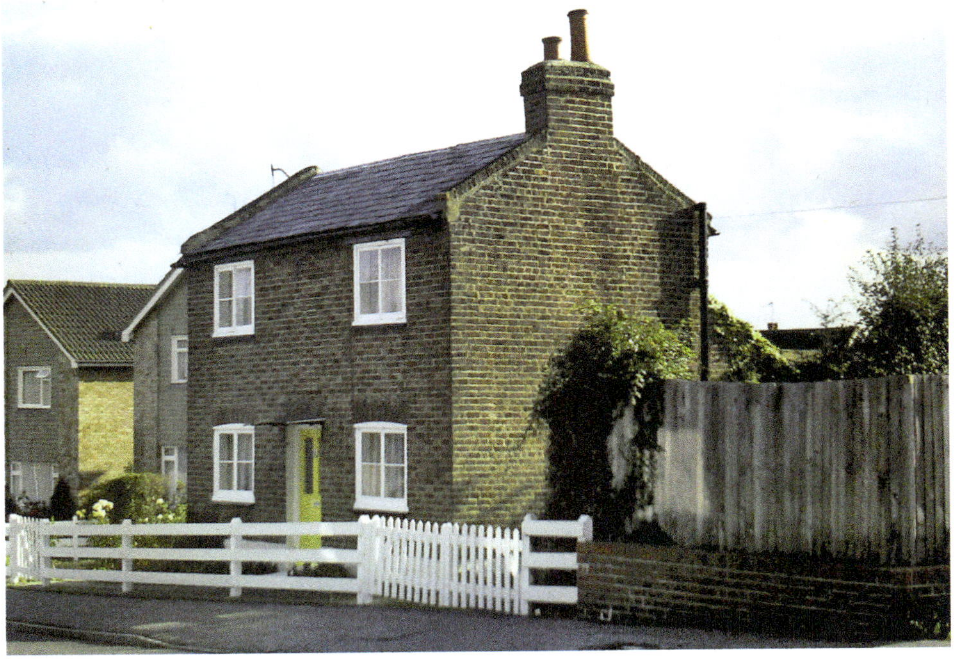

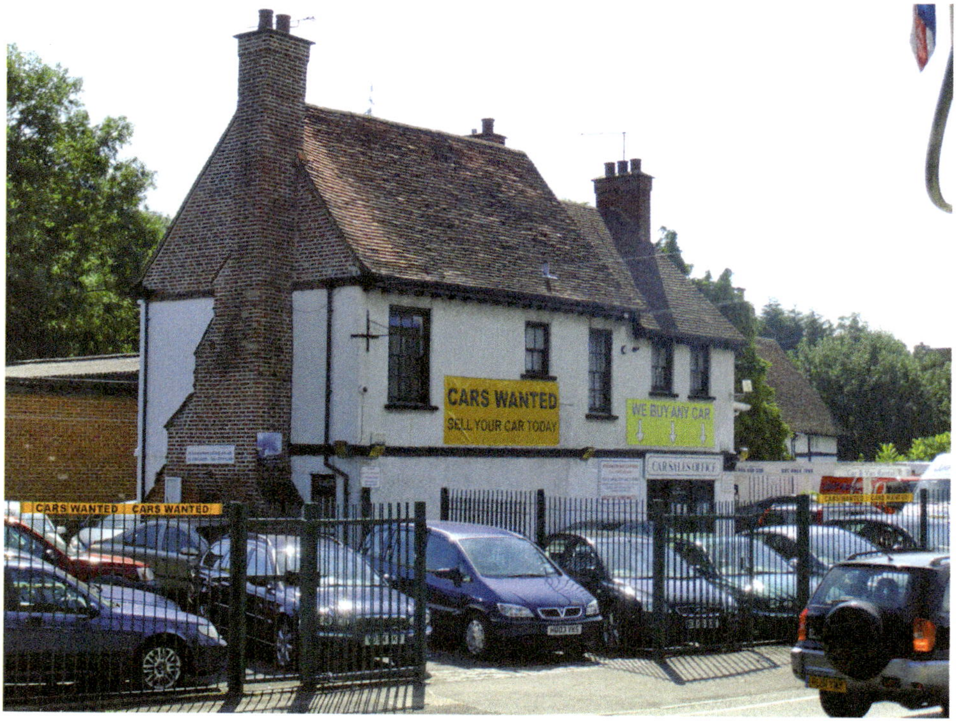

Breakspear Garage and Rose Cottage 2012

Breakspear Road was originally a track from Cannons Bridge along the edge of common land and several cottages were built upon it as encroachments in the sixteenth or seventeenth centuries. The land behind these two buildings, which stretches to the canal feeder, was sold to Hillingdon Borough Council in the 1970s, partly for council house development. The road frontage has been developed as an industrial estate since the war.

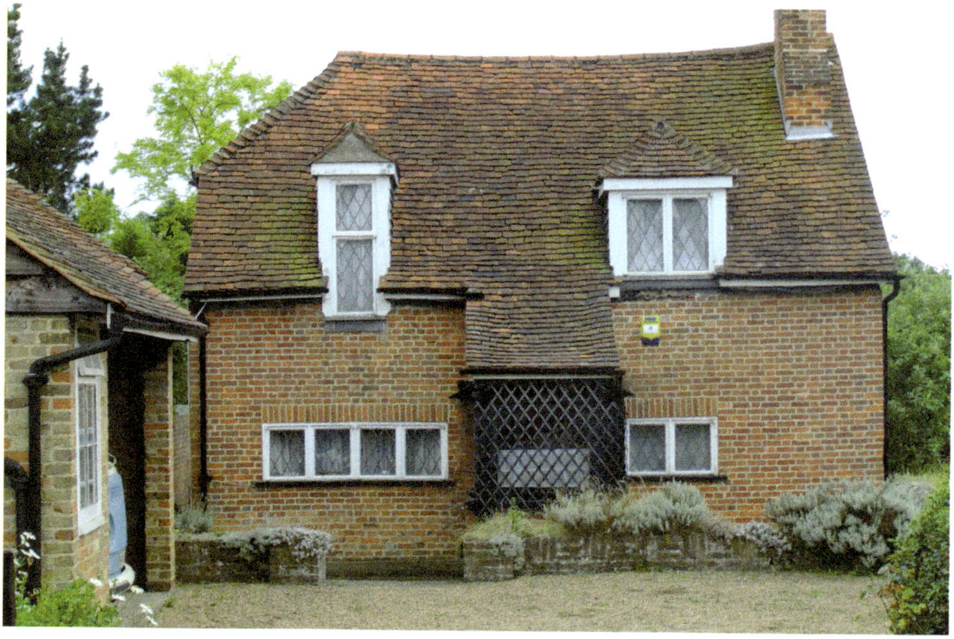

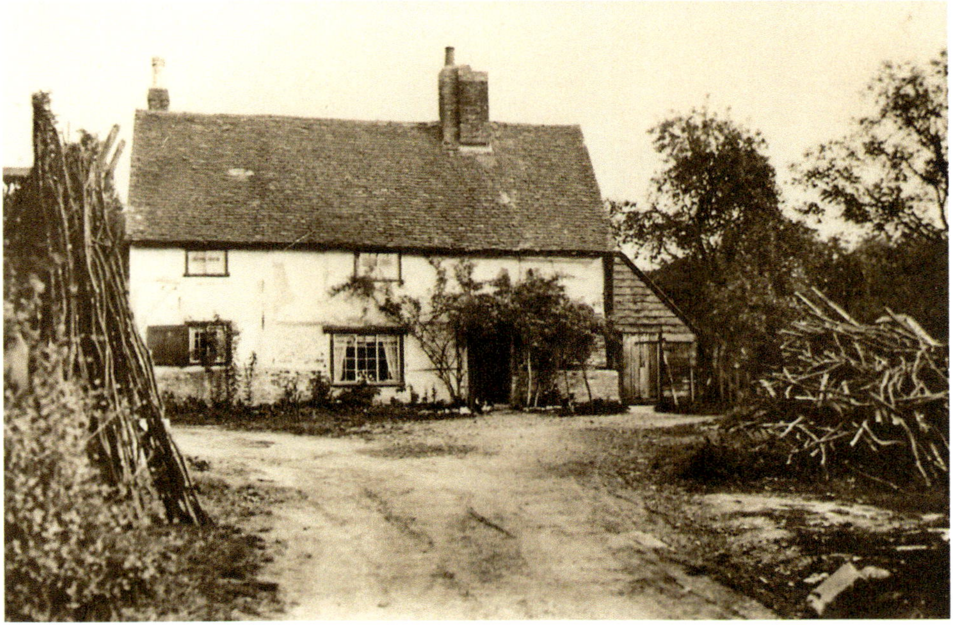

Brill Cottage, 1940 and 2012

The cottage was owned by a London poulterer in the eighteenth century. By the 1840s Thomas Collins ran a shop there. The present name seems to have been applied to it when 'Shorty' Brill, a woodward, inhabited it around the time of the First World War. The house has been beautifully restored, but, as can be seen in the lower picture, the commercial buildings around obscure it from public view.

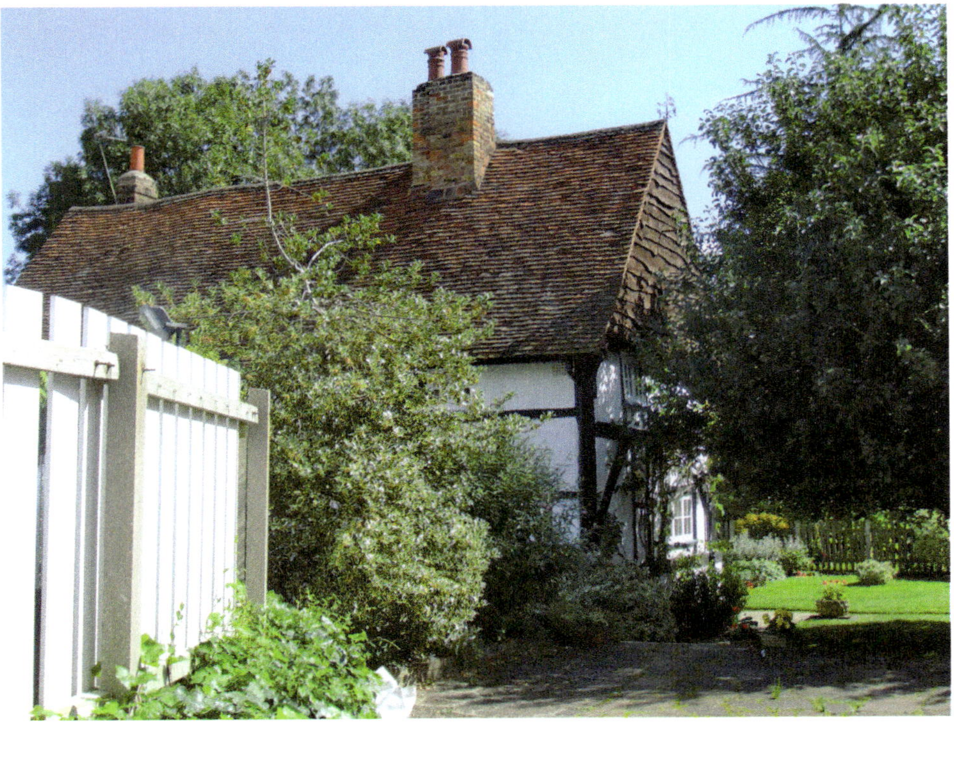

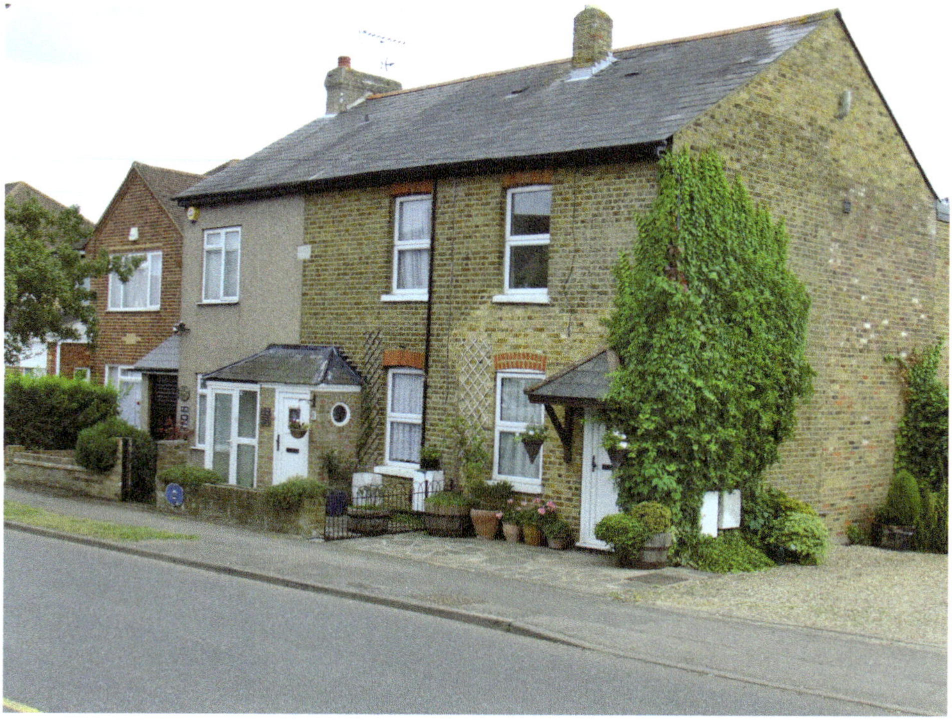

Hope Cottages, Built 1885, Pictured in 2012

No. 3 Hope Cottages, having been a shop, became a private house again in 1989. During building operations the child's boot seen below was found hidden in a recess at the back of the chimney. The well-worn ankle boot has been patched; it has a hobnailed sole and peaked toe cap and may have belonged to a girl. Boots and shoes were often 'buried' in houses for luck. This example could date from the 1860s to the 1880s.

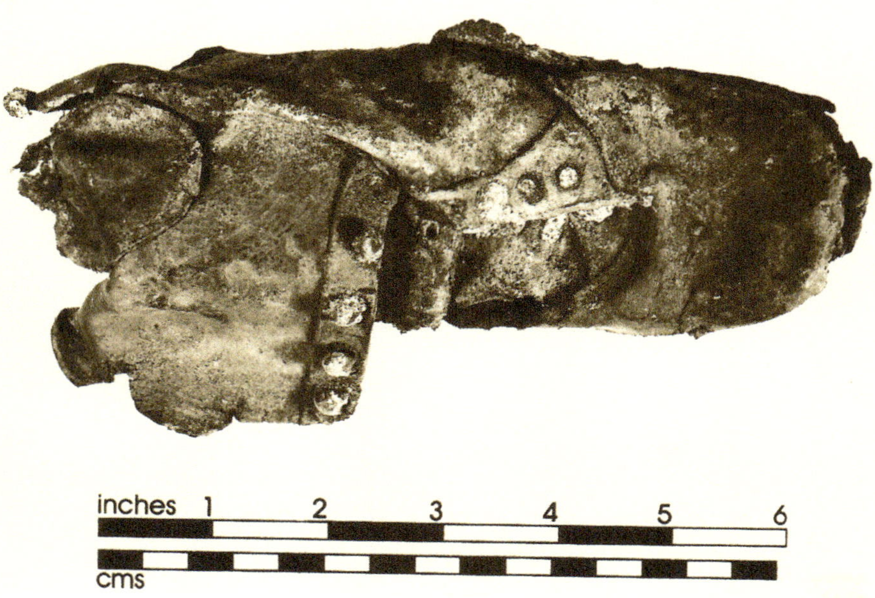

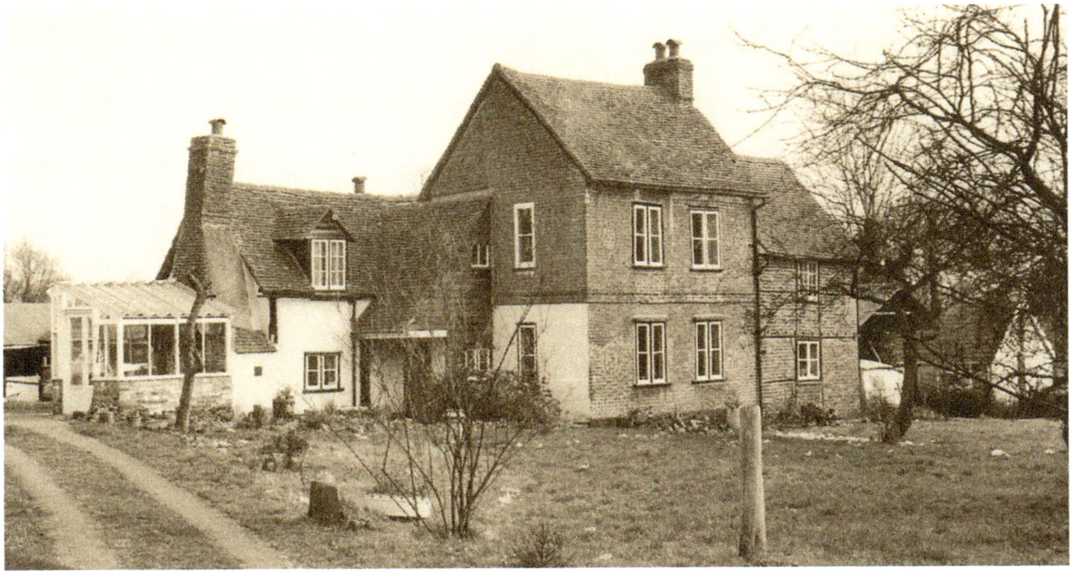

Woodbine Cottage at Tile Kilns

Tile-making was associated with St Catherine's from 1448. This cottage is probably one of the three tile houses mentioned in a survey of 1587, when the tenants were to have 'loam and clay for their necessary uses', but 'every tenant that keepeth a tile kiln must pay to the lord every year when he diggeth earth upon the said common and maketh brick or tile therewith in respect of the said earth one thousand of tiles besides his rent renewed'.

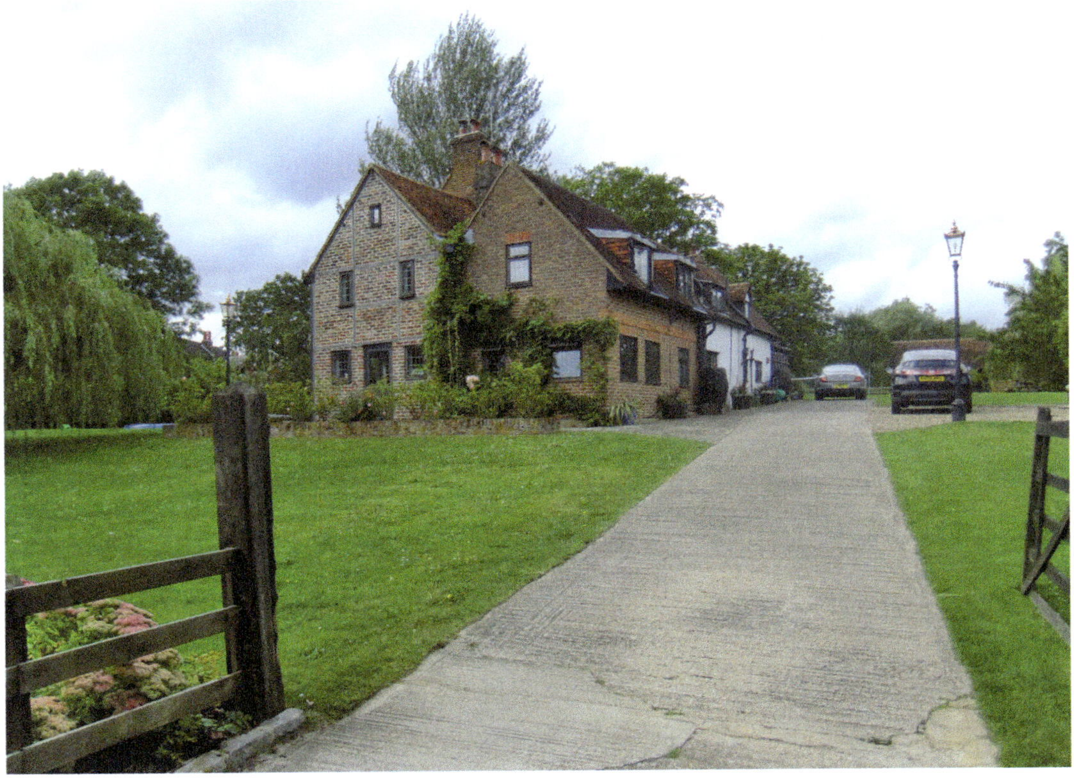

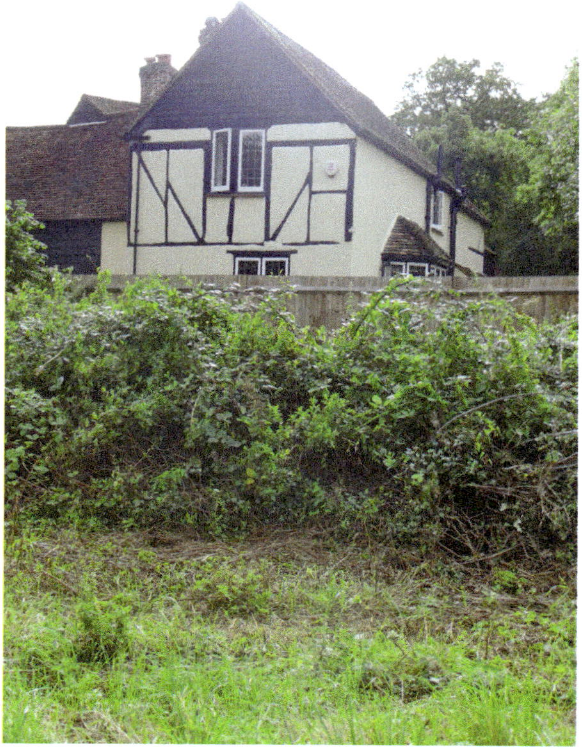

Clack Farm and Tile Kiln Hamlet, Now Known as Old Priory

Mrs Vera Ada Esme Davis, wife of Captain Davis, purchased Clack Farm (above) in 1928, and they restored it with the help of Thomas Downey, a Hertfordshire craftsman. They planned a 'Tudor' hamlet on the adjoining field. The prototype, called Friars Pardon, was built 1934/35, incorporating some old materials. The star house, seen here and now called Lantern House, was built in 1938 for Mr Alfred Crowther, who was associated with architectural salvage. Some of the materials came from Eridge Castle, Kent.

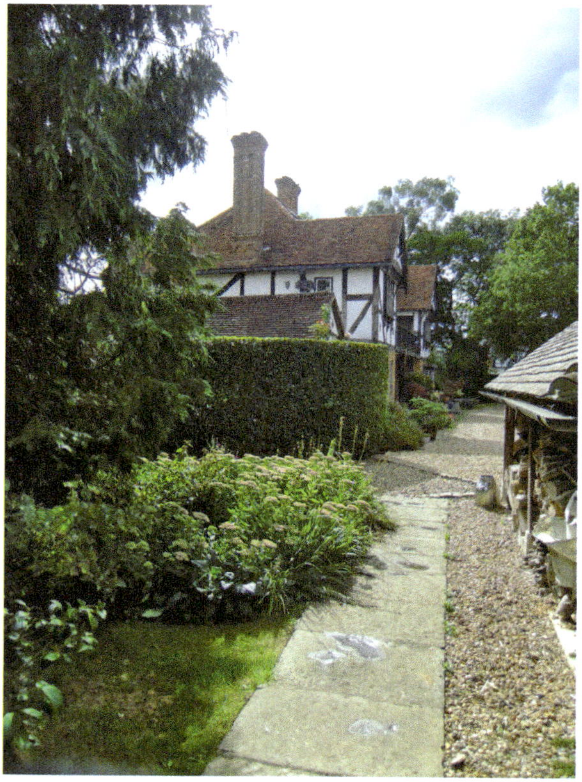

Great and Little King's End

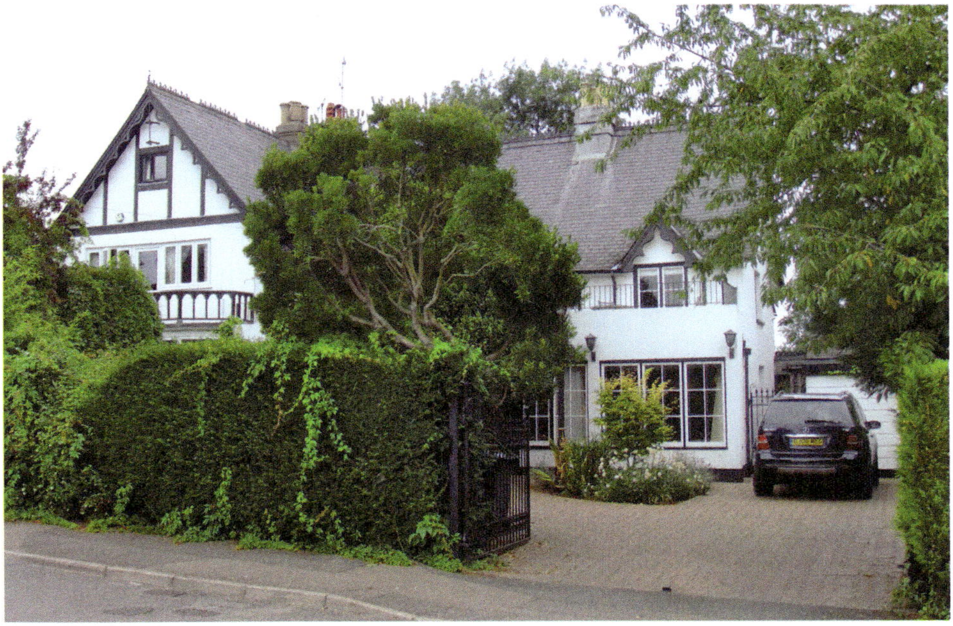

Little King's End, Junction of Hills Lane and Sharps Lane

Old Orchard on the right is an old house that belonged to large landowner, John Walleston in 1565. Walter Morford, a director of Swan & Edgars, lived there in the early years of the twentieth century and extended and gentrified the building, calling it The Laurels. The new wing was separated from the old house in 1927 and was named White Lodge. It became a doctor's surgery in 1958. Kerr's barn stood opposite Old Orchard and the picture shows the view down the lane towards Bury Street.

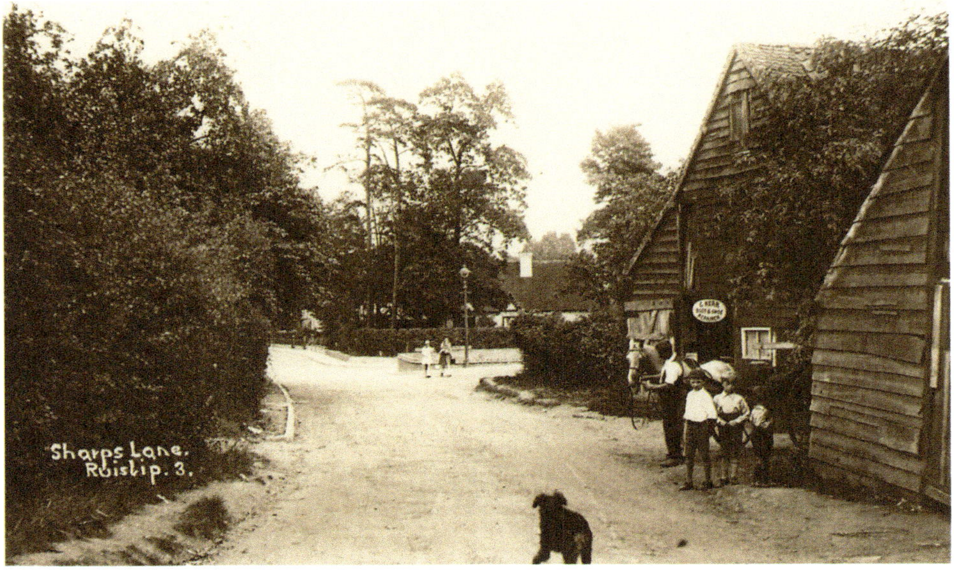

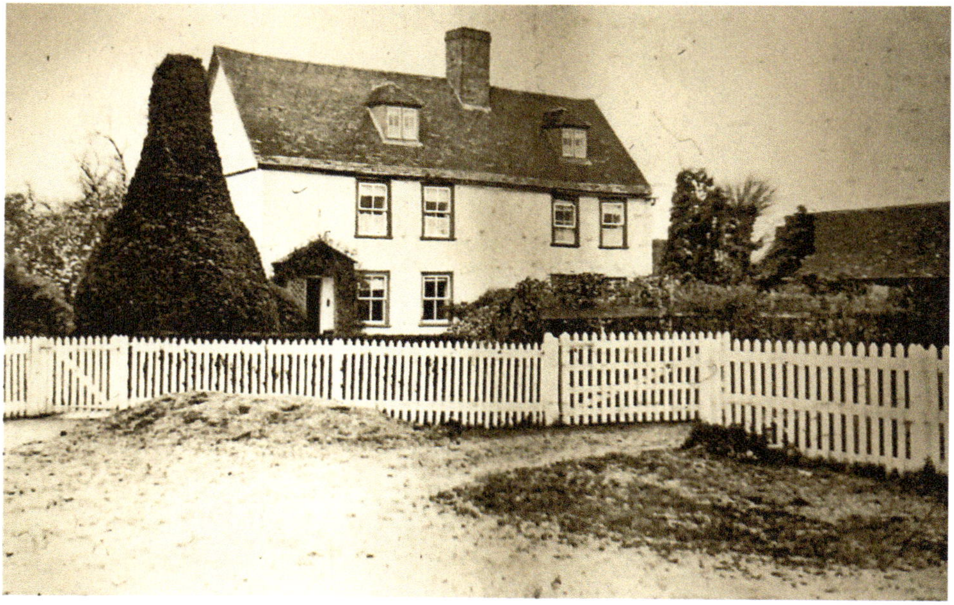

Hill Farm, 1922 and 2012

Hill Farm belonged to Ralph Timberlake in the mid-seventeenth century. He was a yeoman, but some of the family were surgeons, which may be why the property was sold to a London druggist Thomas Serocold in 1713. Mr Clarke of Swakeleys bought the farm in 1758. There were nearly 40 acres of fields around the house as well as land in the common fields. When the Swakeleys estate was auctioned in 1922, tenant James Ewer bought it. Housing development followed.

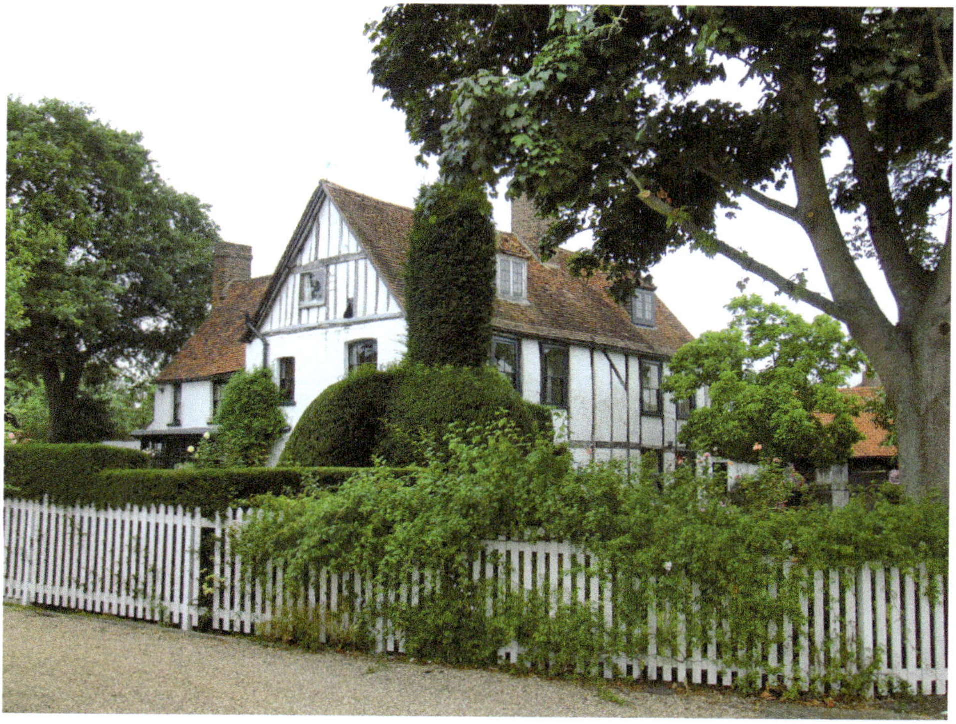

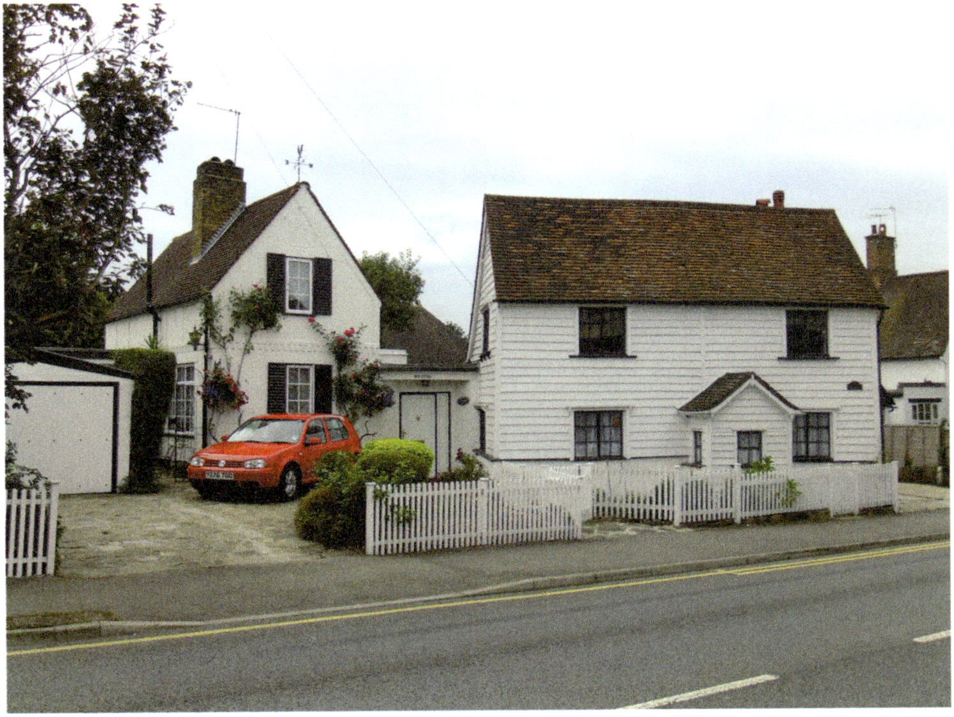

Great King's End: Ickenham Road and Wood Lane Junction

Green Cottage stood at Great King's End Green and survived precariously when the new King's End Avenue was built from the station in 1906. Unusually for the Ruislip area it is weatherboarded. Agricultural labourers and hay binders lived here until Maxwell Scott, a well-known architect, took it and built on Beth Cottage in 1923. The two are now separate houses. The view down the new road towards the High Street shows the type of houses built in the early years of the twentieth century.

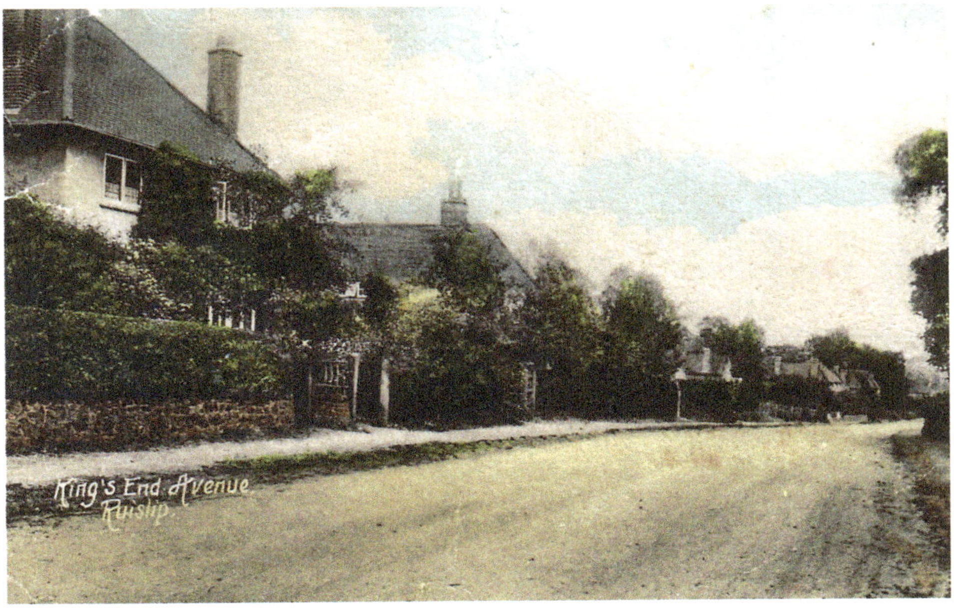

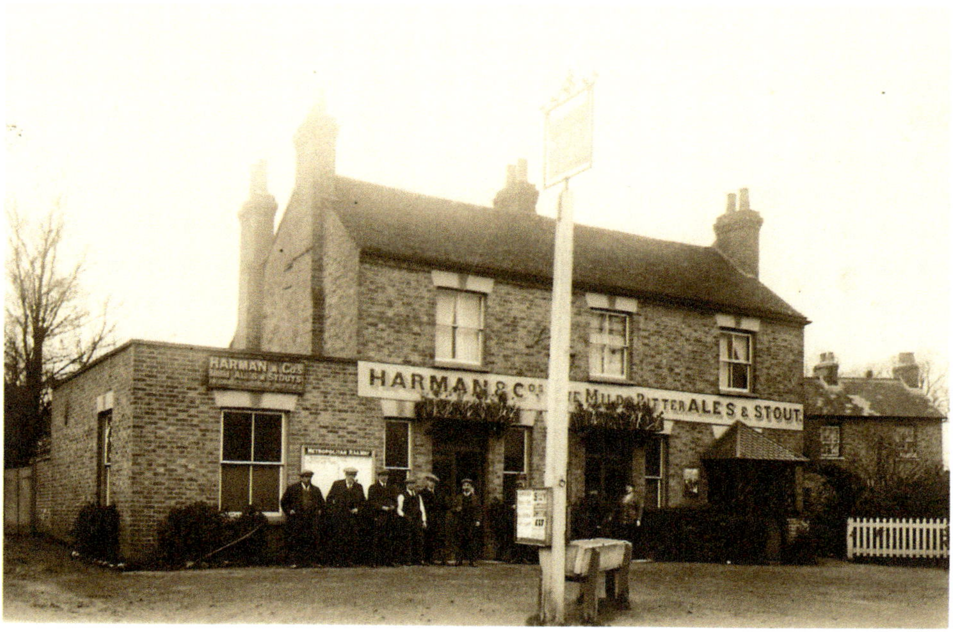

The White Bear

John Weedon held the licence in the 1850s, at a time when there were so many of his kin in the vicinity that the area was referred to as 'The Garden of Weedon'. The extension on the left, built in 1914, has a sign pointing to the Metropolitan Railway, a source of increased trade. Charles Henwood, clerk to a timber wharf, lived in one of King's End Cottages on the right with his wife and five children. The cottages were demolished in 1954.

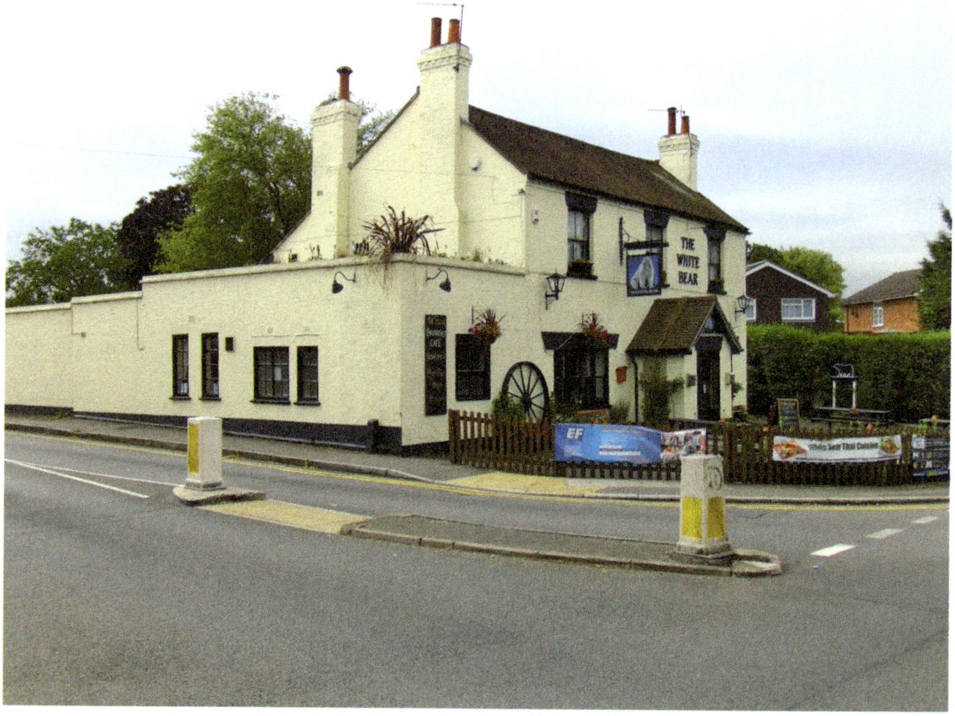

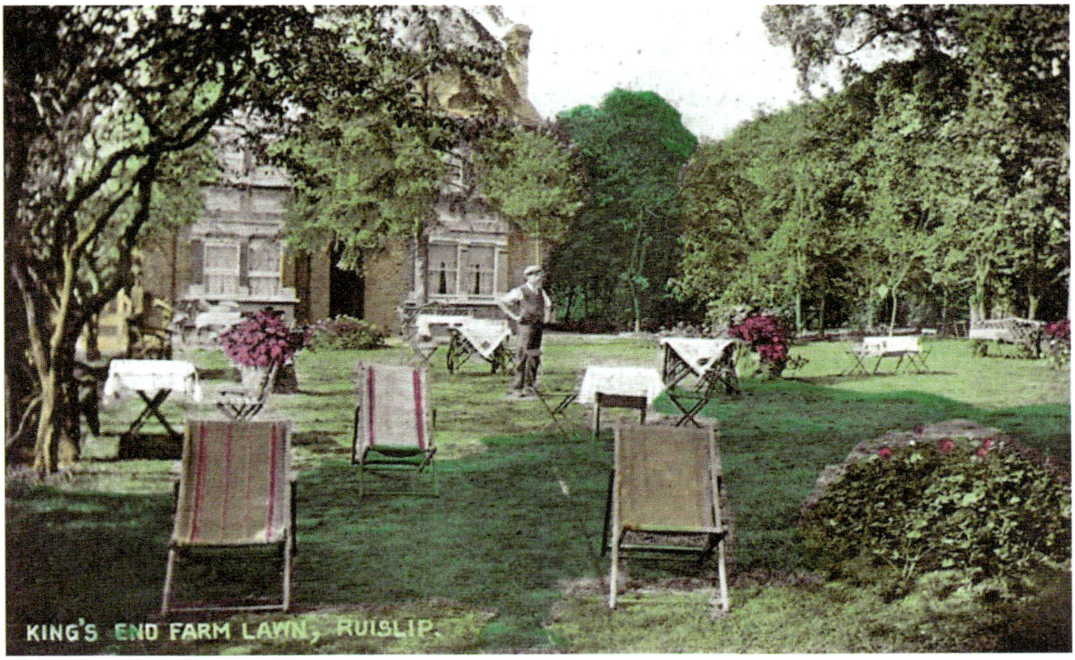

King's End Farm and the Poplars Sports Fields

George Weedon, a man with an entrepreneurial flair, established the Poplars Sports Fields here, with swing boats, donkey rides and cricket pitches, to cater for Sunday School Treats. At the same time he was drawing a higher class of clientele to The Poplars, at the corner of Ickenham Road and the High Street. From 1910 there was an 18-hole golf course that became Ruislip Golf Course. The farmhouse survived as Club House until 1951, when the site was developed.

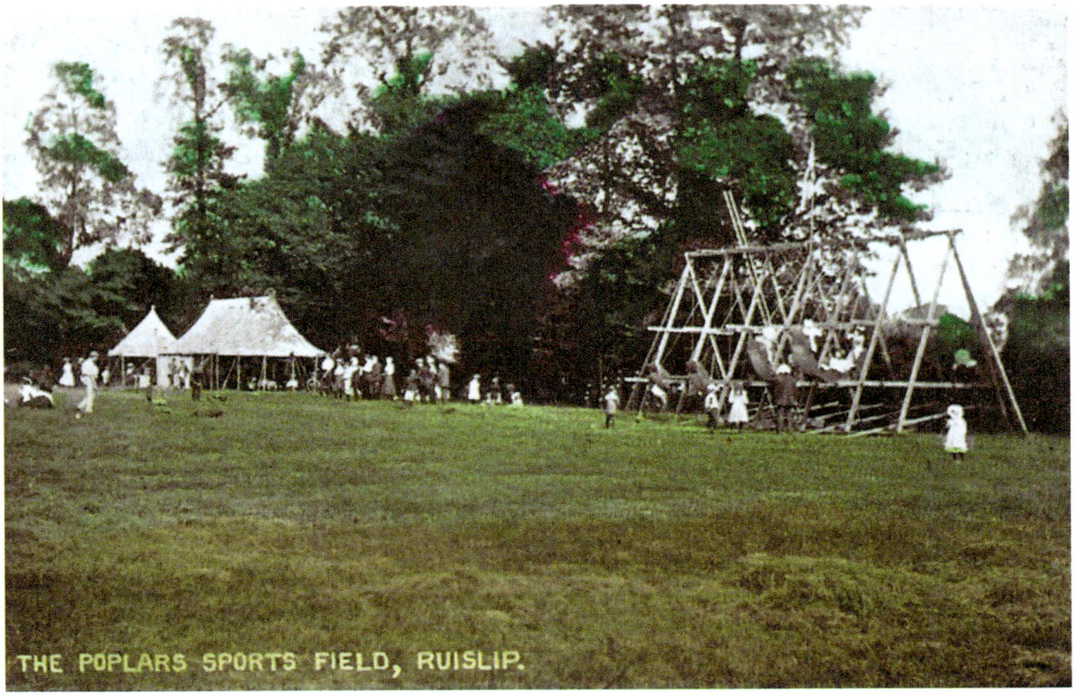

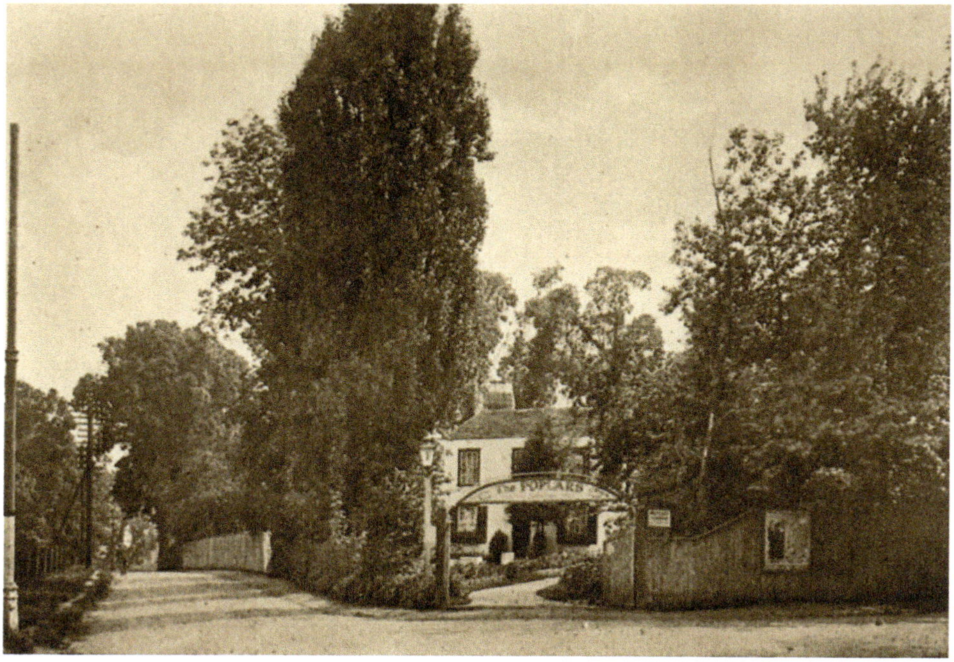

Entrance to the Poplars and the Waitresses

As many as 3,000 trippers arrived at the Poplars on summer weekends. George Weedon stands beside the waitresses in the lower picture. They are wearing bunches of artificial flowers, denoting their names. 'And we spend the day with Rose, you see, At the Poplars where sweet Bluebell serves the tea, And Lily's white hand brings cakes and jam, And don't we enjoy Miss Pansy's cold lamb,' runs the chorus of the Poplars Waltz, which was sold in sheet form, along with other souvenirs.

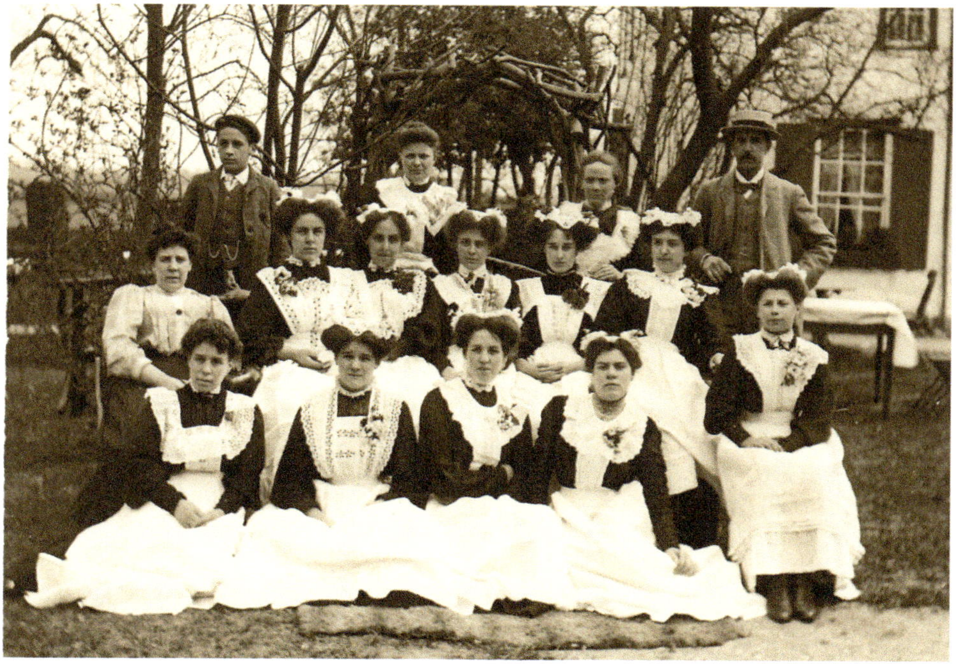

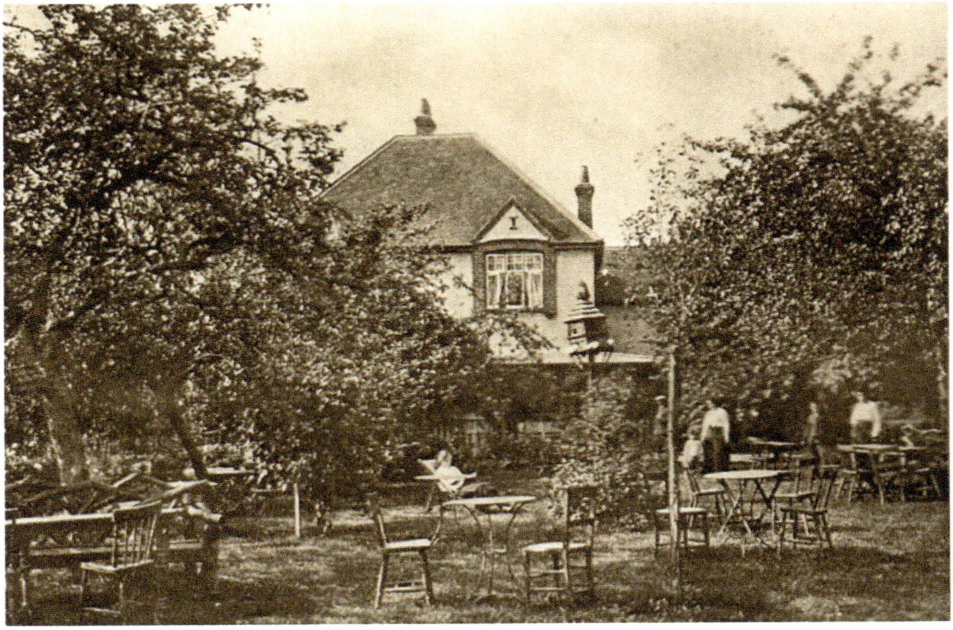

The Orchard Bungalow Hotel to Premier Inn

The Orchard Bungalow, a simple single-storey structure, opened in Easter 1905 to capture the tourists pouring out of Baker Street for a day in the country. Mr and Mrs Rayment, the proprietors, soon added another storey and the next owners ran it as a hotel. It was a high-class restaurant, famed for its dinner dances throughout the Home Counties from 1933–71. RAF men frequented it during the war years.

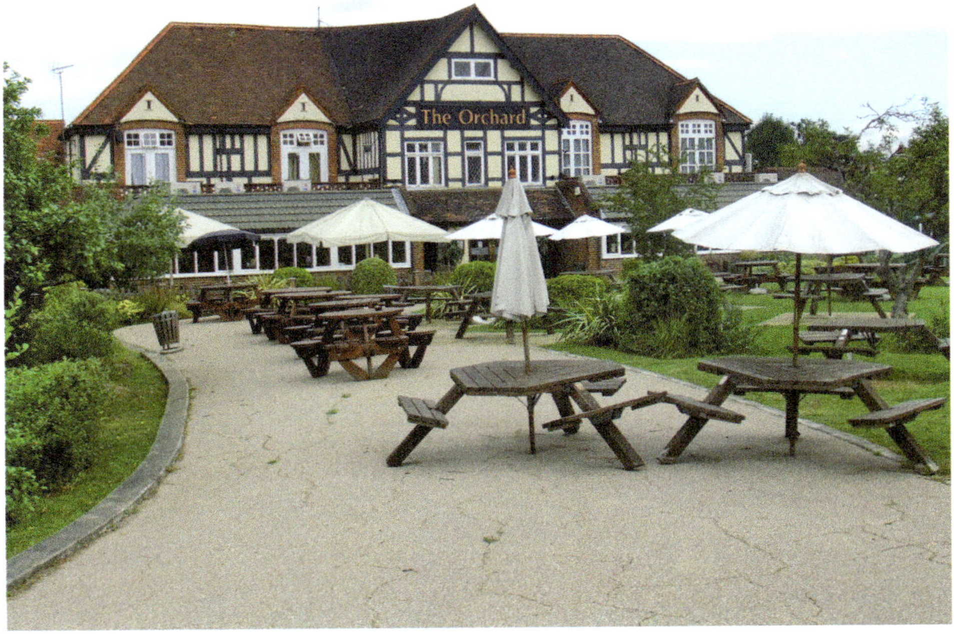

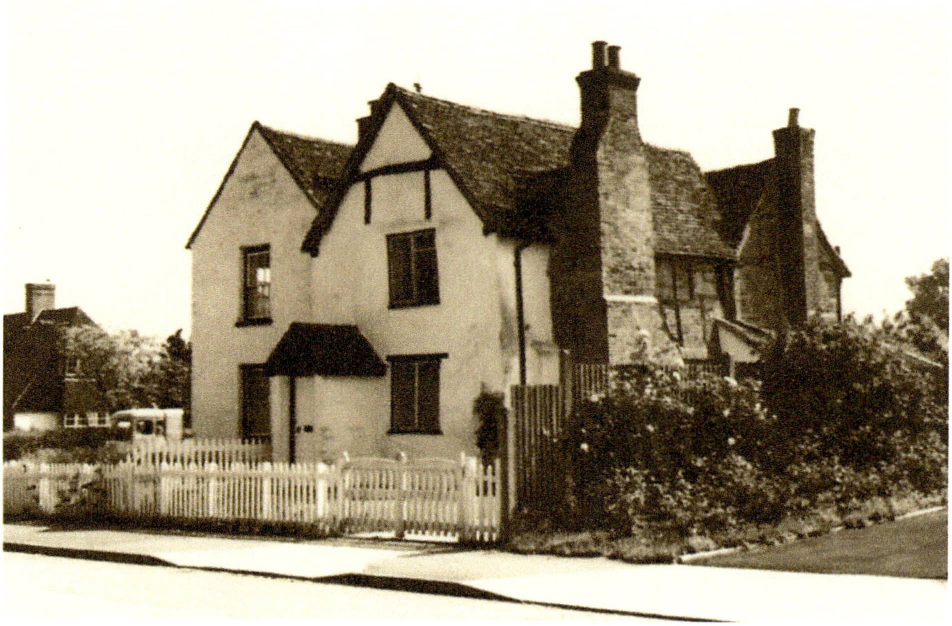

Primrose Hill Cottages

In 1971, the cottage on the right shows its timber framing on two sides and has a splendid chimney. There is a wing at the back. On the left is an eighteenth-century addition, while around the corner out of sight is a small Victorian extension. The building had long been divided into three separate dwellings. Soon after the top picture was taken, a new wing and garage covered the timber and brick nogging, and modern houses have further encroached upon this once rural scene.

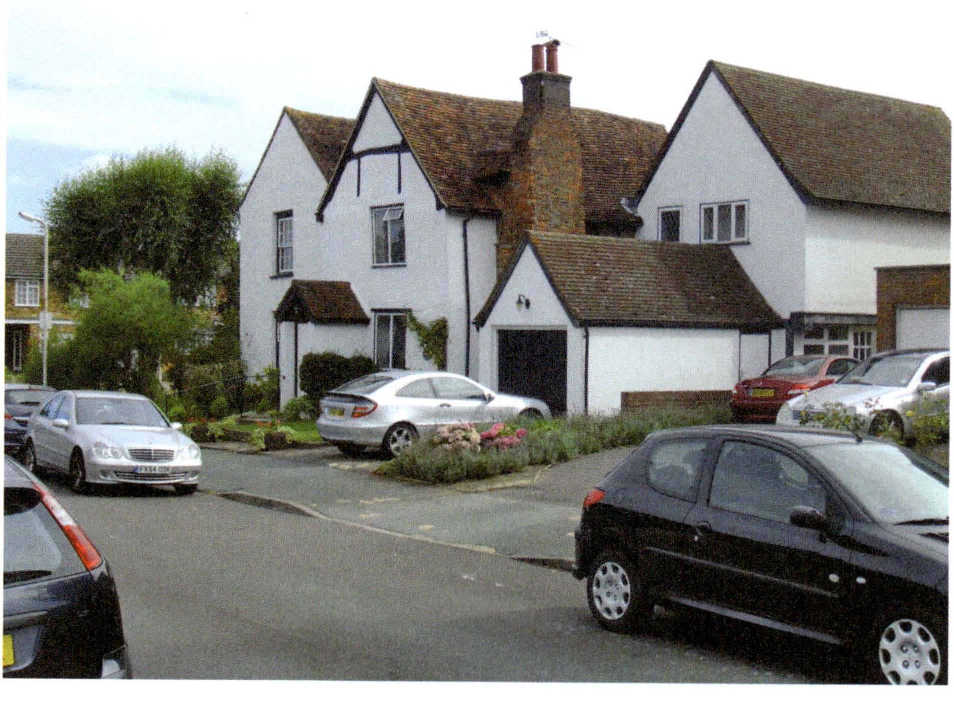

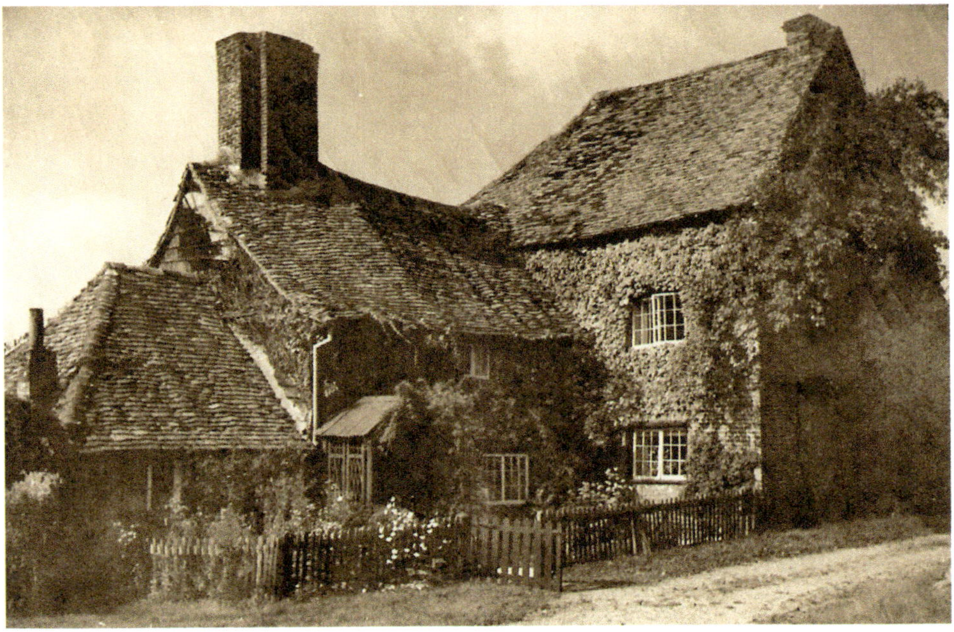

Primrose Hill Farm and the Site in 2012

William Weedon lived at Primrose Hill with his wife and ten children in 1851. Edwin Ewer of Wilkins Farm purchased the farm before 1902, and a new farmhouse was built in 1910, when his son, Shatford Ewer, married. The old farmhouse became a farm cottage, in which Daniel and Alice Collins lived. Shatford Ewer's widow sold the farm to Glaxo around 1960, but it was sold on to Wimpey's. The land north of the railway line was developed in 1962.

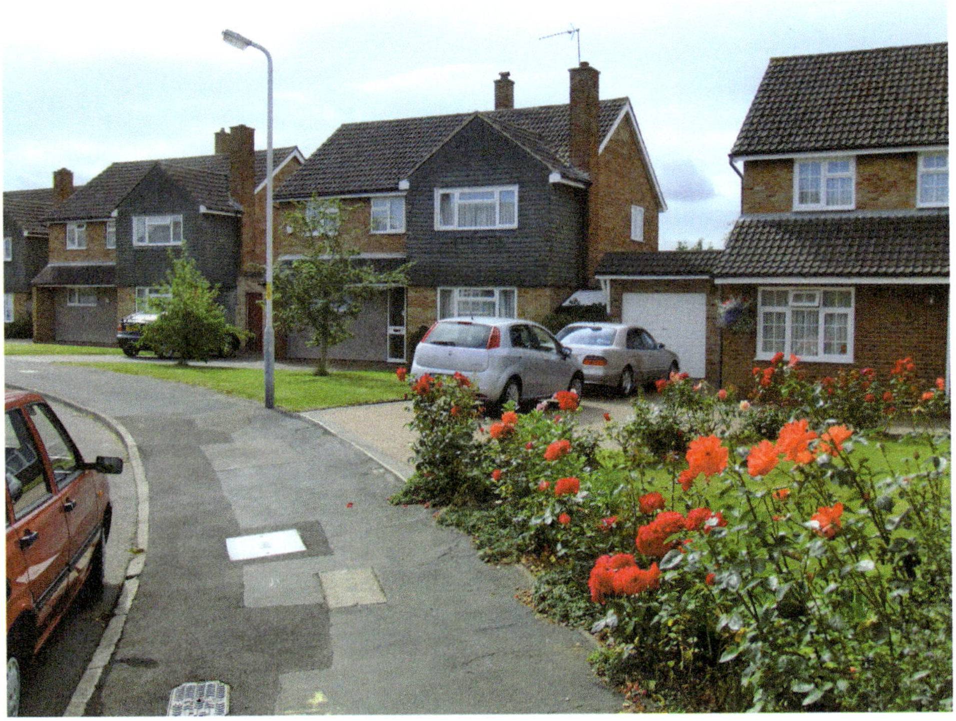

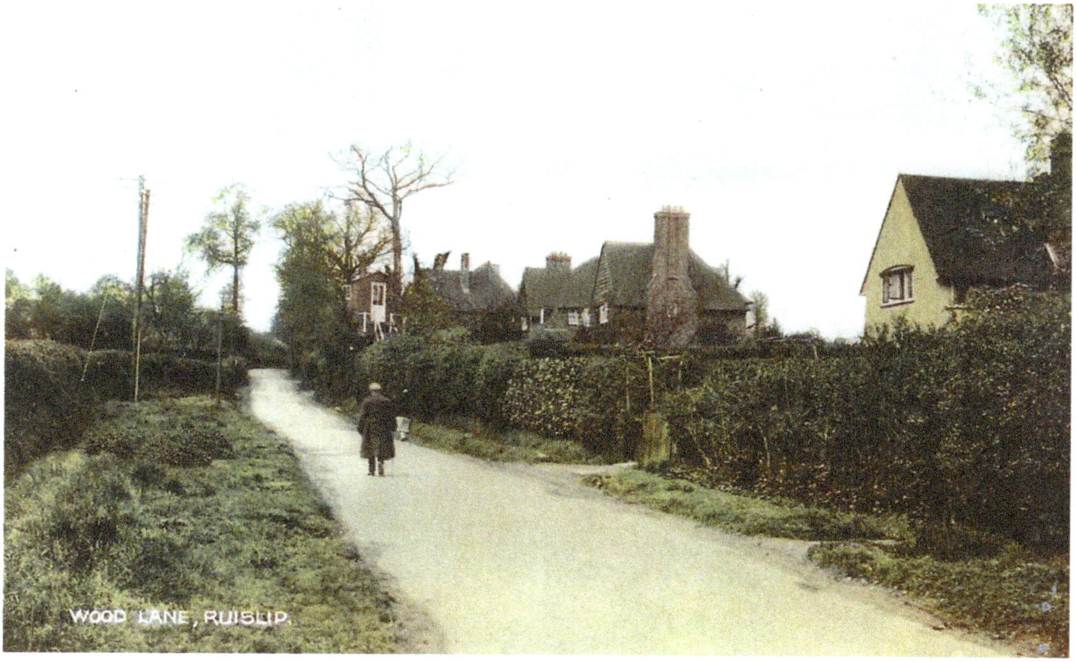

The Tree House in Wood Lane

Wood Lane is a medieval lane connecting Great King's End with Field End Green and the open fields. New detached houses were built between 1911 and 1913 and spasmodically after the First World War. A few more were added in the 1950s and there has been some infilling since. The tree house seems to have aroused much interest and became the subject of postcards. In the modern picture, the tree remains, but the tree house is long since gone.

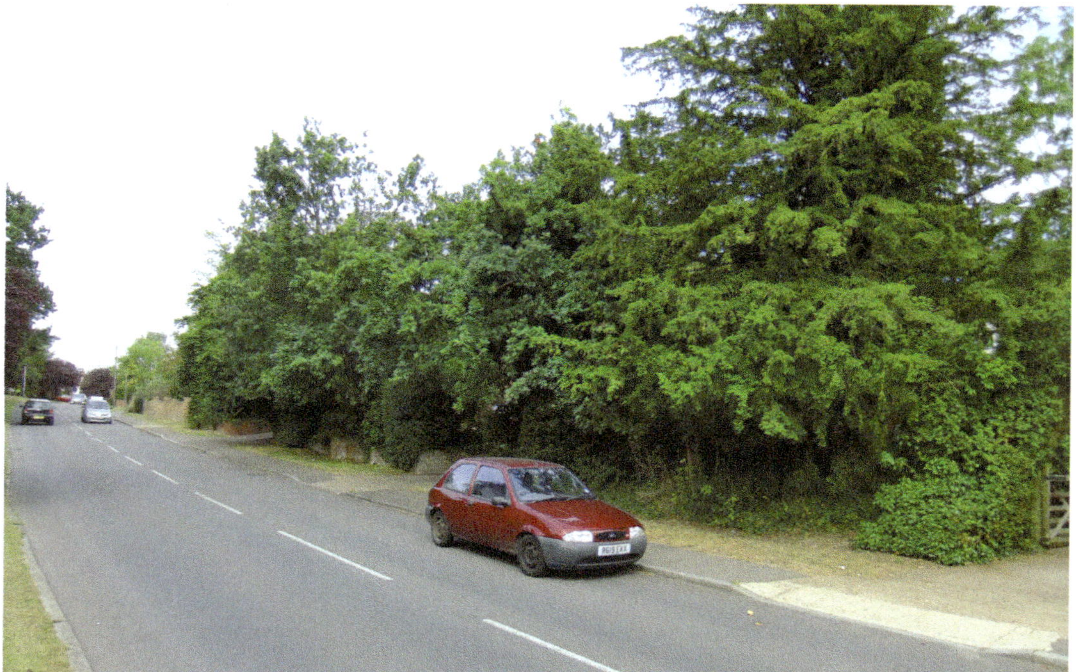

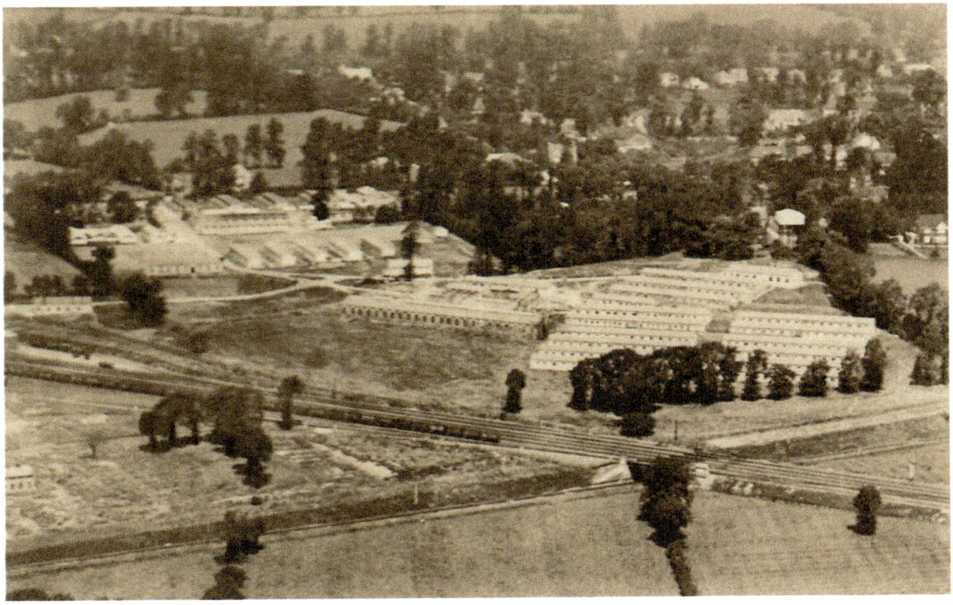

RAF Records

RAF records were established between Primrose Hill and West Ruislip station. A two-year apprenticeship scheme, to train boys in general clerical duties and accountancy, was run there from 1925 to 1945. They helped in the Records Office and a significant number became aircrew. The site also contained barracks, sports facilities and married quarters. Part of the area is now used by Sea Cadets.

West Ruislip station opened in April 1906 as Ruislip & Ickenham station on the Great Western & Great Central Joint Railway.

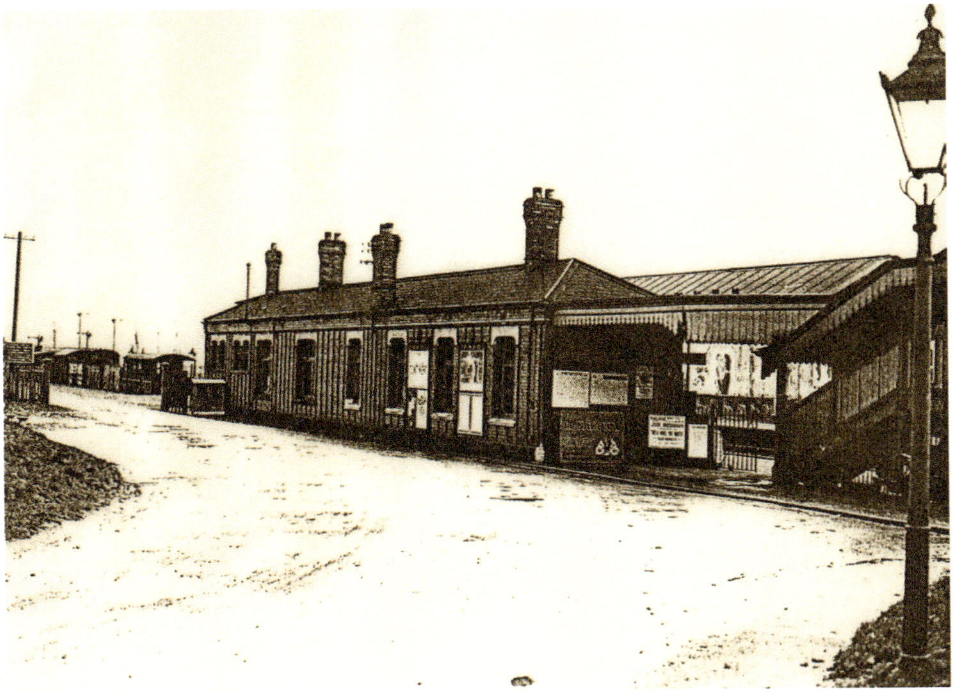

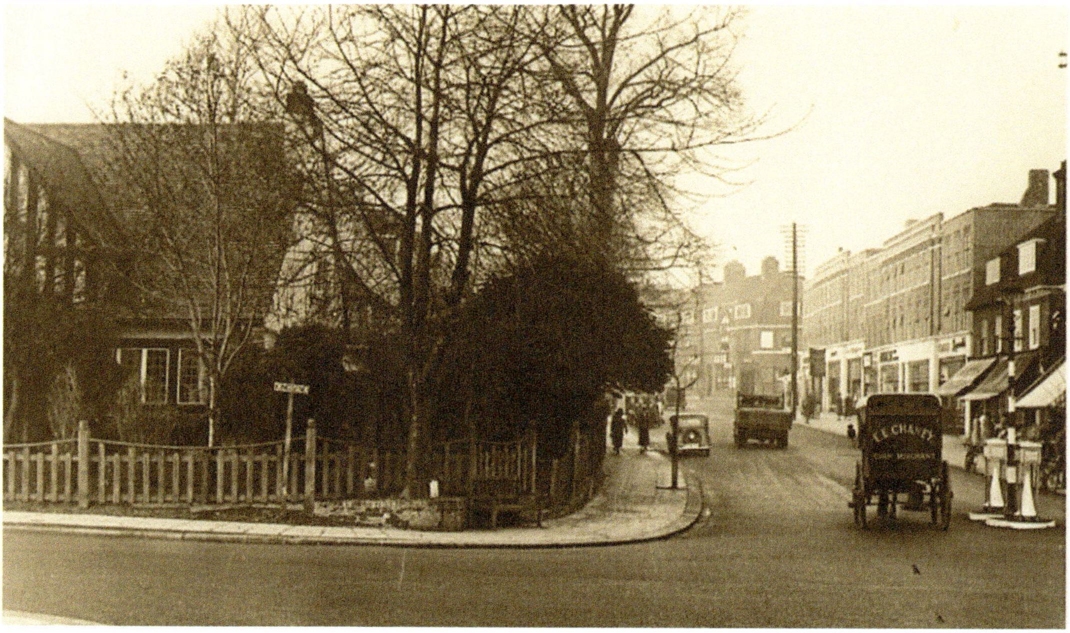

Daily Mirror Cottage and Quilters

This cottage first appeared at the Ideal Home Exhibition at Olympia, resembling an 'old world' cottage with polished tiles on the floor and window sills. It was re-erected at the corner of King's End and the High Street in 1910. Mr Dicky, who was in films, was the first owner and used to make films around this corner, turning the camera handle by hand. Quilters furniture store was built on the site in 1954.

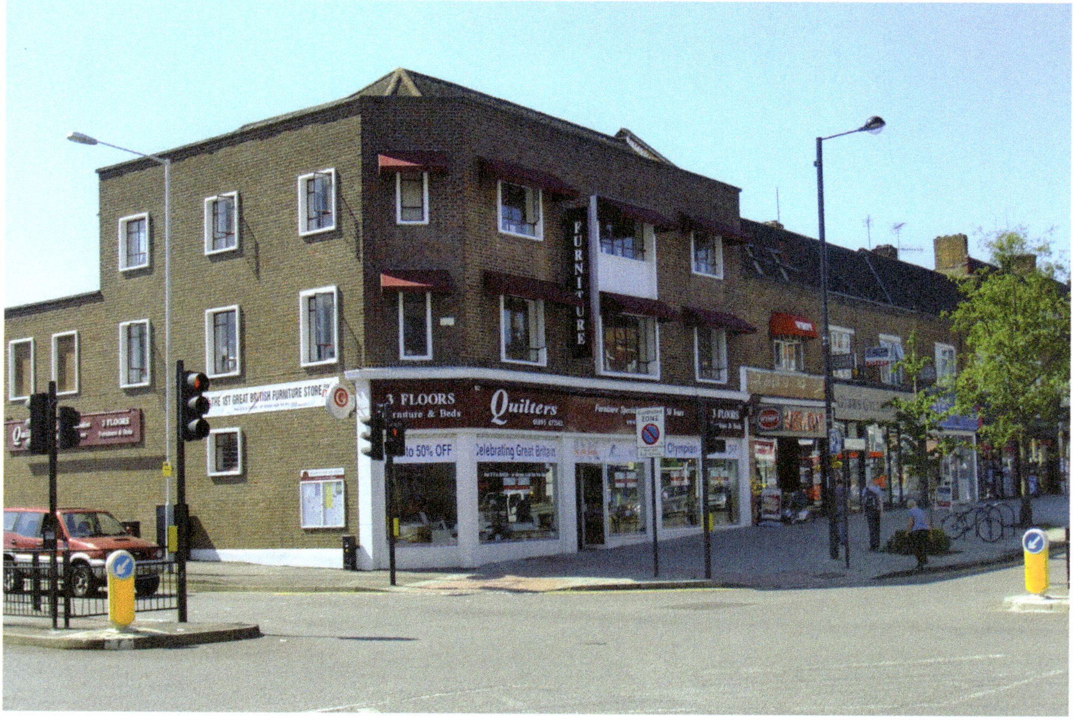

Field End and the Open Fields

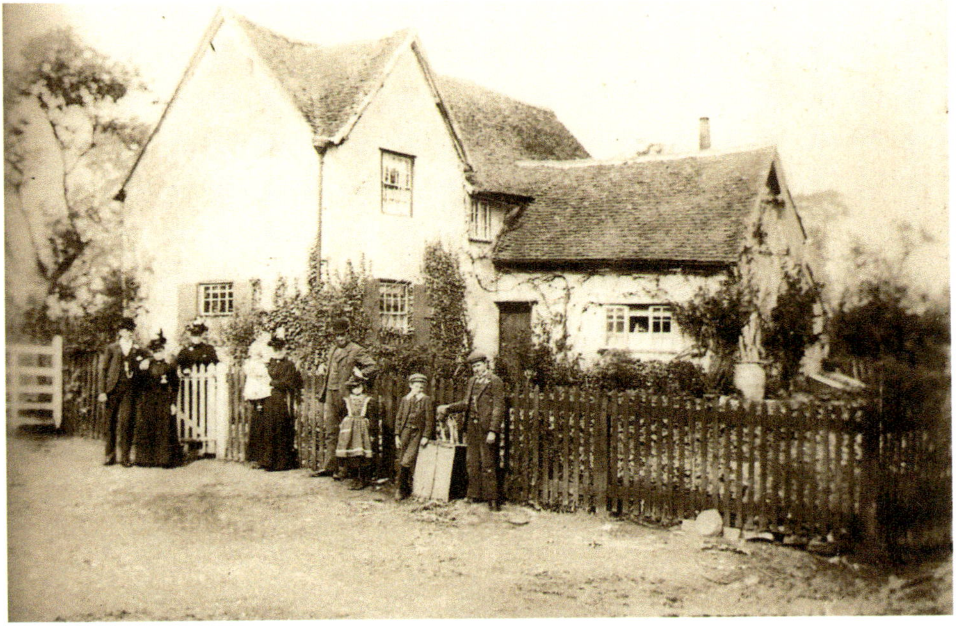

Sherley's Farm with Members of the Collins Family Outside

Frederick Sherley bought this old farmhouse from the Hilliards around 1860, and his name was long associated with it, despite Henry James Ewer becoming owner in 1894. The Collins family lived here as tenants for generations. 'Old' Harry Collins let the barn and stables to a riding school, living alone in such squalor that the house was condemned when he died in 1947. Restored by Mr Saunders, it is now a flourishing hotel and restaurant, as seen below.

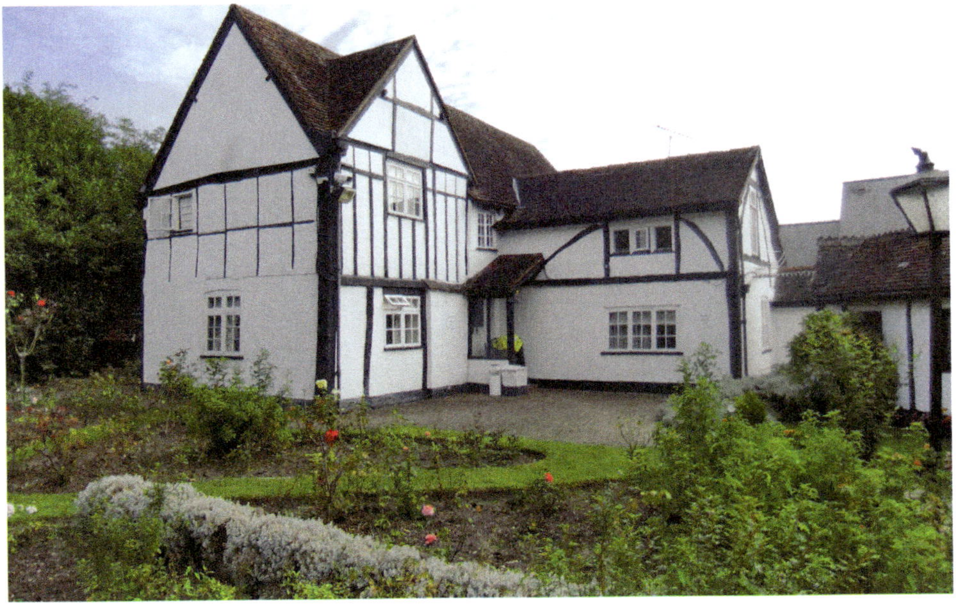

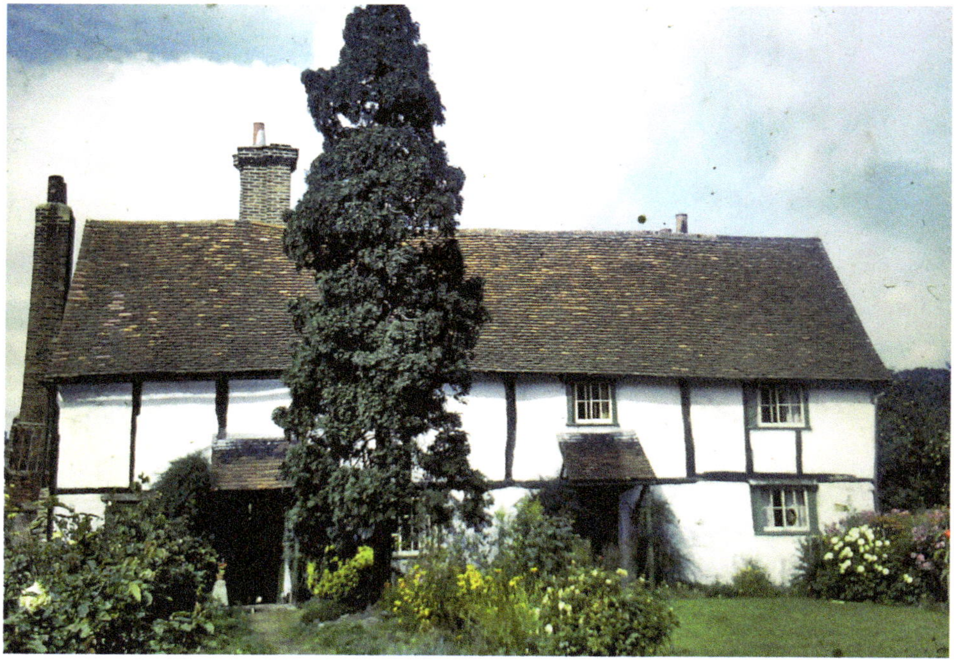

Field End Farm Cottages and Demolition in the Early 1960s
Shown before and during demolition, the timber-framed house with fine brick chimney and jetty was divided into two farm labourers' cottages and farmed from Primrose Hill Farm. According to Alice Hood *née* Weedon, who was born there in 1898, there was no division between the two parts of the building upstairs. The Metropolitan Railway line cut through the farm land and accommodation bridges had to be built to allow cattle free access to the fields on either side. Pond Green is now on the site.

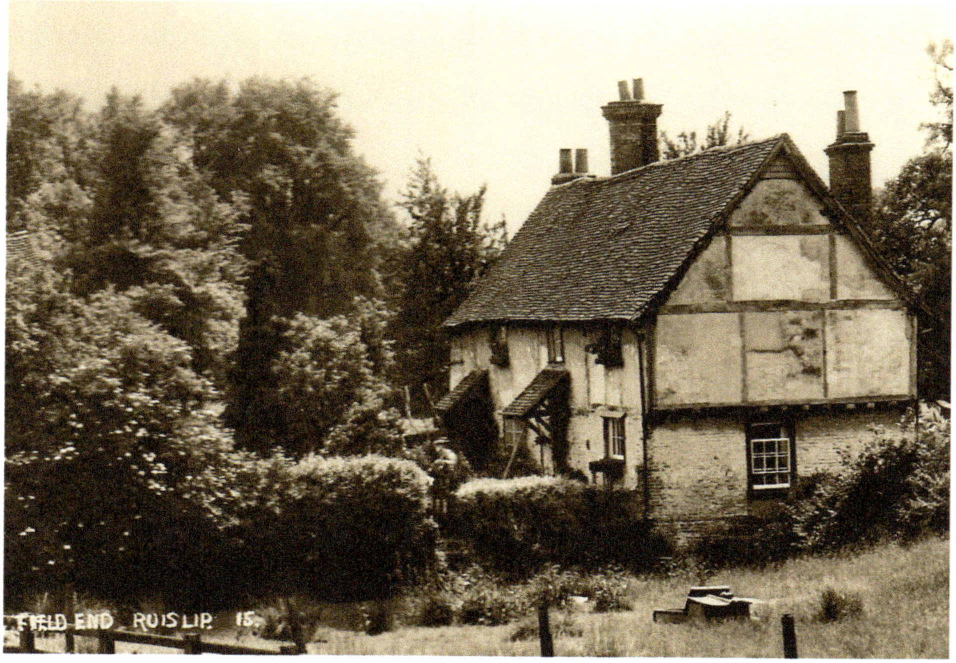

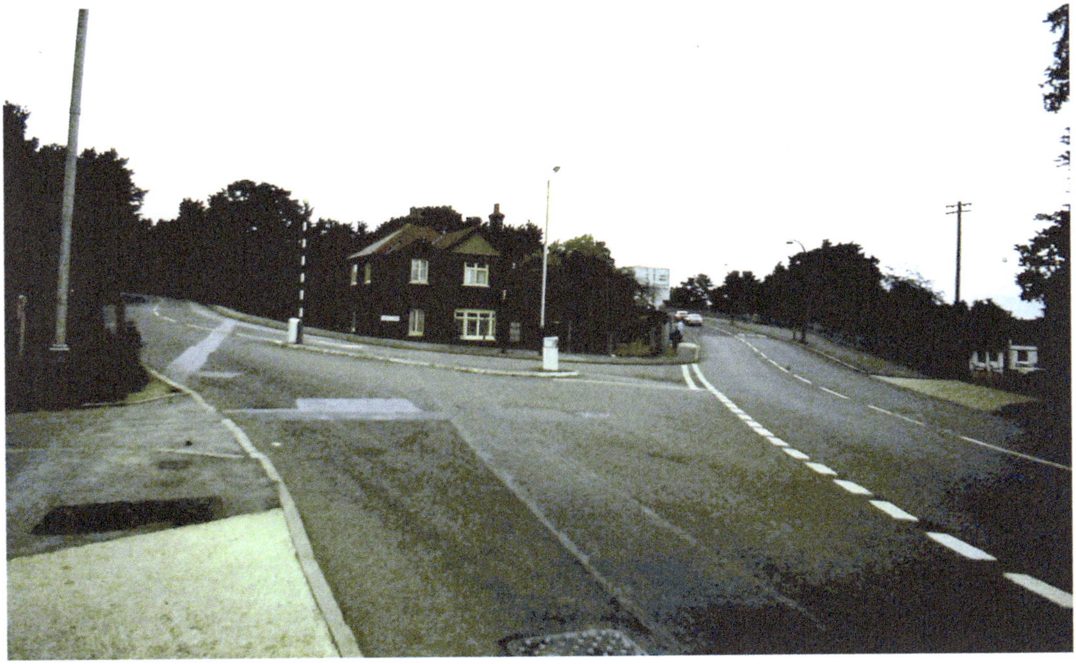

Stationmaster's Cottage and Master's Court Retirement Homes, *c.* 1970 and 2012

The railway station opened in 1904. Mr Smith, the stationmaster, complete with top hat, had his own house at the junction of Wood Lane and West End Road between the slopes of the two bridges, on a triangular plot of land owned by the railway company. The house was lit by electricity powered by the live rails and consequently lighting levels fluctuated considerably as trains passed. Master's Court and Sherleys Court were built on the site of the house and garden in 1994 and 1996.

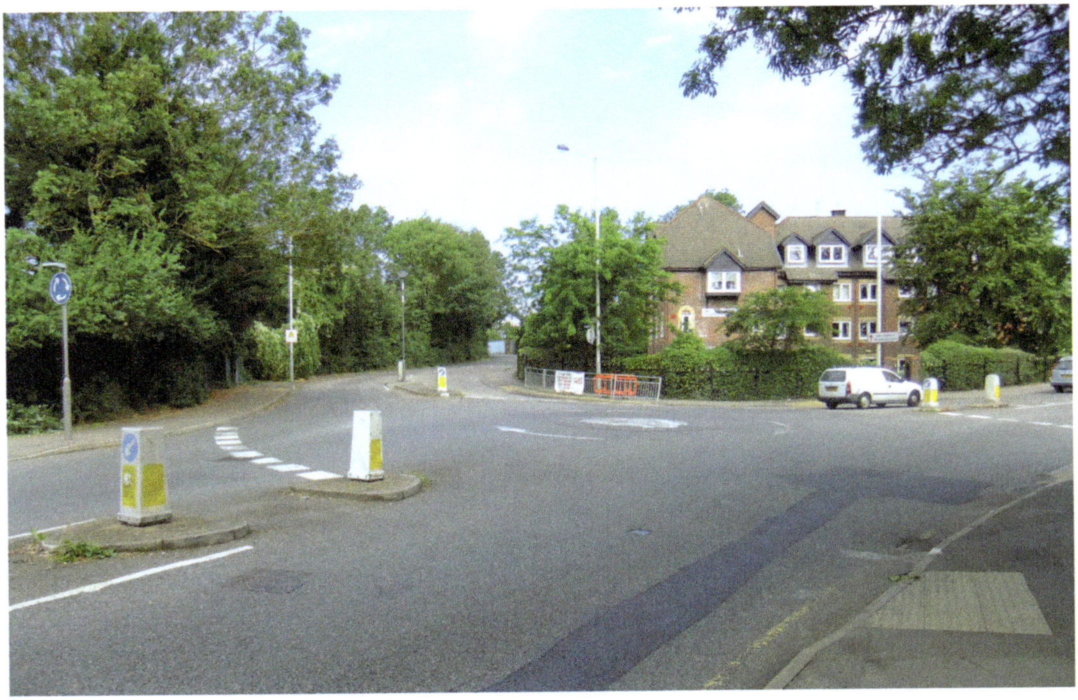

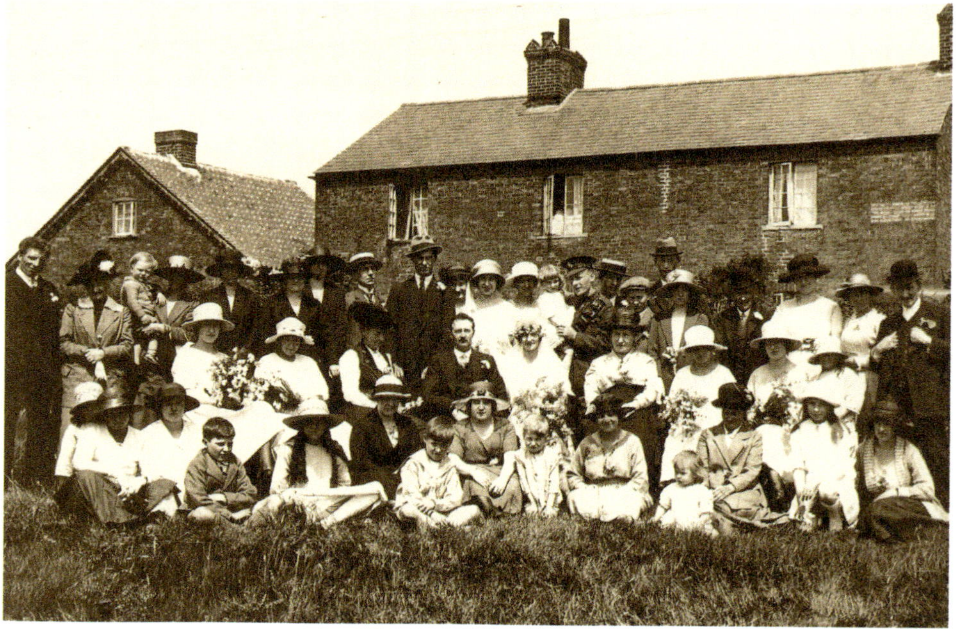

Beddingfield Place, 1922 and 2012

Frederick Sherley built five cottages – a terrace of three and a semi-detached pair – in 1866, apparently using bricks made at a small and short-lived brickworks that he opened near the present Grosvenor Vale. Agricultural labourers, shepherds and hay binders lived here over the years. The view of the cottages on Elizabeth King's wedding day in 1922 shows the brickwork. The cottages were modernised and covered in pebble dash, and the semi-detached pair was completely rebuilt in 1984.

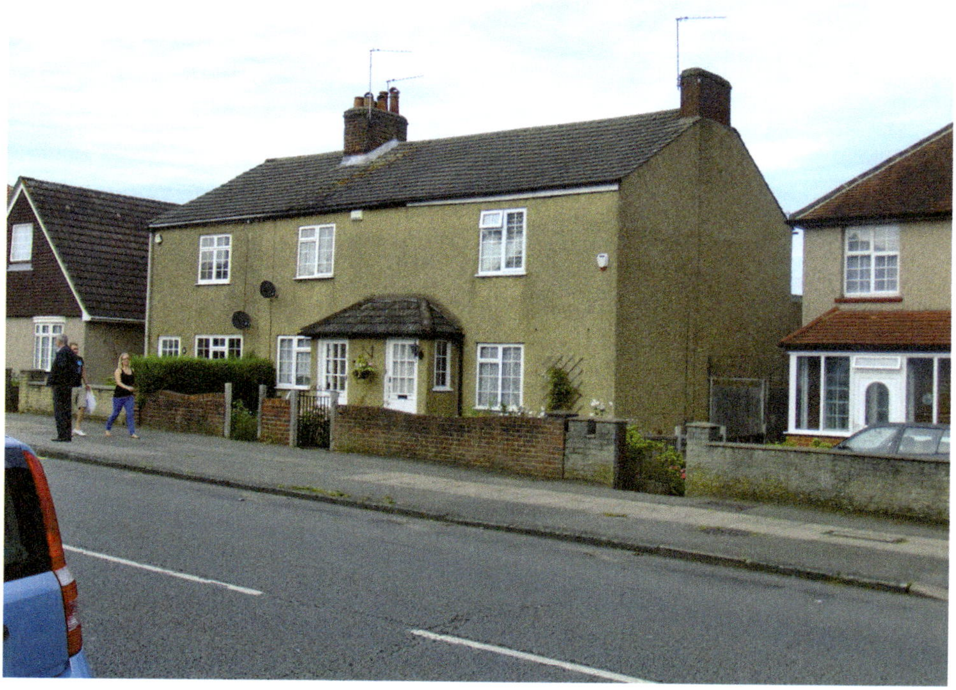

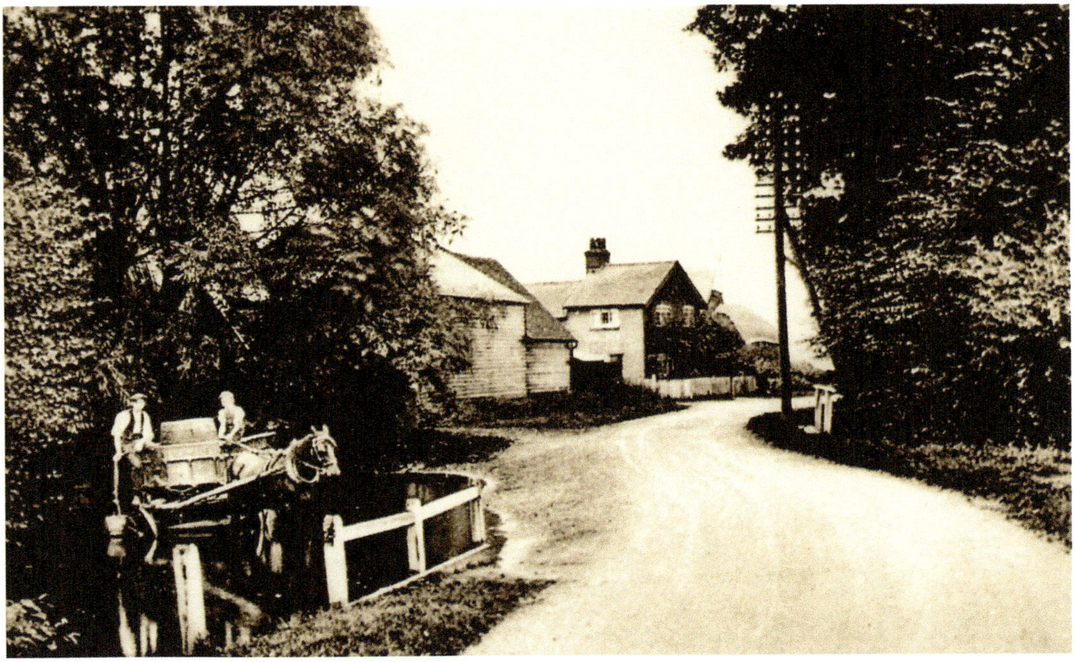

Old Pond Farm, Early Twentieth Centur,y and New Pond Farm, 2012

Ralph Deane, who leased Manor Farm and the demesne from King's College, erected a cottage and farm buildings beside a pond in West End Road, around 1850, on a piece of his own land. In 1872 King's College built a new farmhouse on the other side of the college land. The two became known as New Pond and Old Pond Farms. The land was sold to Southern Estates Ltd in 1930. New Pond Farm is now Ruislip Nursing Home.

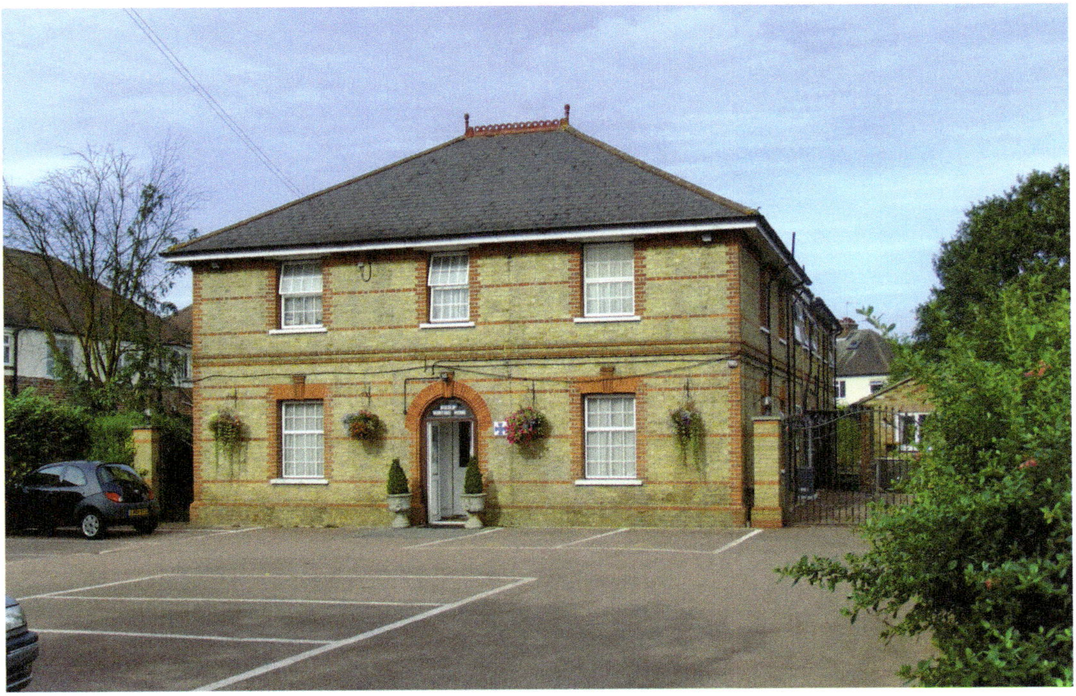

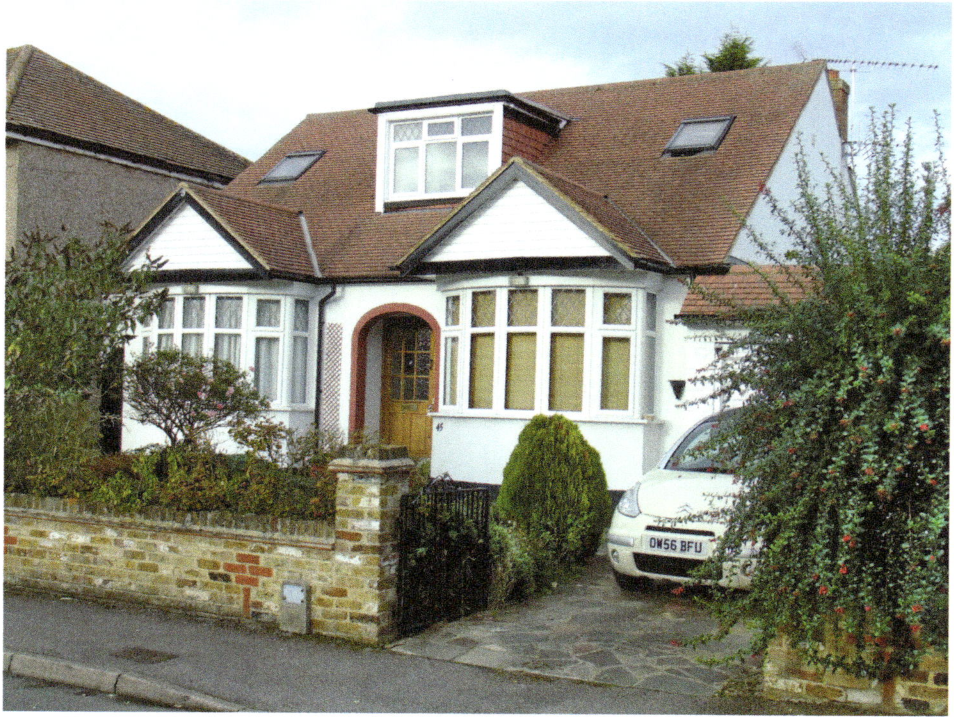

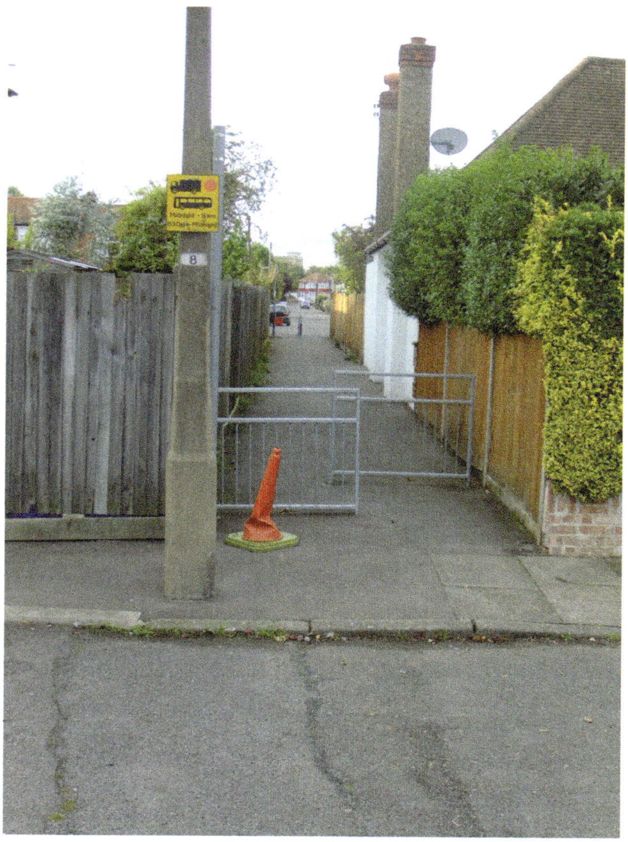

45 Cranley Drive and the Alley

Helen and Peter Kroger, Soviet agents posing as antiquarian booksellers, moved into 45 Cranley Drive in 1955. They were arrested in 1960 after a surveillance operation, conducted from a house in Courtfield Gardens that overlooked their bungalow and belonged to neighbours with whom they had made friends. Gordon Lonsdale, a Russian spy, parked his car in Willow Gardens and slipped down this alley to bring secrets from the Underwater Weapons Establishment at Portland, for the couple to transmit abroad in microdots hidden in full stops.

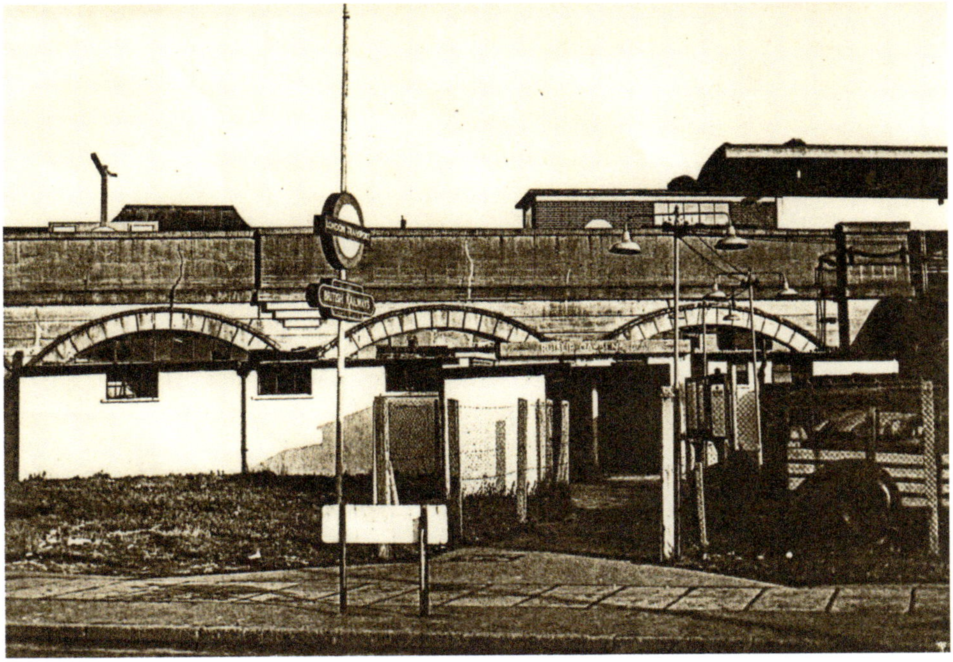

Gaily into Ruislip Gardens Runs the Red Electric Train

The station opened in July 1934 as a halt on the GW & GC Joint Railway. A pagoda-style 'waiting hut' can be seen on the platform in the top photograph. Main Line trains stopped here until 1958. The Central Line running on adjacent lines was planned from 1934, but only opened here in 1948. The lower picture shows the Central Line station in 2012. The booking hall built in 1962 echoes the temporary wooden structure erected in 1948.

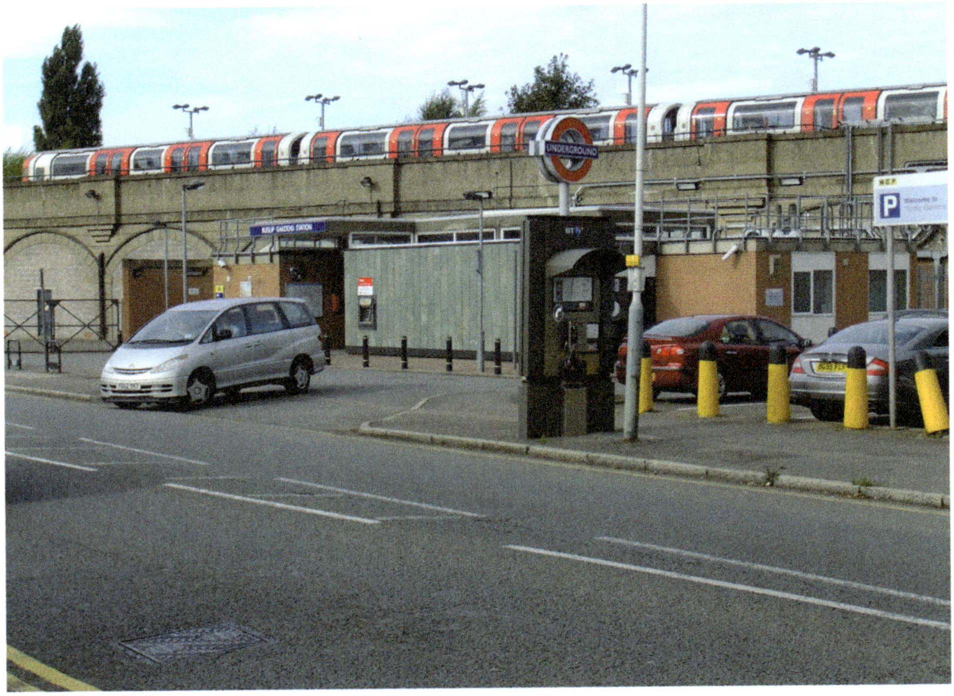

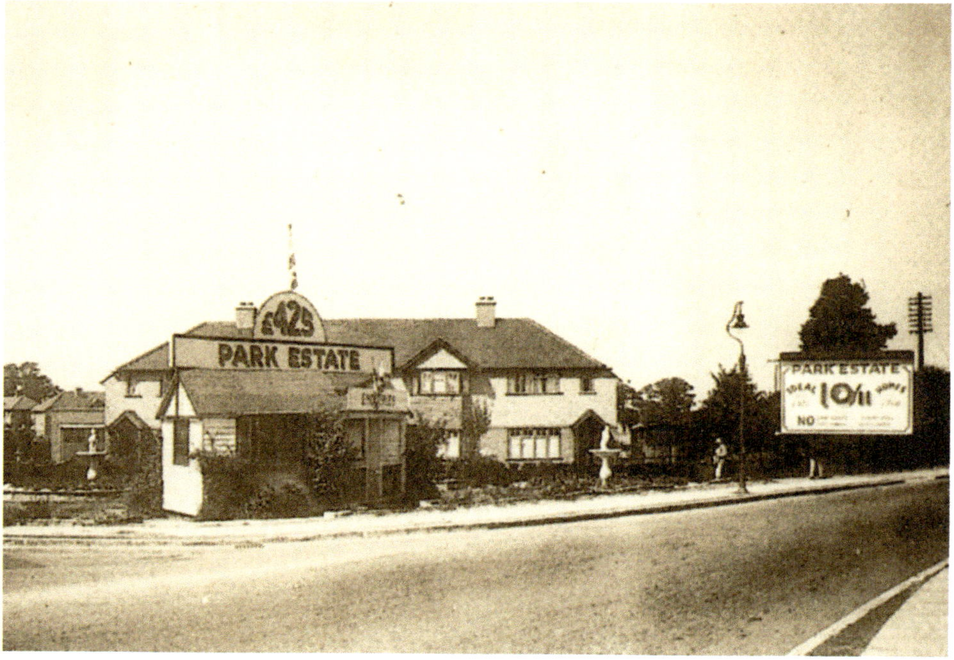

Suburban Development at Ruislip Gardens

Houses soon sprang up on the Park estate opposite the new station, where 'Ideal Homes' were selling for £425. Jack (Kid) Berg, lightweight champion of Great Britain, was 'personally selling' them in 1935 as an inducement to hesitant buyers. Shops and the handsome Tudor-esque Bell public house, built on the north side of the station bridge, served the new suburb.

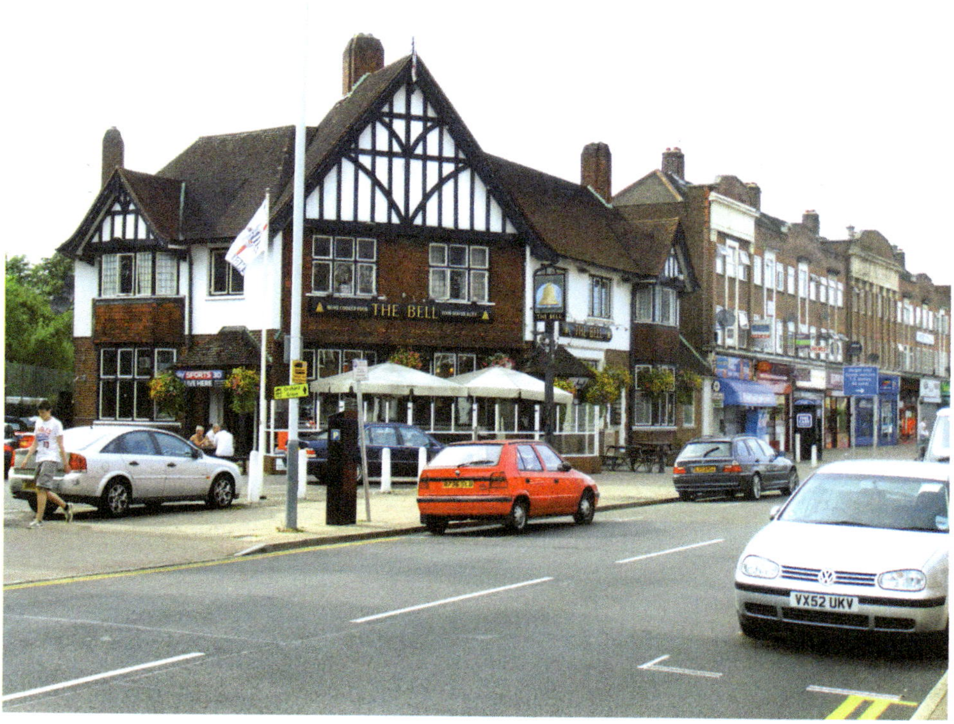

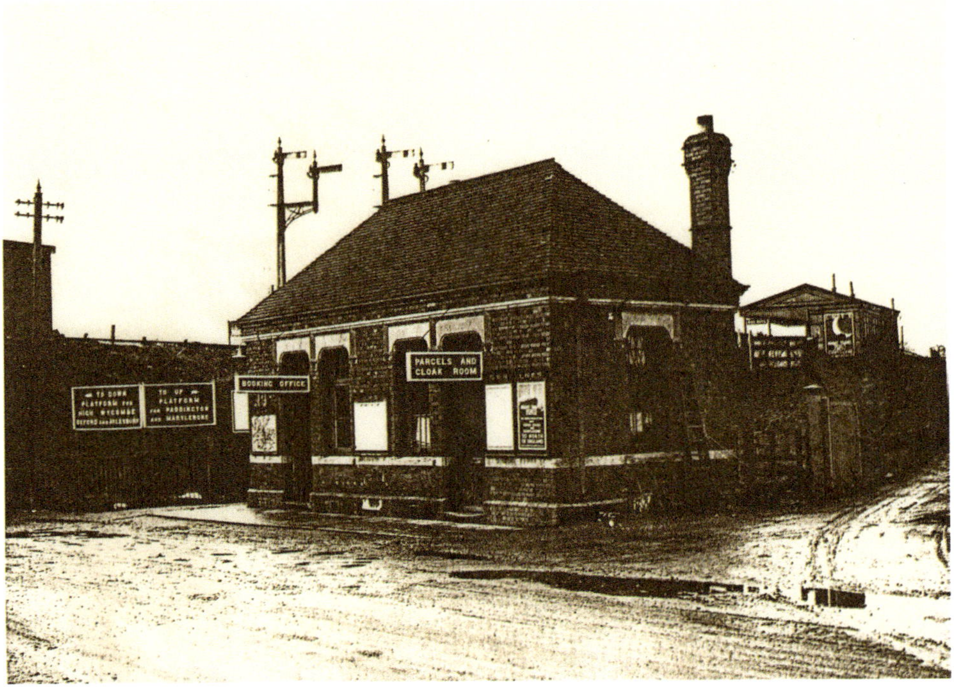

Northolt Junction & South Ruislip Station 1937 and Station Approach 2012

Northolt Junction station opened on the GW & GC Joint Railway in 1908. South Ruislip was added to the name in 1932, after petitioning by the RNUDC. The Central Line ran through from 1948, but the new booking hall was not completed until 1960. The lower picture shows a typical traffic queue slowly wending its way past the modern station.

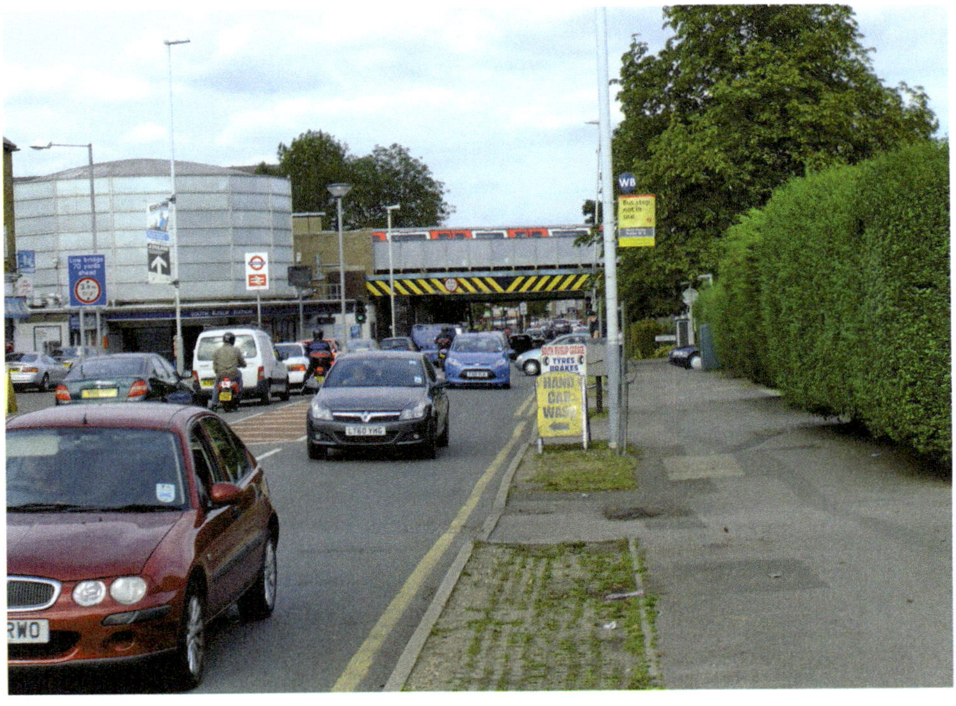

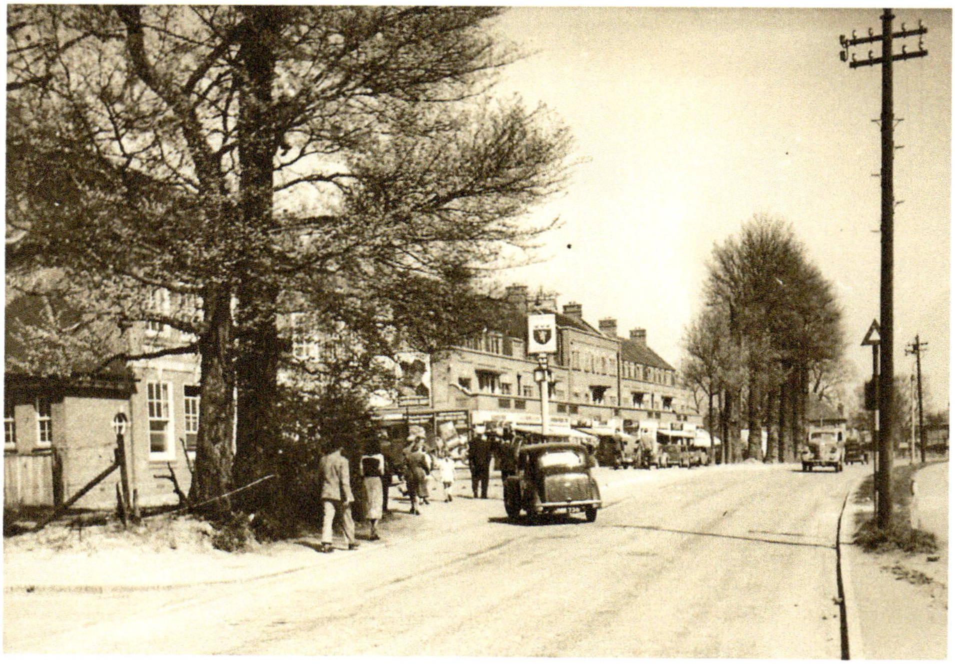

Long Drive

Ralph Hawtrey-Deane sold fields near South Ruislip station to developer Robert Masson-Smith in 1910/11. Haphazard development followed, displeasing to the new RNUDC. The public house seen on the left behind the trees was named the Deane Arms after him. The line of trees beyond was preserved at the request of Mrs Kim Brown, the architect's wife. The pub is now the Middlesex Arms and the trees have long since gone.

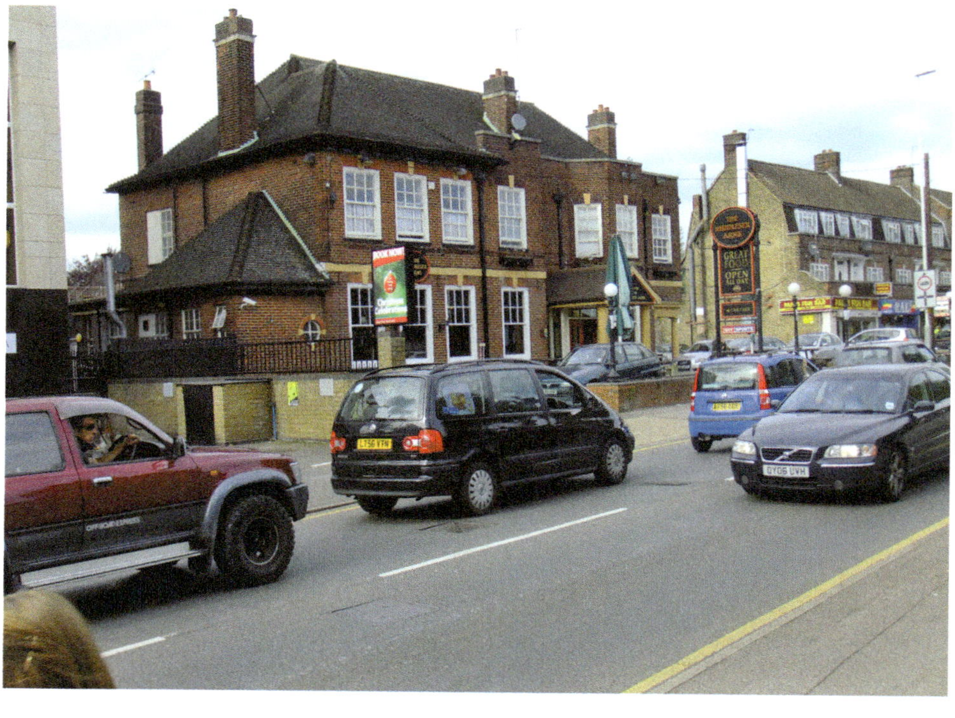

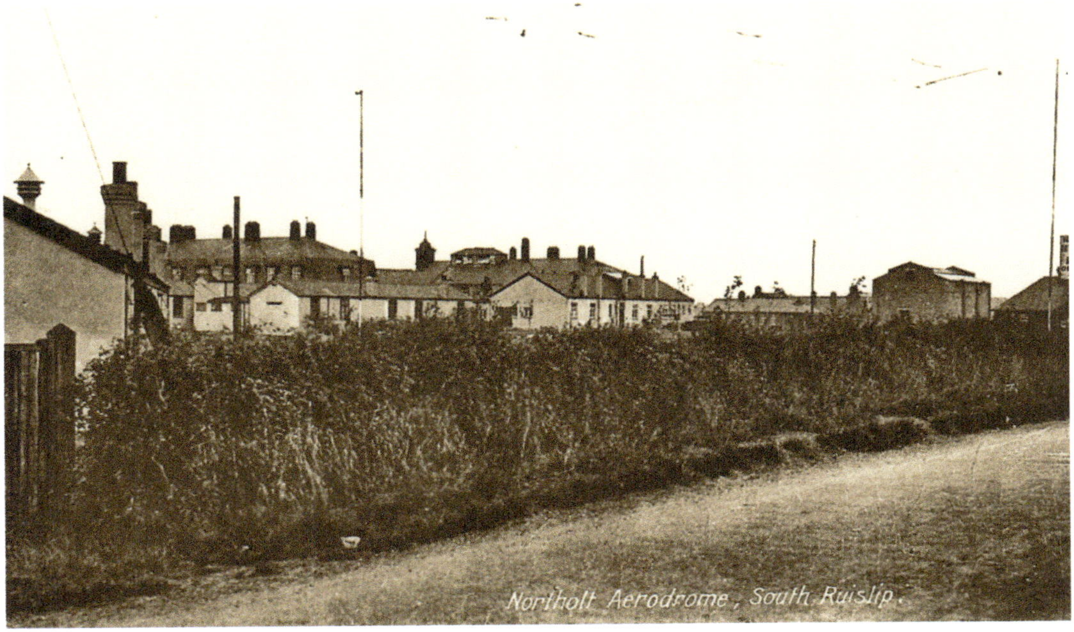

Northolt Aerodrome, 1920s and 2012

Hundred Acres Farm, Glebe Farm and part of Down Barnes Farm were requisitioned for the aerodrome, which opened on 3 March 1915, being named after the nearest railway station, following the convention of the time. It was one of seven Home Defence Night Landing Grounds. Americans and White Russians (from June 1917) trained there, and girls from the village spent pleasant evenings chatting to them at White Butts (where the road crosses the Yeading brook). Only the Americans were invited home to Sunday tea.

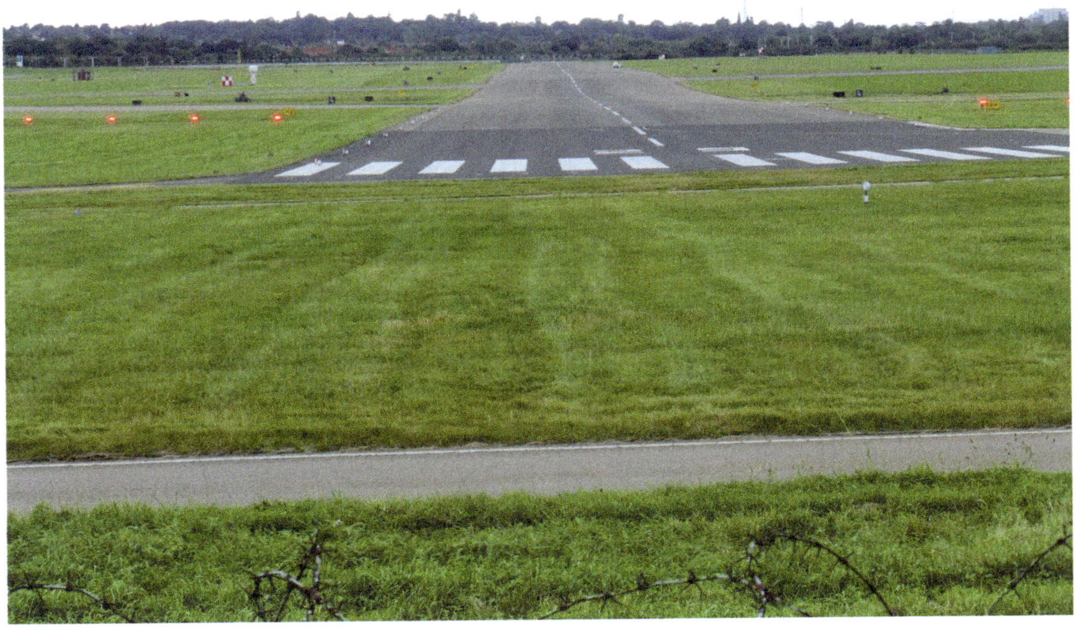

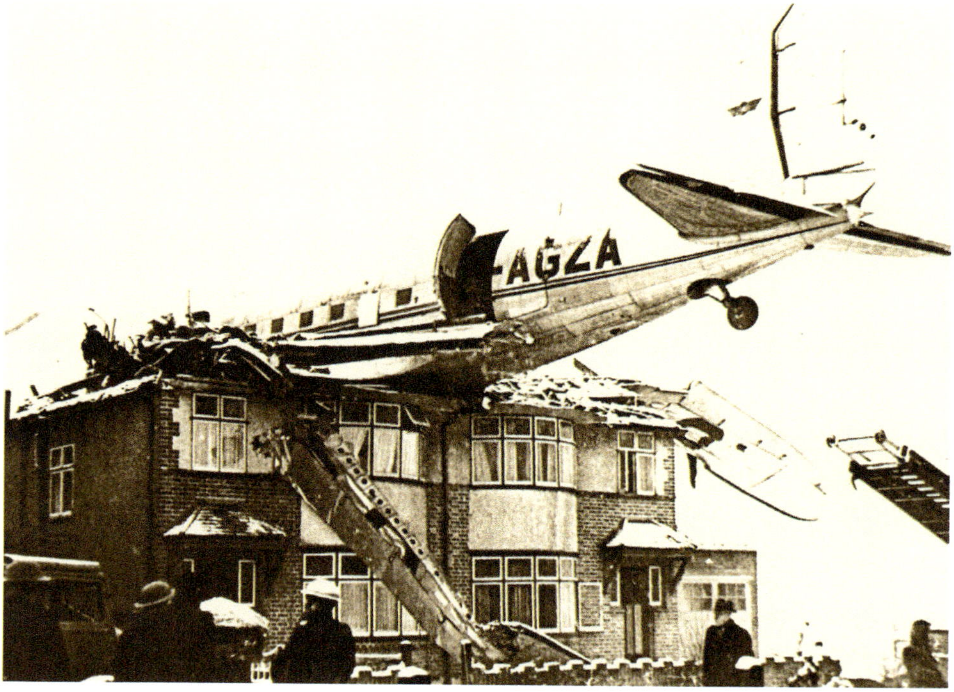

'Dakota Rest'

A BEA Dakota tried to take off from Northolt in a snowstorm on 19 December 1946, but got no further than Angus Drive, where it crash-landed on the roofs of Nos 44 and 46. Passengers and crew climbed onto the roof of No. 46, through the skylight into the loft and emerged from the front door. The house was renamed 'Dakota Rest' for a time. There is no sign of the near-calamity in this quiet scene taken sixty-six years later.

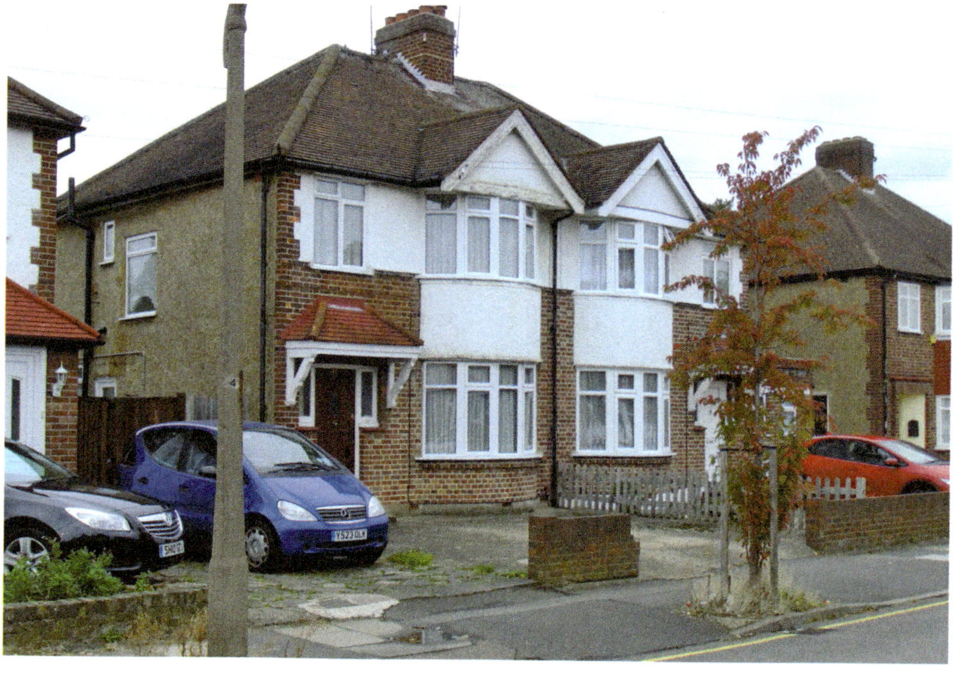

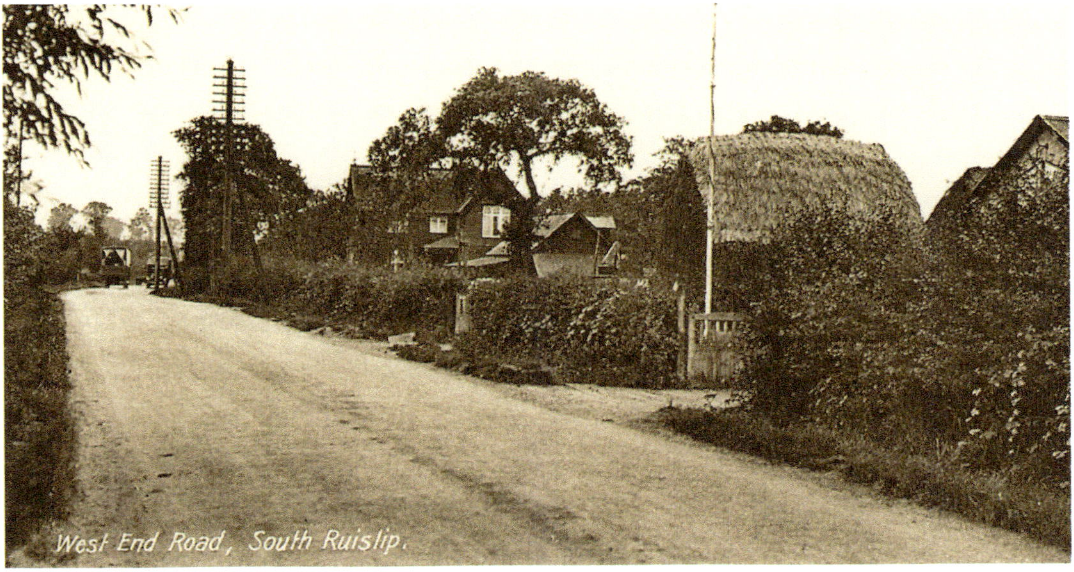

Glebe Farm in its Glory Days and 2012, Inset Plaque

Sir Charles Henry Mills, wishing to link Hundred Acres Farm with another of his properties, Down Barnes, bought the glebe land that protruded between them from Revd Christopher Packe, Vicar of Ruislip. He built the attractive neo-Gothic-style Glebe Farm in 1882. It became famous for the horses that Jack Rock kept here for filming in the 1950s and '60s. Later it was taken over by a religious sect. Now used for storage and despite having locally listed status, it is in an absolutely appalling state.

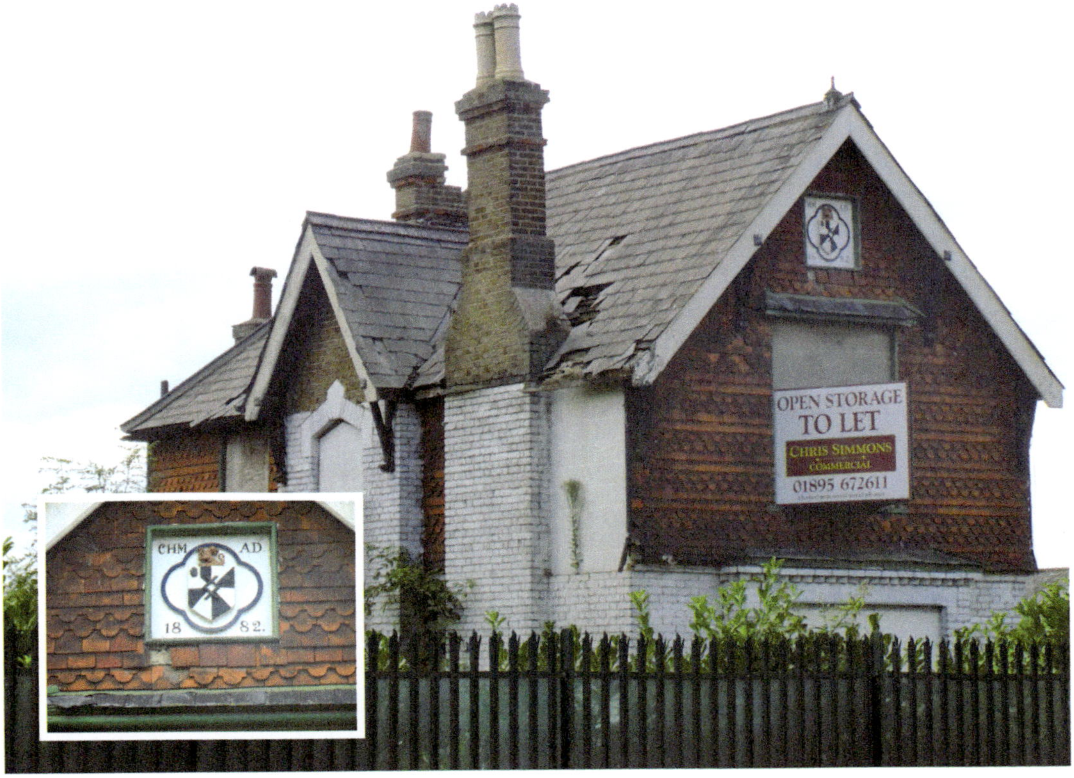

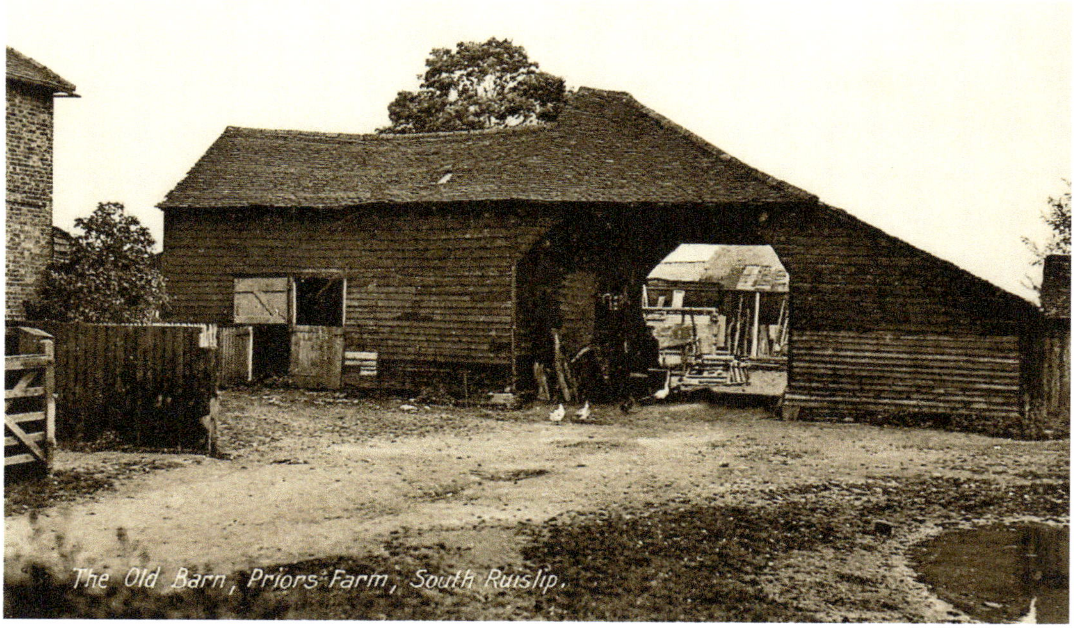

Priors Farm

In the thirteenth century, the prior of Ruislip had a grange at Bourne, where a boy looked after the oxen used for ploughing. Its exact position has not been determined, but the open field crossing the southern end of the manor was always called Priors Field. Ralph Deane built a new farmhouse before 1835, seen here with its picturesque barn in 1957; it was replaced in 1964. The Jones family have farmed here since 1926.

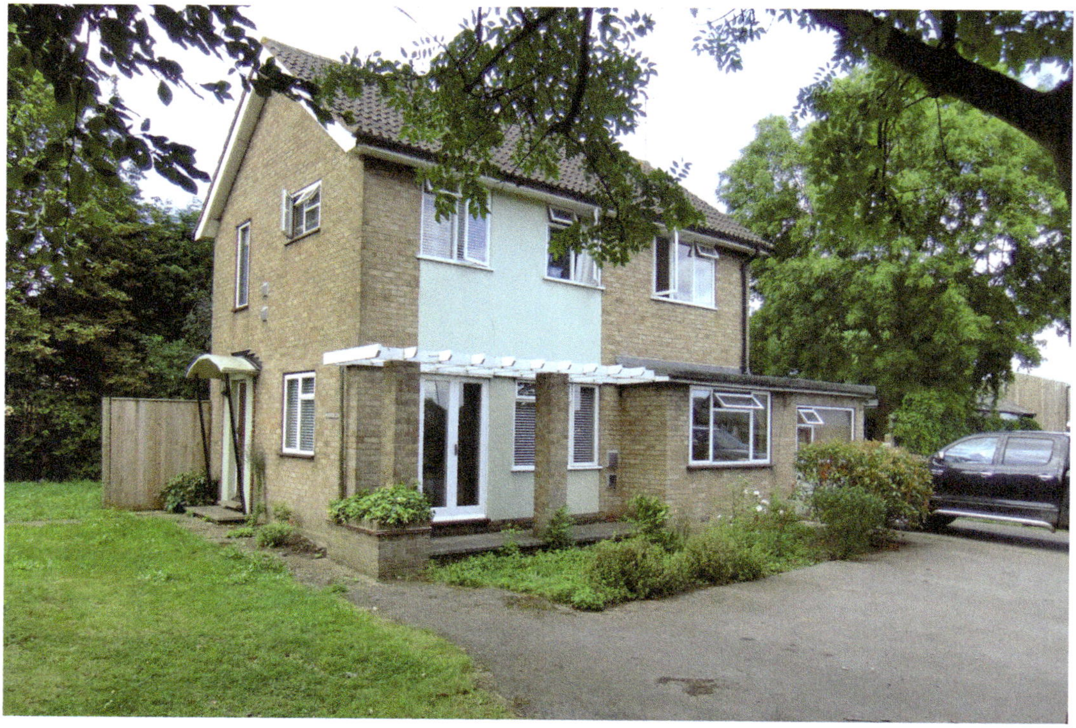

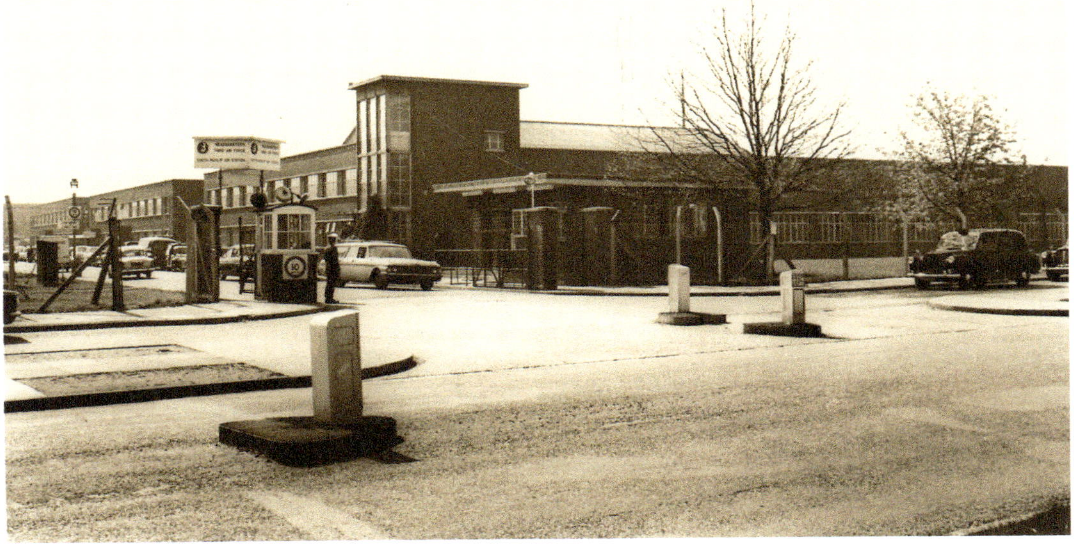

American Base 1949–72

During the Cold War the American 3rd Air Force, European forces, had a base between Long Drive and Stonefield Way. Troops arrived in Easter 1949 as simple warehouse-like buildings were being divided and done up inside 'like a palace' – in the eyes of the young women who attended dances – with draperies and carpets unobtainable in post-war England. There was a baseball diamond reached by a tunnel beneath the railway, a gymnasium and ten-pin bowling. The Americans moved in October 1972. The site became a business park, seen below in 2012.

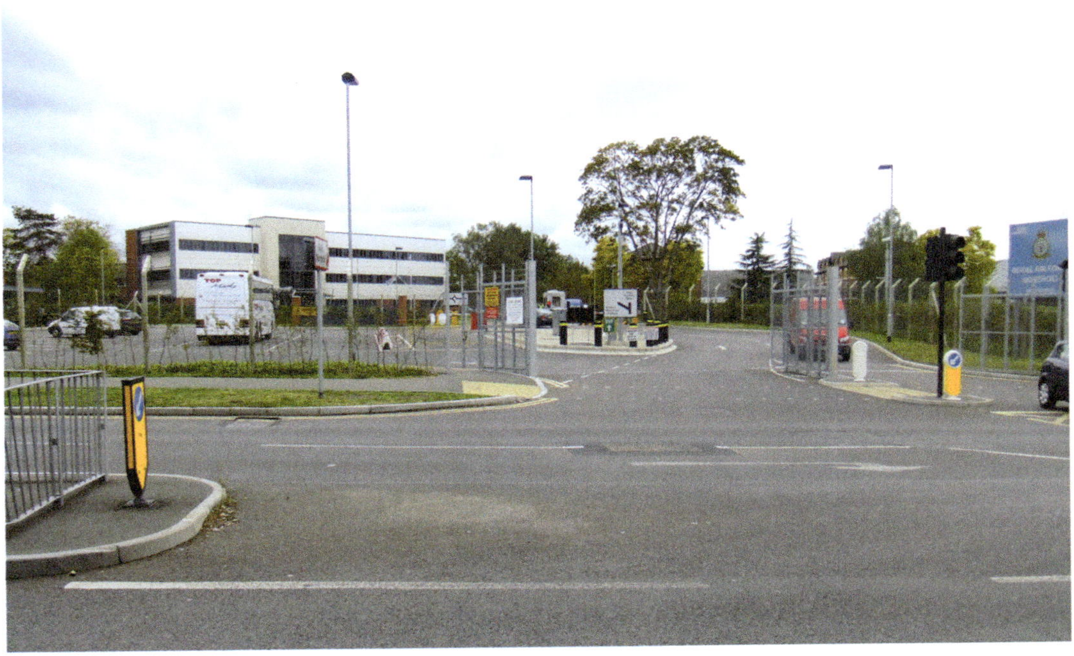

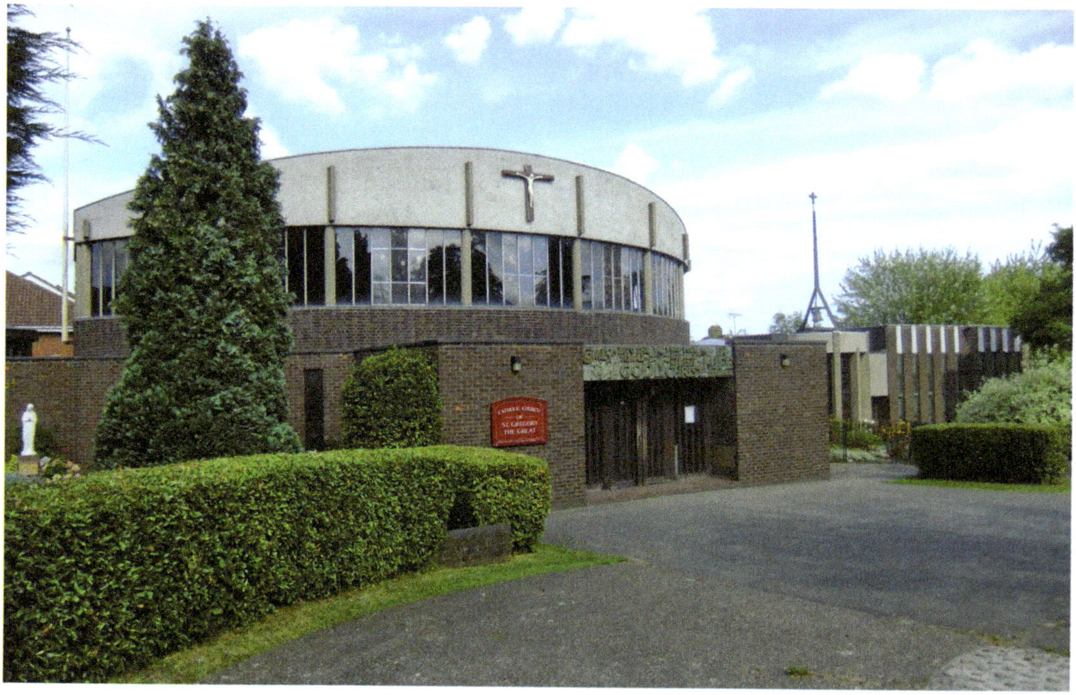

St Gregory's Roman Catholic Church and New Library

South Ruislip is well served by churches. St Mary's Church of England was built in 1959, replacing the wooden building that preceded it. Roman Catholics waited until 1967 for St Gregory's, although there was a Mass centre from 1958. The architect Gerard Goalen designed the modern-style church to meet post-Vatican II liturgical requirements. Close by is the brand-new South Ruislip Library and Adult Education Centre, opened in October 2012.

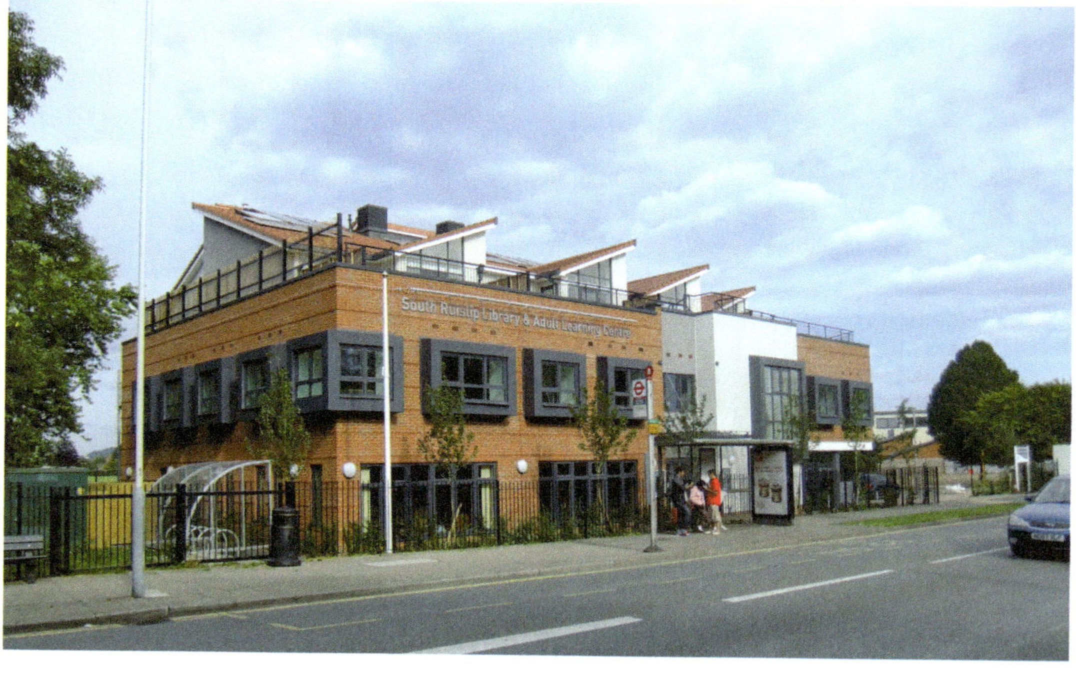

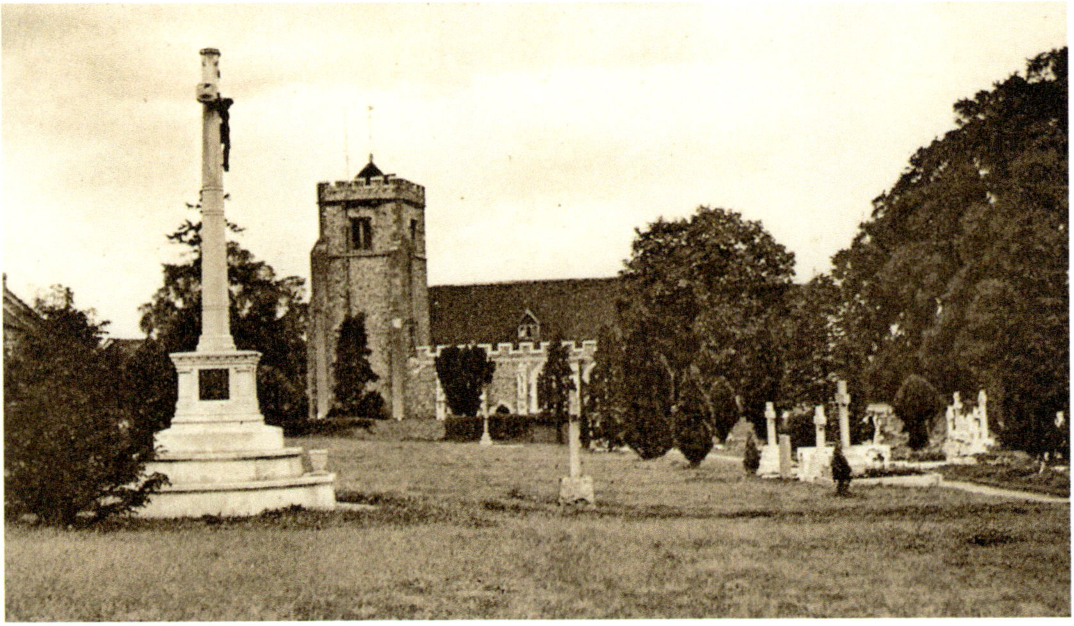

Ruislip War Memorial Erected 1920, Polish War Memorial Unveiled 1948

There were numerous deaths at Northolt during training between 1915 and 1918, and the victims were buried in St Martin's graveyard, seen here with the war memorial in its original position. Many other war dead from both world wars are also interred there. The Polish airmen who took part in the Battle of Britain have a special place in the public's hearts. The Polish war memorial sited between Glebe Farm and the A40 was designed by the Polish sculptor Mieczysaw Lubelski shortly after his release from a German labour camp.

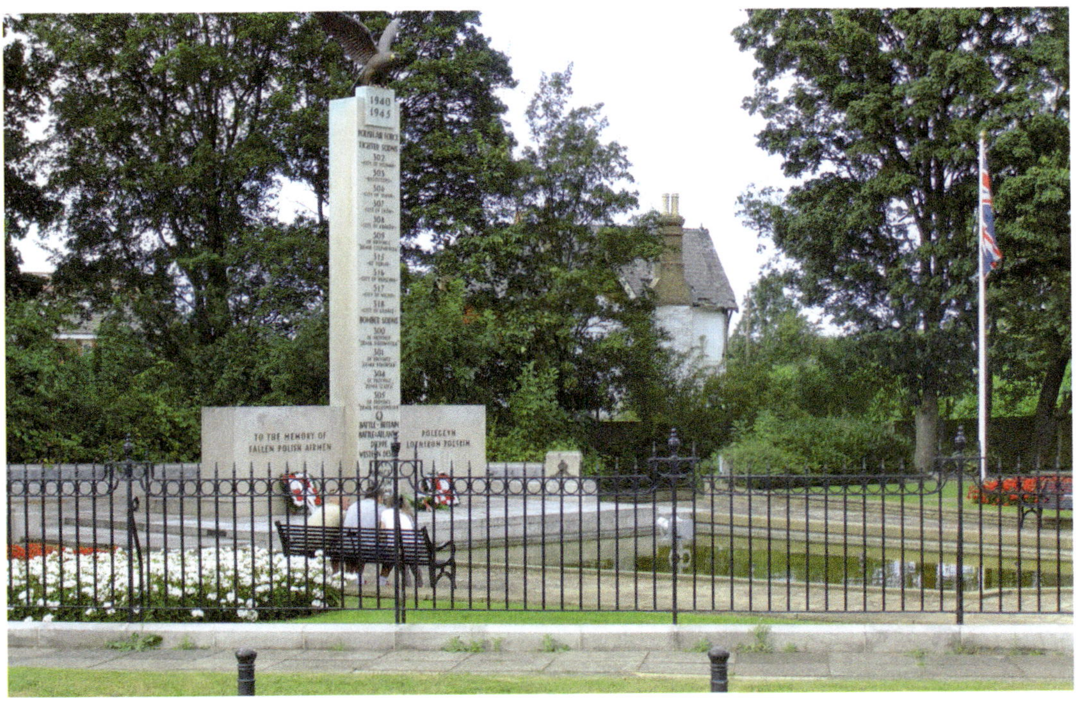

And Finally...

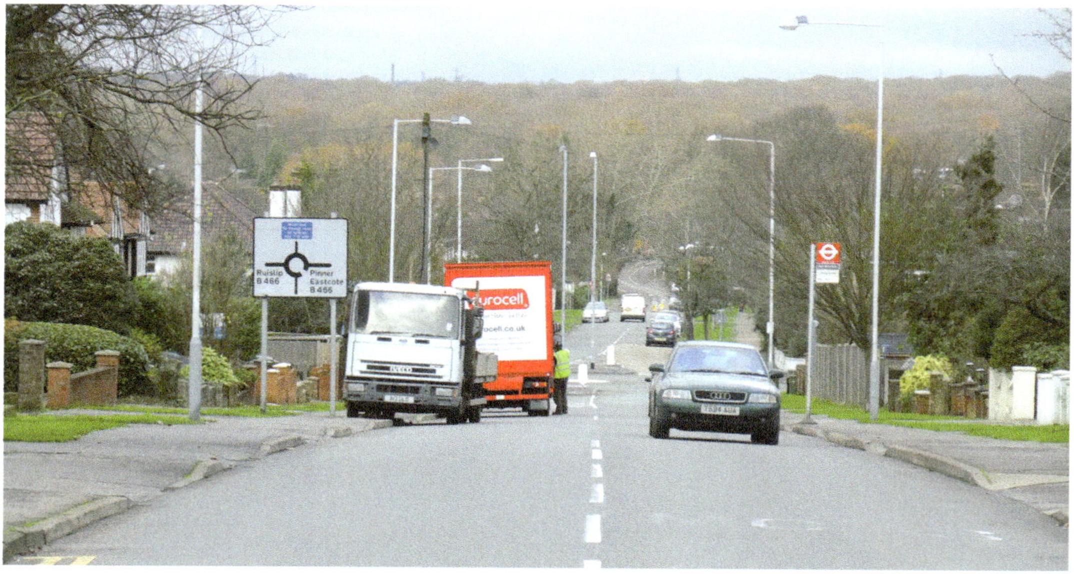

The View from Windmill Hill, North and South

The windmill mentioned in 1294 stood near this spot. To the north, the hill runs down to the Pinn valley. The trees of Park, Copse and Mad Bess Woods on the opposite hillside remind us that there, at least, little has changed since medieval times. How different is the busy scene to the south, across the former quiet open fields where the villagers once grew their crops.

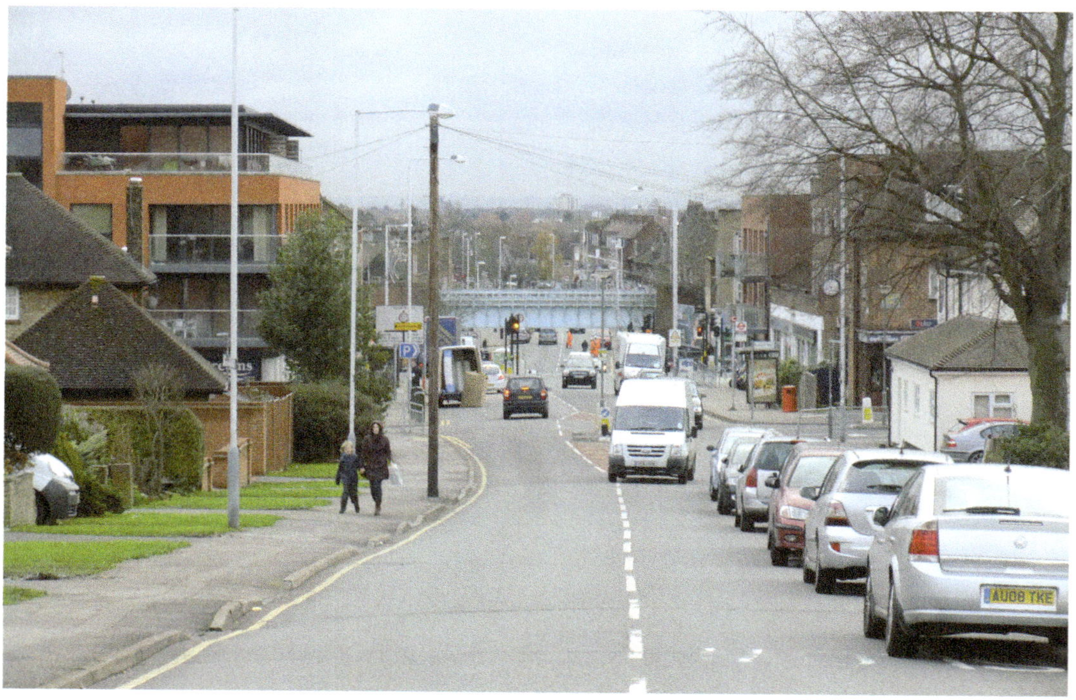